SALVATION

Based on the
Basic Bible Studies Course
Series 1

By
Roger D G Price

"Let the word of Christ dwell in you richly"
(Colossians 3:16)

ISBN 0 9527633 0 3

Published by BBS Books in co-operation with CCF Tapes

Further copies of this book are available from:

CCF Tapes, 30 Crescent Road
Bognor Regis, West Sussex, PO21 1QG (England).

A full list of Bible studies by Roger Price available on audio cassette is given at the back of this book.

Unless otherwise stated, Scripture quotations are from:

The Holy Bible - Revised Authorised Version (RAV)
Copyright ©1982 Thomas Nelson, Inc., USA
(published by Samuel Bagster & Sons Ltd.)

This is the British usage edition of the
New King James Version (NKJV) of the Bible
Copyright ©1983 Thomas Nelson, Inc., USA.

The following versions are also quoted occasionally where indicated:

The Authorized (King James) Version (AV)

New American Standard Bible (NASB)
Copyright ©1960, 1962, 1963, 1968, 1971, 1975,
1977 The Lockman Foundation, USA.

The Holy Bible, New International Version (NIV)
Copyright ©1973, 1978, 1984 International Bible Society,
published by Hodder & Stoughton.

Written by A. Manchester, based on tapes by Roger Price.

Page make-up assisted by Paul Shearing, Software Development Services, Caterham.

Cover make-up by Neill Blume. Cover picture from a painting by Nigel Purchase.

Printed in England by Stanley L. Hunt (Printers) Ltd., Rushden.

Copyright of this edited version only (but not any original tapes or other source materials) ©A. Manchester, 1996.

All rights reserved. No part of this publication may be reproduced, stored in a retrieval system or transmitted, in any form or by any means, electronic, mechanical, photocopying or otherwise, without the prior permission of the publisher or editor.

INTRODUCTORY VERSES

Jesus said:
"Come to Me, all you who labour and are heavy laden, and I will give you rest. Take My yoke upon you and learn from Me, for I am gentle and lowly in heart, and you will find rest for your souls. For My yoke is easy and My burden is light."
(Matthew 11:28-30)

"Let not your heart be troubled; you believe in God, believe also in Me. In My Father's house are many mansions; if it were not so, I would have told you. I go to prepare a place for you. And if I go and prepare a place for you, I will come again and receive you to Myself; that where I am, there you may be also. And where I go you know, and the way you know." Thomas said to Him, "Lord, we do not know where You are going, and how can we know the way?" Jesus said to him, "I am the way, the truth, and the life. No one comes to the Father except through Me."
(John 14:1-6)

ACKNOWLEDGMENTS

Roger Price read widely and drew from a number of sources for these studies. He gave no detailed bibliography for his tapes, on the basis that it would have to be extremely long and that truth ultimately belongs to and originates from God Himself. However, a short bibliography is given at the back of this book which names some of the known sources he used for these early studies, as well as works that were referred to frequently during compilation of this book, or from which information has been included in the footnotes or appendices.

A number of people have helped in the production of this book in various ways: by providing transcripts of the tapes, contributing their own notes, making useful suggestions or by helping proof-read successive versions of the text. The contributors share a high regard for Roger Price's teaching and the conviction that its publication will be of benefit to the Church as a whole. David Gordon and Martin Emerson in particular helped by carrying out additional research and made very useful suggestions.

Valuable contributions to points of linguistic interest in relation to New Testament Greek were made by Mr Bruce Sherdley, visiting teacher of New Testament Greek at Capernwray Bible School (Carnforth, England), to whom sincere thanks are given for his thorough replies to many specific questions.

Paul Shearing is also thanked for help with page design, use of computer equipment and software configuration to enable the production of pages to be completed successfully.

Alan Manchester (Compiler and Editor)

CONTENTS — MAIN CHAPTER HEADINGS

    INTRODUCTORY VERSES III
    ACKNOWLEDGMENTS IV
    TABLE OF CONTENTS—IN DETAIL... VI
    PREFACE.. XI
    NOTES ON STYLE... XII
    SYNOPSIS OF THE BOOK... XIII
    OPENING REMARKS ABOUT THE COURSE BY ROGER PRICE XIV

1.   INTRODUCTION: THE WORD OF GOD 1

THE BARRIER AND GOD'S ANSWER—SALVATION

2.   THE BARRIER 13
3.   THE VIRGIN BIRTH 27
4.   REDEMPTION 43
5.   CHRIST DIED FOR OUR SINS—ATONEMENT AND EXPIATION 55
6.   WHY MUST WE BE BORN AGAIN?... 69
7.   THE BARRIER REMOVED
     —PROPITIATION, JUSTIFICATION AND ETERNAL LIFE IN CHRIST 85
8.   THE UNFORGIVABLE SIN 103

ETERNAL SECURITY

9.   OUR MOTIVATION TO HOLINESS—ETERNAL SECURITY (PART 1).......... 119
10. OUR SECURITY IN CHRIST—ETERNAL SECURITY (PART 2) 131
11. RESPONSES TO THE CASE AGAINST ETERNAL SECURITY
     —ETERNAL SECURITY (PART 3) 145

TWO IMPORTANT PRINCIPLES FOR CHRISTIAN LIVING

12. WALKING IN THE LIGHT WITH GOD— 1 JOHN 1:9 165
13. ALL THINGS WORK TOGETHER FOR GOOD—ROMANS 8:28 183

HOW JESUS ADDRESSED A LEGALISTIC PERSON

14. THE RICH YOUNG RULER.. 201

    APPENDIX 1. THE ORIGINAL LANGUAGES OF THE BIBLE 217
    APPENDIX 2. CONDITIONAL SENTENCES IN GREEK 223
    APPENDIX 3. CHRIST IN THE OLD TESTAMENT................................ 231

    BIBLIOGRAPHY 237
    BIBLE STUDY TAPES BY ROGER PRICE 239

TABLE OF CONTENTS — IN DETAIL

1. INTRODUCTION: THE WORD OF GOD 1
  The Importance of the Bible 1
  The Canon of Scripture 3
    The Old and New Testaments 4
  Original Languages 5
  Archaeology 6
    The inconsistency of some Bible critics 7
  History of Koine Greek 7
    The suitability of Koine Greek for New Testament revelation 10
  Summary—Applying the Word 11

2. THE BARRIER 13
  No other Name than Jesus Christ 13
  MAN'S PROBLEM—THE BARRIER 14
  SALVATION — GOD'S PLAN TO OVERCOME THE BARRIER 16
  GENESIS 3: THE FALL OF MAN 17
    Satan deceives Eve by his craftiness 19
    Eve and Adam disobey God 21
    The effects of the Fall 22
    Adam and Eve realize they are naked before God 23
    Adam and Eve are shown grace 24
    Summary 25

3. THE VIRGIN BIRTH 27
  Body, spirit and soul 27
  Spiritual death and the old sin nature 28
  Grace and judgments 30
  Salvation first revealed in Genesis 3:15 32
  The Virgin Birth foretold in Genesis 34
  Jesus Christ: God and man 35
  The Virgin Birth foretold in Isaiah 36
  Jesus' Victory on the Cross 38
  What Jesus' Victory means to us 40
  Conclusion 42

4. REDEMPTION 43
  SIN: THE FIRST BRICK IN THE BARRIER 43
    1. The old sin nature 43
    2. Death reigned following Adam's sin 44
    3. Personal sins 44
  Slavery to sin (John 8:30-36) 44
  Redemption 47
  Jesus Christ: the only Free-man 47
  The significance of Blood 48
  Knowledge of Redemption in the Old Testament 49
    Adam and Eve 49

  Cain and Abel 50
  Noah 51
  Job 51
  David 52
 The Good News—Redemption through Jesus Christ 52

5. CHRIST DIED FOR OUR SINS—ATONEMENT AND EXPIATION 55

 ATONEMENT 55
  Christ died for all 55
  The Gospel message 57
  Noah's Ark: a picture of salvation 58
 THE SECOND BRICK: THE PENALTY OF SIN 61
  Jesus' Cry of dereliction on the Cross 62
   "Jesus the Nazarene" 63
  Jesus fulfilled the picture of the Bronze Serpent 66
  Jesus, a "worm" on the Cross 66
  Our debt has been paid and cancelled 67
  Conclusion 68

6. WHY MUST WE BE BORN AGAIN? 69

 BRICK THREE: SPIRITUAL DEATH 69
  The unbeliever's problem – Spiritual Death 69
   The unbeliever's problem described in 1 Corinthians 2:9-14 70
  The work of the Holy Spirit 71
  The New Birth: Regeneration 72
  Jesus' conversation with Nicodemus (John 3) 73
  Signs of the Messiah 74
   The Messiah's miracles 74
   Jesus' healing of a Jewish leper 75
  Jesus tells Nicodemus he must be born again 77
  Nicodemus hears the Gospel message 81
  Nicodemus was born again 82
  Conclusion 83

7. THE BARRIER REMOVED
—PROPITIATION, JUSTIFICATION AND ETERNAL LIFE IN CHRIST 85

 BRICK FOUR: THE CHARACTER OF GOD 85
  Appeasement in other religions 85
  Propitiation 87
  What the Old Testament tells us about propitiation 88
   The Ark of the Covenant 89
   The mercy seat 90
 BRICK FIVE: MAN'S GOOD DEEDS 92
  Imputation 93
  Justification by Faith 95
 BRICK SIX: TEMPORAL LIFE 98
  Eternal Life in Christ 98
  All shall be made Alive 100
 THE BARRIER HAS GONE 101
  Reconciliation 101

8. THE UNFORGIVABLE SIN **103**

Faith versus Works *103*
   1. The law proved that all people are sinners 104
   2. The law was a shadow of Christ 104
   3. The law provided a basic set of rules to give peace in Israel 105
Boasting and the law of Faith *106*
   The example of Abraham 108
   The example of David 109
Faith, not sin, is the decisive issue in salvation *110*
Sin will not be the decisive issue on the Day of Judgment *111*
THE UNFORGIVABLE SIN 114
  Blasphemy against the Holy Spirit *115*
  Conclusion *117*

9. OUR MOTIVATION TO HOLINESS—ETERNAL SECURITY (PART 1) **119**

The Purpose of the Christian life *120*
Calvinists and Arminians *121*
The Intercession of Jesus *122*
The basis of our eternal security *123*
Our Motivation to holiness *124*
Holiness requires a new nature *128*
Summary *130*

10. OUR SECURITY IN CHRIST—ETERNAL SECURITY (PART 2) **131**

Two views of salvation *131*
   What does the Bible say? 132
FOUR PRINCIPLES 133
Principle 1: God's omniscience *133*
Principle 2: The nature of a Gift from God *136*
Principle 3: The work of the Father, Son and Holy Spirit in our salvation ... *138*
   The work of the Father 138
   The work of the Son 139
   The work of the Father and Son together 140
   The work of the Holy Spirit 141
Principle 4: The family or kindred relationship *143*
Conclusion *144*

11. RESPONSES TO THE CASE AGAINST ETERNAL SECURITY
    —ETERNAL SECURITY (PART 3) **145**

Errors made in interpreting the Bible *146*
SCRIPTURE PASSAGES USED TO OPPOSE ETERNAL SECURITY 147
Group 1: Passages dealing with fruit and the judgment of believers' works ... *148*
   The Parable of the Sower 148
   Hebrews 6:7-10 150
   1 Corinthians 9:27 152
Group 2: Passages about God disciplining believers *152*
   Ananias and Sapphira 154
   King Saul 154
Group 3: Passages or verses taken out of context *156*
   Matthew 24:13 156

>   Matthew 7:21-23 157
>   *Group 4: Passages exhorting believers to live in fellowship* *158*
>   Hebrews 6:1-6 158
>   Hebrews chapter 10 160
>   *Miscellaneous scriptures*...*161*
>   Revelation 3:5—'Overcomers' 161
>   2 Timothy 2:11-13..162
>   *The Joy set before Him* *163*
>
> **12. WALKING IN THE LIGHT WITH GOD— 1 JOHN 1:9 ....165**
>   *Walking in Agreement with God* *165*
>   *The Discipline of a Father (Hebrews 12)*...*167*
>   *The Spiritual and the Carnal Christian* *169*
>   *1 John 1:9 — A great promise for us to claim*...*171*
>   The example of David 171
>   *Repentance*...*172*
>   *Confession*..*173*
>   *The Parables of Luke 15* *175*
>   The Parables of the Lost Sheep and Lost Coin.................................176
>   The Parable of the Prodigal Son..177
>   *Conclusion* *181*
>
> **13. ALL THINGS WORK TOGETHER FOR GOOD— ROMANS 8:28 ......183**
>   *Anticipating difficulties*...*183*
>   The trials of Elijah 184
>   Simon Peter's denial of Jesus 185
>   *The Promises of God*..*185*
>   The example of Moses...187
>   *Romans 8:28 – All things work together for good* *187*
>   The example of Simon Peter again..188
>   *Three principles that apply to all believers*...*189*
>   *The Romans 8:28 principle seen in the lives of Joseph and his family*..........*190*
>   Reuben 190
>   Simeon and Levi..191
>   Judah, Issachar, Dan and Benjamin..191
>   *The story of Joseph* *192*
>   *Conclusion* *199*
>
> **14. THE RICH YOUNG RULER 201**
>   *The importance of living a godly life* *201*
>   *How to witness* *202*
>   THE RICH YOUNG RULER 203
>   *The religious leaders and the law* *206*
>   *Jesus showed the rich young ruler how he was breaking the law*.................*208*
>   "The Corban gimmick" 210
>   *Jesus' challenge to the rich young ruler* *211*
>   *Lessons for Jesus' disciples* *212*
>   *The issue of Rewards* *213*
>   *Conclusion* *214*

IX

APPENDIX 1. THE ORIGINAL LANGUAGES OF THE BIBLE 217
- *Hebrew* *217*
- *Aramaic* *219*
- *New Testament Greek* *220*

APPENDIX 2. CONDITIONAL SENTENCES IN GREEK 223
- *Types of Conditions* *224*
- *Examples from the New Testament* *226*
- *Conclusion* *230*

APPENDIX 3. CHRIST IN THE OLD TESTAMENT 231
- *Can a man or woman see God?* *231*
- *Christ's appearances in the Old Testament* *232*
- *The Angel of the LORD* *234*

BIBLIOGRAPHY 237

BIBLE STUDY TAPES BY ROGER PRICE 239

PREFACE

Roger Price was a gifted Bible teacher, who dedicated his life to being a channel for discovering and communicating the truths and principles of the Word of God. He died in January 1987, aged 39. He travelled widely, teaching and encouraging the saints, inspiring them to love the Lord Jesus and to study the Word of God for themselves.

Between 1974 and 1986 he recorded approximately 280 Bible studies on audio cassette tape, in the context of providing teaching for his own local church and for those he visited during the course of his ministry. They comprised a course of 100 Basic Bible Studies, about 150 Special Topic Studies, studies relating to church life and instruction for local church elders, etc. He always maintained that the teaching of the principles of the Word of God provided a 'springboard' for people to search out more truth for themselves. It was his desire that the Basic Bible Studies course should be made available in written form so that the material might become more accessible.

Each chapter in this book represents one of the 14 studies in Series 1 of the Basic Bible Studies course (BBS 1 to 14). The studies are called "Basic", not because they deal with topics superficially or require no thought or effort, but rather because they cover topics which are *foundational* and which are essential for Christians to understand. The truths and principles covered are necessary to a sound and balanced understanding of salvation and provide a firm basis for further study of the Scriptures.

This book has been produced to provide a useful reference for those already familiar with the tapes, as well as to make the teaching available to a wider audience, both in English and through translation. It is envisaged that it might be the first volume in a series covering all the material in the course.

These particular studies were recorded at the very beginning of Roger's ministry, and it has therefore been necessary to modify or update some of the material by making minor additions and amendments. The purpose of any changes has been to make this book consistent with Roger's later, more detailed teaching on certain subjects or to improve clarity. Some extra information has been included in a few places from other studies, some slight reordering of material has been necessary in several chapters to complete the logic, and repetition has been avoided where possible.

It is the purpose of these studies, now in written form, to provide a clear understanding of how God's wonderful grace has been revealed in the salvation He has provided. The aim of those involved in the production of this volume has been faithfully to represent Roger's teaching, and his gift of communicating the truth with liveliness and clarity.

NOTES ON STYLE

This book was first compiled from notes taken from the audio tapes of BBS 1 to 14. Additions were then made from transcripts of the messages and from Roger Price's own brief updated notes on BBS 1 to 8, prepared with a view to future publication. The resulting text was then edited extensively, with much additional research being carried out to verify the material.

Footnotes are indicated by superior numbers in the text. Some contain information on the tapes which constitutes a diversion from the main logic. Others are to help clarify a point, to explain terminology or to provide additional information or cross references.

Three appendices have been included on subjects of particular interest which warranted more detail or explanation in written form.

Roger Price used the Authorized (King James) Version of the Bible (AV) in his studies. Scripture quotations in this book are based on the Revised Authorized Version (RAV), which is the British usage edition of the New King James Version (NKJV). This modern version is based on the AV and is therefore closest to it. The translators of both used the Greek Received Text (*Textus Receptus*) for the New Testament. The AV is sometimes quoted or given as a helpful alternative rendering. The New International Version (NIV) and New American Standard Bible (NASB) are also occasionally quoted.

All Scripture quotations are shown in bold type. Lower case letters have occasionally been changed to upper case to fit in with the sentence structure of these notes. Quotations have sometimes been slightly extended or shortened in comparison with the tapes. Brackets are used around a name, phrase or alternative translation when it has been inserted to make a biblical quotation more easily understood. Occasional underlining indicates a word that is discussed. Italics and special layout of poetic passages have been omitted in biblical quotations. In some places where a verse was quoted or alluded to on the tapes, but the Bible reference was not given, the reference has been included. Additional references are also given.

Throughout the text and within biblical quotations, personal pronouns and nouns have been capitalized when they refer to God. The covenant name of God in the Old Testament, YHWH (often transliterated as 'Jehovah' or 'Yahweh' with added vowels), is rendered LORD or GOD.

Greek and Hebrew words have been transliterated into English, with the Greek vowels eta and omega being indicated by $\bar{e}$ and $\bar{o}$ respectively.

SYNOPSIS OF THE BOOK

The Bible reveals how we can have fellowship with God only through the Lord Jesus Christ, who died on the Cross for us. His is the only name given by which we must be saved, and salvation is a gift of God by grace which is available to whoever will believe on Him. Understanding this grace of God is essential if we are to live lives dedicated to Him and if we are to have assurance of our salvation.

Roger Price firmly believed that the Bible is its own best commentary and so he dealt with the various aspects of salvation by reference to illustrations found within the Bible itself and by explaining some historical customs. For example, redemption is explained in terms of an ancient slave-market, atonement is discussed in relation to Noah's ark, and propitiation is explained by reference to the mercy seat found in the Book of Exodus.

Based on the early chapters of Genesis, the first half of this book outlines the problems mankind faced as a result of the Fall and our inability to earn any favour with God. These are then examined in terms of the 'Barrier' which exists between God and man apart from the Cross.

Our utter dependence on God Himself to provide a way of salvation becomes clear as we see how the glorious gospel of Jesus Christ was first revealed, and why His virgin birth was essential. We then see how Christ's work on the Cross dismantled the barrier brick by brick and, on the way, we gain an understanding of terms such as 'regeneration,' 'atonement,' 'propitiation' and 'justification.'

The second half of the book goes on to examine the so-called "unforgivable sin", and dispels the fears that come from misunderstanding this subject. Three chapters are then devoted to the important issue of whether a Christian can ever lose his or her salvation. The importance of holiness is emphasized and the principle of "eternal security" is established, firmly founded on the nature of God's character.

There follows a study of two important promises from which all Christians can derive comfort and encouragement. The promise of God's faithfulness and forgiveness to repentant sinners (1 John 1:9) is illustrated by three of Jesus' parables; and, the principle that all things work together for our good (Romans 8:28) is studied by tracing remarkable events in the lives of several Old Testament characters.

The Series concludes with a fascinating look at how Jesus dealt with a rich young man who was convinced he could earn his own salvation.

OPENING REMARKS ABOUT THE COURSE BY ROGER PRICE

The Basic Bible Studies course will include about 100 studies, covering most of the major topics in the Bible. It is a foundational course of Bible instruction. For convenience, the studies are in series, covering: Salvation, Judgments, Fulfilled Prophecy, Unfulfilled Prophecy, the Character of God, the Word of God, and Essentials for Growth as a Christian.

This first series concerns Salvation. It deals with some of the aspects of salvation that are often mentioned but rarely explained, for example: regeneration (that is, the new birth)—and its far-reaching effects, propitiation, reconciliation, atonement, and other such terms.

We go on to do an extensive study of eternal security and, then, to some basic principles of Christian living. We discover two wonderful promises found in the New Testament: 1 John 1:9, which tells us how to stay in unhindered fellowship with God, and Romans 8:28, which deals with the marvellous principle that everything works together for your good if you are a believer in the Lord Jesus Christ.

The aim of the course, and of every study, is that we should be effective Christians in our individual lives and, moreover, that we should be able to study and understand the Word of God for ourselves and apply it in our lives. Once we have grasped the basic principles, we should be able to build on them and go on to a thorough knowledge of the Word of God.

I have become convinced that the Word of God is *the* essential ingredient in a Christian's life. It is the key that will unlock everything we need to know as Christians. It will also help us become what the world needs to see in ambassadors of Jesus Christ.

Roger Price

(from introductory talk given at the start of BBS 1)

1. INTRODUCTION: THE WORD OF GOD

This study provides a foundation for the whole Basic Bible Studies course. In it, we look at the importance of the Bible to us, and see a little about the Bible itself and how we should apply it in our lives.

THE IMPORTANCE OF THE BIBLE

"**All Scripture is given by inspiration of God**" (2 Timothy 3:16a). The authors "**were moved by the Holy Spirit**" (2 Peter 1:21b). We believe, therefore, that the Bible is God's Word and that it is thus without error and is historically and scientifically true.[1] As such, it is the supreme authority for both life and conduct.

The purposes of this Basic Bible Studies course are to cover the major subjects in the Bible, to help make us effective Christians in everyday life, and to enable us to understand and read the Word of God for ourselves. God wants us to know His Word and to have a thorough grasp of the principles it contains.

Acts 11:26b tells us that it was the non-Christians who first called the believers "Christians", that is, 'followers of Christ,' or 'Christ's ones.' This was because they saw the principles of Jesus Christ's own life being lived out in them. (Before this time, believers had been called "followers of the Way" or simply "disciples".) The principles in God's Word will similarly enable us to show forth the life of Christ.

It is through the Word of God that we can become mature believers, who are stable and content, and who have peace, self-control and poise no matter what the circumstances. Such mature believers can radiate joy when others are 'cracking up' under the strain. Only the Word of God can do this, because it reveals to us how *God* views a particular situation.

---

[1] Reasons why we can trust that the Bible is the Word of God, and can trust that it is inspired, infallible and inerrant (in its original manuscripts), are dealt with in detail in the sixth series of Basic Bible Studies, entitled "The Word of God" (BBS 78 to 86). These studies also discuss how God has preserved and protected His Word throughout the centuries.

Once we come to see things from His viewpoint, we will find peace descending in our lives. For example, in a political crisis many people may become agitated and worried, but God is not anxious!

The Word of God continually speaks about itself, and frequently stresses how important it is for us to study it and apply it. Unfortunately, some Christians seem to ignore these passages. Here are a few examples; ask yourself, "Is this really true of me? Am I applying the Word of God as I should?"

- "**Let the word of Christ dwell in you richly in all wisdom, teaching and admonishing one another in psalms and hymns and spiritual songs, singing with grace in your hearts to the Lord**" (Colossians 3:16). Note the word "**richly**"; God's Word should dwell richly within us—not poorly.

- "**Be diligent to present yourself approved to God, a worker who does not need to be ashamed, rightly dividing the word of truth**" (2 Timothy 2:15). We should be diligent in studying the Word of God. Are you a worker who is approved? This scripture tells you whether or not you are.

- "**All Scripture is given by inspiration of God** [literally: **God-breathed**], **and is profitable for doctrine, for reproof, for correction, for instruction in righteousness, that the man of God may be complete, thoroughly equipped for every good work**" (2 Timothy 3:16-17).

- "**As newborn babes, desire the pure milk of the word, that you may grow thereby**" (1 Peter 2:2). I immediately imagine a picture of a lamb. A lamb almost attacks its mother in its desire for milk. It is so urgent about being fed on her milk that it nearly knocks her over; it's hard to know how the ewe puts up with it! Calves do the same. Similarly, if a baby misses its milk, it screams the house down; it does not just whimper quietly in the corner!

Oh that all Christians would be like that! If only Christians would start screaming the moment they are taken away from the Word of God. But it is not generally true of Christians today. Do you know why?

1 Peter 2:2 explains that the purpose of feeding on the Word is "**...that you may grow thereby.**" Satan knows that we need the Word of God in order to grow and reach maturity, to attain "**to the measure of the stature of the fullness of Christ**" (see Ephesians 4:13b). He will therefore do all he can to discourage or prevent Christians from studying the Word. Unfortunately, teachers of the Bible sometimes make the

Word of God seem dry and thus aid him very effectively. Every one of us should be urgent about the Word of God. Studying the Word, to deepen our relationship with Christ, should be the greatest quest in our lives.

Acts 17 gives an indication of what our attitude should be. It is interesting what is said about some *non*-Christians because of their attitude to the Word. "**Then the brethren immediately sent Paul and Silas away by night to Berea. When they arrived, they went into the synagogue of the Jews. These were more fair-minded than those in Thessalonica, in that they received the word with all readiness, and searched the Scriptures daily to find out whether these things were so. Therefore many of them believed**" (Acts 17:10-12a). God thus, through the writer Luke, commended these Bereans as more "**fair-minded**" (or literally, "**noble-minded**") than the Jews from Thessalonica in Macedonia. Why? It was because they were receiving the Word of God "**with all readiness**" and they were eager to search out the truth.

The word for "**readiness**" in Greek means 'eagerness (of mind),' and suggests the Bereans were willingly receiving the Word of God. The word translated "**searched**" means 'to investigate,' 'to examine,' 'to sift through,' or actually 'to dissect.' Note that they did this *daily*.

Christians today should have this same readiness of mind and should daily search the Scriptures. One of the aims of this course is to bring the Word of God alive, so that people may develop a hunger and thirst to understand the Word of truth.

THE CANON OF SCRIPTURE

The 66 books gathered in the Bible form "The Canon of Scripture." This term has been used for centuries to describe the Bible. The word 'canon' comes from the Greek word *kanon*, which had a very specific meaning. It was a straight edge used in building in the ancient world, a measuring rod or a ruler. It was used by a surveyor to see if a builder's wall was straight, upright and correctly proportioned. It was equivalent to today's plumbline or spirit-level. Weavers also used a *kanon* to check if woven lines were straight in a carpet or in cloth. The word thus came to mean a standard rule by which things were judged.

So why is the Word of God called "The Canon of Scripture"? It is because the Word of God is just such a standard or measure—a straight edge against which we should test our lives. *We* may have certain ideas; but what we need to do is take the canon of Scripture and lay it alongside them. If there is a discrepancy, and we seem to be veering off at an angle, the teaching of Scripture will tell us how to get back on to the true and on to the straight. We must measure our ideas against it, and change our ideas in accordance with God's revealed viewpoint.

After I became a Christian, I found that many of my ideas differed from God's, since I had had a non-Christian education and had developed some humanistic ideas. As I searched the Bible, I came across many passages that contradicted my own thinking. I had to be careful not to bend the canon to suit my ideas, but instead to admit that *I* was wrong. It is important for us to realize that, if our ideas do not fit the canon of Scripture, then *we* are always the ones who are in error; it is *we* who must change our thinking to agree with God's Word.

We live in a day when even many Christians are saying things that are not in line with the Word of God. We must know the Bible and use it effectively, so that we can judge what we hear. There will always be those who will preach what people want to hear. Such spiritual gimmicks come and go, and they can occupy our attention for several years if we are not watchful. We must be careful not to be distracted by them, wasting precious time that we can never retrieve.

Paul used the Greek word *kanon* in Galatians 6:16, where it is translated "rule": "**And as many as walk according to this rule, peace and mercy be upon them, and upon the Israel of God.**" Many preachers had gone to the Galatians and had given them different teachings. One in particular had told them that, to be Christians, they needed to be circumcised; and so, many of them were being circumcised. Paul therefore wrote to them and said, "**O foolish Galatians! Who has bewitched you...?**" (Galatians 3:1). He then told them the truth: that circumcision was not necessary. Paul was saying in Galatians 6:16 that he had given them a canon or rule in his letter with which they could test other people's teaching. If anyone came teaching circumcision, they could use his letter as a canon. If the preacher's teaching matched up to this canon, they should listen; if not, they should ignore the teaching.

We have to do the same today. We should always test what we hear against the canon of Scripture, and ask ourselves whether ideas being presented to us are biblically based or not? All gifts of prophecy should be tested in a similar way.

The Old and New Testaments

The Canon of Scripture is divided into two major sections, the Old and the New Testaments. God used about 40 main authors in total to write all the books of the Bible. (Additional authors also wrote parts of some books—in particular, the Psalms and Proverbs.) However, there was only one supreme author, God Himself, who inspired the writings through those who actually wrote the books.

The 66 books in our Bibles today all correspond to natural divisions and to differences in authorship. However, the chapter and verse divisions were not put there by God. The first 39 books, Genesis to Malachi, were written before Christ came, and constitute the Old Testament. The other 27 books, Matthew to Revelation, were written after Christ died and rose again, and constitute the New Testament. Both the Old and the New Testaments are necessary, and we should study them both. We must be balanced in reading them. I spend at least twice as long studying the Old Testament, because there are many more books in it, and it is much longer than the New Testament. If we only read the New Testament, we are ignoring more than three-quarters of the Canon of Scripture.

ORIGINAL LANGUAGES [2]

There is another basic difference between the Old and New Testaments, besides the times at which they were written: they were also written in different languages.

The Old Testament was almost entirely written in Hebrew, the language of the Jews. This is a language that remained substantially unchanged throughout the period of the Old Testament, and which has developed only slightly since then. Daniel 2:4b-7:28 was an exception, being written in Aramaic. These historical chapters in the Book of Daniel deal with Nebuchadnezzar, the Chaldean king of the Neo-Babylonian Empire, as well as the rise and fall of other Gentile empires. Aramaic was a widely used language, and would have been known by the Jews who were in exile in Babylon at that time. It was therefore a fitting language for Daniel to convey his message in.[3]

The New Testament manuscripts are in the 'Koine' dialect of Greek: a wonderful language, also known as "New Testament Greek" or "common Greek". *Koinē* in fact means 'common' in Greek, and this Greek was the common, everyday language of most of the civilized world for several centuries, including the 1st Century AD, when the New Testament was originally written. It differs from both classical Greek and modern Greek.

---

[2] More information about the original languages of the Bible is given in Appendix 1.

[3] Sections of the Book of Ezra and Jeremiah 10:11 were also written in Aramaic.

ARCHAEOLOGY

Until last century, Christians unfortunately made a big mistake about Koine Greek. Some of them said that, because there had been no remains discovered in Koine Greek apart from New Testament texts, Koine Greek must have been a special divinely-inspired language known only by Jesus and His converts. But this would have been very strange if Jesus and His disciples intended to use it to spread the truth!

The Christians were quite wrong, as shown by the huge number of Koine Greek papyri[4] that have now been found. Several finds of major significance were made at the end of last century during excavations at the site of Oxyrhynchus, on the west bank of the Nile in upper Egypt, by Dr B P Grenfell and Dr A S Hunt from Oxford—scholars who went searching for valuable art treasures in Egyptian tombs.

At Tebtunis, they found a tomb containing about two thousand stuffed mummified crocodiles. This was quite a common discovery and indicated that the next tomb should contain treasure. They therefore asked the natives to take the crocodiles out. However, when one of the crocodiles was accidentally dropped, it was found to be stuffed with inscribed papyri.

These papyri were found to be a whole library of texts, written during the 2nd or 3rd Centuries AD in Koine Greek; they were some of the greatest finds ever to be discovered in Egypt. The writings included legal agreements, missing Greek plays, children's notes, shopping lists—and New Testament fragments. The latter included nearly the whole Gospel of Matthew. Far more importantly, however, a complete grammar of Koine Greek was discovered which has provided scholars with a much fuller understanding of how sentences were constructed.

Much has also now been learned about the vocabulary as well as the grammar of Koine Greek, and we now have a very good understanding, not only of the syntax, but of the way in which certain words were used. Some words in the New Testament which were never understood before can now be understood plainly, helping greatly in our understanding of the New Testament.

---

[4] Papyrus was an ancient type of paper made from the papyrus reeds which grow along the banks of the River Nile. The pith was soaked and put in strips to form a very enduring and hard-wearing 'paper', which people used to write on. The inks were so powerful that the writing on papyri can be clearly read today. God designed it so to protect His Word!

The inconsistency of some Bible critics

It is interesting that while the Christians wrongly assumed Koine Greek to have been a special language, many Bible critics replied that this was utter nonsense and that archaeologists would soon discover other Koine Greek manuscripts. This demonstrates the inconsistency of many such critics.

The critics had themselves made assumptions about other matters, based on a similar lack of evidence. For example, until the 20th Century, many scholars criticized Isaiah 20:1 mercilessly, because it was the only record of a certain Assyrian king called Sargon. They said that, because there was no archaeological record of this king, it was clear that the Bible was "full" of inaccuracies. (Christians could of course have replied that archaeological remains would soon prove that Sargon indeed had been an Assyrian king!) Bible critics at that time also said that the Hittite empire, for which the Bible was the only major source of information, had either never existed or must have been very small, in view of the absence of archaeological remains. Consequently, before about 1916, history books actually stated that the Hittites were a small hill tribe;[5] this was in direct contrast to the Bible, which suggests they were once a vast nation, comparable in size and might with the Egyptian empire.

Much of the Bible has now been vindicated by archaeology.[6] In fact, it is amusing that more tablets have now been found relating to Sargon than about any other Assyrian king, and more tablets have been found on the Hittites than on any other ancient empire! It is now known that the Hittites indeed were a vast empire in Asia Minor for many centuries BC.[7]

HISTORY OF KOINE GREEK

With hindsight, we can see the wisdom of God in choosing Koine Greek as the language in which He would reveal His New Testament truth! For Koine Greek was a remarkable language, one of the most concise and

---

[5] See Encyclopædia Britannica, 1909 edition, for example. (Those who had ridiculed the Bible over the existence of the Hittite empire included the 18th Century French writer Voltaire.)

[6] We are extremely privileged today, as far as the Word of God is concerned. There has never been a time with more scientific and archaeological evidence in favour of the Bible. Sadly, many Christians never take the time to find out about it. For example, I know of only one Old Testament battle for which there is yet no archaeological evidence. I feel sure that it will not be long before archaeological proof will be found!

[7] Important archaeological evidences of the once great Hittite kingdom were first uncovered in 1906, but were not translated until about 10 years later. It is now understood that the Hittites dominated Asia Minor between about 1700 and 1200 BC, being at their zenith from about 1500 to 1200 BC.

flexible ever in the whole world. To help us understand why it was such an appropriate vehicle for God's revelation, it is interesting to look at its history.[8]

The kingdom of Macedon was at the northern edge of ancient Greece. Around 360 BC, Philip II King of Macedon fell in love with and married the red-headed princess Olympias of Epirus, a neighbouring state in Greece. Their son was Alexander the Great,[9] one of the greatest geniuses in world history. From the age of 13, he was trained by the great Greek philosopher Aristotle in every branch of human learning, and, by the age of about 16, he became a general in his father's army—a position which he fully deserved. He soon proved himself to be an extremely able and fearless leader.

At that time, Greece was divided into many city-states, which had formed various alliances in the past and fought against each other. They were all independent, not only in policy, but also in dialect: Epirus, Thebes, Attica, Arcadia, Achaea and Sparta, etc. The most beautiful dialect was Attic Greek, spoken by the Athenians, which was a flowing 'intellectual' language. There were other more 'primitive' dialects, among which was Doric Greek, spoken in the south by the Spartans.

Many of the Greek states considered the Macedonians to be uncivilized barbarians, but the Macedonian rulers claimed Greek ancestry. When Philip II became King of Macedon, he determined to do what no one had ever done before—to unite the whole of Greece, and become ruler over it.

By the time Alexander was 18 years old, his father had conquered the outlying regions of Macedon and had established control over most of Greece, managing to unify the Greek city-states quite successfully. Philip II did not treat the Greeks as conquered enemies, but rather he organized a league of city-states, because he wanted them to join him in his next ambitious plan—conquest of Persia. (Persia had dominated Greece for several centuries, causing great damage, and was seen as a lasting threat.)

However, Philip II was assassinated in 336 BC, and the unity of his "Hellenic league" rapidly began to disintegrate. Alexander, about 20 years old, ascended the throne—determined to secure the unity of the Greek city-states so that Greece could conquer the Persians. He also

---

[8] This section includes some additional information from "World History and Cultures—in Christian Perspective" (A Beka Book Publications, USA). More details about the history and characteristics of Koine Greek are given in Appendix 1.

[9] The dates of Alexander the Great's life are usually given as 356 to 323 BC.

INTRODUCTION: THE WORD OF GOD

resolved to use his conquests to spread Greek culture, which he had grown to love and admire, throughout the world.

First, Alexander marched to Epirus and proclaimed himself king, based on the fact that his mother had been one of its princesses. The people agreed. He then took over Thebes, and other city-states, expanding his control and unifying them into a viable empire. However, as he developed his army, which comprised not only soldiers but also engineers and surveyors etc. from many states and regions, he had great difficulty. The problem of language came to the fore, because he needed them all to understand his orders quickly and clearly.

As Alexander the Great extended his empire, he therefore carried his Greek language throughout the then-known world, and differences between the various Greek dialects were slowly eliminated. The dialect of Greek which came to predominate was called the "common dialect" (*koinē dialektos*), which we now call Koine Greek.

Koine Greek was able to express ideas very concisely. A good example is its compact commands: if soldiers were told to "Fire!" they could tell from the verb form alone whether they were expected to fire once or continuously![10]

With extraordinary genius, Alexander conquered and acquired Anatolia (present day Turkey), and then turned south to subdue Syria, Palestine and down into Egypt. (The Egyptian city of Alexandria was named after him, as well as about 15 other cities.) He then turned his attention eastwards and marched against the Persian empire. He decisively conquered the forces of Persia, and subdued what is modern-day Iran, Afghanistan and Pakistan. Very soon, the whole vast Persian empire became his.

Alexander could not resist further conquests and so he acquired parts of India and territory right up towards Tibet and China, before returning westwards. Then, at the age of 33, having conquered most of the known world, he died: not because of exhaustion, but of a fever—several days after a prolonged banquet and over-drinking.[11]

God had used him: in every place he had been, Alexander had diffused the language and culture of Greece. By the time of his demise, most of the then-civilized world was learning Greek and, by the time of Jesus

---

[10] See the section on the brevity of Greek verb forms in Appendix 1.

[11] There are several accounts of how Alexander the Great died, but most authoritative records say he died of a fever, perhaps as a result of malaria.

some 300 years later, Koine Greek was the everyday language of the common people. It was understood by almost everyone, and continued to be widely used until the 5th Century AD.

The suitability of Koine Greek for New Testament revelation

Jesus and His disciples would of course have known Koine Greek. And as soon as the disciples began to preach the gospel and the New Testament had been written down in Koine Greek,[12] everyone from India to Macedonia and down into Egypt could immediately understand the message. As a result, the gospel spread like wildfire throughout these regions. It only slowed down a little when it got to the borders of the former Greek empire, where other languages were prevalent.

God had thus prepared just the right medium for the gospel message to spread very quickly. Those Christians who believed that Koine Greek had been a special language, known only by a few, were therefore absolutely wrong!

Koine Greek was also extremely well suited for the initial spread of the gospel because it was an outstanding language. It was able to convey precise ideas very accurately and concisely. Being written in Koine Greek, the New Testament Scriptures thus express their meaning very exactly. English, in comparison, is a less compact language, and so our English versions must use more words to express the original meaning. But the Greek text is still available. Therefore, if a passage is not clear, it is possible to refer to the original Greek, which can sometimes provide a fuller understanding.[13]

---

[12] Jesus and His disciples would almost certainly have known Koine Greek and used it in many situations, although they probably would have spoken Aramaic more regularly and would have known the Hebrew used in the synagogue. Some people have suggested that a few New Testament books may originally have been written in Hebrew or Aramaic before being translated into Koine Greek, but there is no conclusive evidence for this. (See Appendix 1.)

[13] In the audio tape of this study, Roger Price gave a brief exposition of conditional statements in Greek (which he called "the four ifs"), and discussed how it may sometimes be possible to learn more about a conditional sentence from the Greek of the New Testament than is immediately apparent in most English translations. In view of the complexity of this subject, a fuller explanation of conditional sentences is given in Appendix 2 at the back of this book.

Summary—Applying the Word

The whole Bible is God's Word; every part of it was inspired by God, and it has been given to us for our edification. God has protected every sentence and letter of His Word,[14] and it is our heritage. He has given it to us so that we may benefit from it and glory in it.

The Bible is inerrant (in its original manuscripts)—that is, it contains no inaccuracies—and it is the canon by which we should measure ourselves to see if our path is straight. We therefore have much to learn from careful Bible study, including the text in its original languages. In particular, we can learn from the precise nature of the language of the New Testament, Koine Greek.

In a later study (chapter 4) we will look at the passage in John 8 which contains this verse: **"Then Jesus said to those Jews who believed Him, "If you abide in My word, you are My disciples indeed""** (John 8:31). They had a choice: perhaps they would continue in Jesus' word (that is, His teaching), but perhaps they would not.

We face the same choice today: **"If you abide in My word, you are My disciples indeed."** If we abide in Jesus' teaching, then we are truly His disciples. If we do not abide in Jesus' teaching, we may truly be believers, but we are not His disciples.[15]

The Word of God is absolutely crucial to us; that is why Hebrews 4:12 says, **"The word of God is living and powerful, and sharper than any two-edged sword, piercing even to the division of soul and spirit, and of joints and marrow, and is a discerner of the thoughts and intents of the heart."** The Greek word translated **"a discerner of"** (*kritikos* in Greek) means 'fit for judging' or 'critical of.' God requires that we allow the Word of God to be our judge—a judge of the thoughts and intents of our heart.

---

[14] Jesus affirmed the significance not only of every sentence and word, but of the smallest letter and the tiniest part of each letter in the wording of the law (see Matthew 5:18).

[15] The Greek word translated "disciple" meant a 'learner', and indicated thought accompanied by endeavour and commitment. In those days in Jewish society, 'disciples' were students and apprentices of a particular rabbi or 'master', and 'learners' of Scripture. A disciple's overriding aim and burning desire was to be exactly like his master in thought, word and behaviour. Through memorization of his master's teaching, and through imitation of his lifestyle as a result of close association and friendship with him, a disciple became qualified to become his teacher's reliable witness. To us today, being a disciple of Jesus thus means learning and following His teaching, and seeking to become like Him.

If we allow the Word of God to do its work, we discover that it is indeed living and powerful, and that God uses it to change us. By it, we grow to maturity, and can know peace in every circumstance. However, if we do not read and apply the Word, we cannot be transformed by it, and we shall continue to experience the same misery and spiritual bankruptcy as others who are not believers.

As Paul said in 2 Timothy 2:15, "**Be diligent to present yourself approved to God, a worker who does not need to be ashamed, rightly dividing the word of truth.**"

NOTES

2. THE BARRIER

We have seen how the Word of God is vital to us because it reveals God's thoughts to us. It shows us how we ought to live: **"Your word is a lamp to my feet and a light to my path"** (Psalm 119:105). By obeying the Word of God we learn how to live holy lives, as Psalm 119:9 says: **"How can a young man cleanse his way? By taking heed according to Your word."** We should thank God for giving us His Word. We are like babes or sucklings to whom the Word is milk.

We now turn our attention to the relationship between God and man, and to the first major topic of our course: the barrier between God and man.

NO OTHER NAME THAN JESUS CHRIST

Our first real Bible study of this course begins with Acts 4:8-12. Peter and John were being questioned by the elders, rulers and scribes in Jerusalem about the healing of a lame man at the Beautiful Gate of the Temple:

"Then Peter, filled with the Holy Spirit, said to them, "Rulers of the people and elders of Israel: If we this day are judged for a good deed done to the helpless man, by what means he has been made well, let it be known to you all, and to all the people of Israel, that by the name of Jesus Christ of Nazareth, whom you crucified, whom God raised from the dead, by Him this man stands here before you whole. This is the 'stone which was rejected by you builders, which has become the chief corner-stone.' Nor is there salvation in any other, for there is no other name under heaven given among men by which we must be saved.""

The final verse here makes an amazing statement. It is saying that if you firmly believe in Buddha you are not saved. If you firmly believe in Mohammed it is no good. If you are a follower of Karl Marx, it will not help you in the future. If you really believe that Mary Baker Eddy was sent by God, it does not help you at all. If you follow an Indian guru, that is not the answer. Rather, it declares, **"There is no other name** [than the name of Jesus Christ of Nazareth] **under heaven given among men by which we must be saved."**

Jesus said, **"I am the way, the truth, and the life. No one comes to the Father except through Me"** (John 14:6). He also said, **"I am the door"** (John 10:9)—that is, the way in or the entrance to salvation and eternal life. We talk about something very solemn when we talk about the name of Jesus. We must remember His divinity. He is God; He is the Son of God; and His name is the only name given for salvation.

Those who have difficulties with these verses have failed to recognize the problem man faces and to see why it was absolutely necessary for Jesus Christ, the Son of God, to come and die for us. Why for example was no other good man sufficient? To grasp these issues, the barrier between God and man must first be understood.

Man's Problem — THE BARRIER

The Bible reveals that man is faced with a major problem in his relationship with God. There are at least six obstacles which each form a blockage to that relationship. These obstacles are like six enormous bricks in a wall, and this wall constitutes a barrier between man and God:

GOD		MAN
	1. SIN	
	2. THE PENALTY OF SIN	
	3. SPIRITUAL DEATH	
	4. GOD'S CHARACTER	
	5. MAN'S GOOD DEEDS	
	6. TEMPORAL LIFE	

Each of these bricks in the barrier is insurmountable, and sufficient in itself to separate us from God. No human being could ever get over, round, under or through even one of the bricks by himself; and no other person could ever help you get past any of them. Jesus Christ Himself and His death on the Cross made the only way through. All six of these bricks are explained more fully in later chapters:

1. **Brick One – Sin.** God is absolutely holy. This means that He is absolutely pure, absolutely righteous and just, and in Him there is no sin at all. God is so holy that just ONE small sin[1] in the whole of our lives is sufficient to separate us or 'cut us off' from God forever, and to make us utterly unable to approach Him.

2. **Brick Two – The Penalty of Sin.** God is absolutely just, and so He must judge and punish sin in full; and, **"the wages of sin is death"** (Romans 6:23). So if we have sinned, not only does that sin cut us off from God because He is absolutely holy, but the penalty of that sin is also going to cut us off: God must punish us justly, and the correct penalty for that sin is death.

3. **Brick Three – Spiritual Death.** God is a Spirit,[2] and we can communicate and have fellowship[3] with Him only through our human spirits: **"God is Spirit, and those who worship Him must worship in spirit and truth"** (John 4:24). However, every person is born physically alive, but *spiritually dead*: we are born separated from God's life. Our human spirits are 'dead' and we are unable to commune with God. Instead of being living, functioning channels through which we can receive His life and power, our spirits are like flat batteries—defunct. Spiritual life can only be ours if God is present within our human spirits through His Holy Spirit, and if we are in union with Him there. But we are spiritually dead when we

---

[1] The Bible gives several definitions of sin (for example 1 John 3:4 and 5:17, James 4:17, Romans 14:23). Anything that we do or omit to do in thought, word or deed not in keeping with God's character and will is sin. Several Greek and Hebrew words are used to describe sin, with various shades of meaning (some being translated 'transgression,' 'iniquity,' 'trespass,' 'disobedience,' 'offence,' etc.) The most common Greek word is hamartia, which literally means 'a missing of the mark.'

[2] A spirit does not have flesh and bones (Luke 24:39). This tells us that God is not essentially a physical, material Being. However, God is a personal Being, with intelligence, self-consciousness, will and feeling. He is invisible, unless He chooses to reveal Himself (as He has done in various ways, but particularly through Jesus Christ, the Son of God, made flesh).

[3] A close friendship with God, based on spiritual communion and agreement, and a shared source of life. 'Fellowship' is a translation of the Greek word koinōnia, which means 'common sharing,' and for the Christian this means sharing in the life of Christ. All who thus share His life have fellowship with God and with one another (see 1 John 1:3, 6-7).

are born.[4] (This brick could thus be called either "Physical birth" or "Spiritual death".)

4. **Brick Four – God's Character.** Before we can have fellowship with God, every part of His righteous character has to be satisfied with us. However, His character and our character are fundamentally incompatible, because of the effects of sin in us. Thus we are all excluded.

5. **Brick Five – Man's Good Deeds.** God is absolutely holy and good. In comparison, our own 'goodness' is not enough and can never be enough to satisfy God. Isaiah says that our 'good' works are "**like filthy rags**" to God (Isaiah 64:6)—in other words, any good that we naturally do is totally unacceptable to Him, because it does not originate from God Himself and is inevitably tainted with wrong motives. The more 'good' we try to do, therefore, the more we reinforce our position on the wrong side of the barrier. We thus cannot by ourselves ever do anything to get past this brick.

6. **Brick Six – our Temporal Life.** God is eternal—He has always existed and He lives forever. However, it is certain that we are all going to die physically, unless the Lord Jesus returns first.[5]

SALVATION —
GOD'S PLAN TO OVERCOME THE BARRIER

This is the barrier. However, even before the creation of the world, God knew that the problem of this barrier would exist, and that we would be on the wrong side of it. God wanted fellowship with those He loved, and wanted them on the same side as Him. So God made a plan to overcome this barrier, and that plan was called "*Salvation*". The plan required Jesus Christ, the Son of God, to fulfil it. It centred and focused on Him. Jesus must have been approached (I am speaking in human terms because these

---

[4] Note: Having a dead spirit does not mean that the spirit does not exist. The Book of James tells us, "the body without the spirit is dead" (James 2:26). Therefore, all who are physically alive have a human spirit. The spirit gives life. Any body with a human spirit is alive. However, when we are born, our spirit is cut off from God who is the Source of spiritual life. The spirit is there, but is not able to receive life or power from God. The only solution is a spiritual rebirth, as described in chapter 6.

[5] Incidentally, no Christian should fear death, although some are afraid of how they will die. God will always look after us, even through the moment of death and beyond. Psalm 23 says, "Though I walk through the valley of the shadow of death, I will fear no evil" (verse 4). We will only walk through the shadow of death; we will not go into the domain of death itself. Whether we die or the Lord Jesus returns first, we shall continue to live together with Him (see 1 Thessalonians 5:10, 2 Corinthians 5:8).

things are mysterious and incomprehensible to our finite minds)—and He was willing to carry out God's plan of salvation.

Understanding the details of the barrier will help us to appreciate both our salvation and the uniqueness of the work of Jesus Christ. Later in this book as we study each brick in turn (in chapters 4 to 7), we will examine how Jesus Christ successfully fulfilled God's plan of salvation and dealt with each brick forever.

Understanding the truths given in these studies should give you rest, and make you more equipped to witness to others about Jesus and to provide answers to their questions and problems. If for example you meet people who feel they are not good enough for God, you will be able to *agree*, but tell them that Jesus came to take away their sins on the Cross, and to provide them with *God's* own righteousness!

Now we need to take a step back in time and see what caused the barrier to exist. The Book of Genesis, in chapter 3, provides the explanation. And remarkably, Genesis 3 describes not only the origin of the barrier, but also points to God's answer to it. As we will see later, the necessity for the virgin birth of Christ was also rooted there.[6]

GENESIS 3: THE FALL OF MAN

Genesis 3 is set in the Garden of Eden[7] where, at first, Adam and Eve had constant fellowship with their Creator.

"Now the serpent was more cunning than any beast of the field which the LORD God had made..." (Genesis 3:1a). Who was this "**serpent**", and what was he like? We tend to imagine a scaly black reptile or large snake moving across the ground. But this serpent was probably nothing like creatures we see today.

The Hebrew word *nachash* translated "**serpent**" is probably derived from a word meaning 'hiss' or 'whisper.' A very similar word (meaning 'bronze' or 'copper') comes from an identical root meaning 'shining,' 'brilliant,' or 'sparkling.' Therefore the word for the serpent is associated

---

[6] Psalm 119:160a says, "The entirety of Your [God's] word is truth." This clearly includes Genesis. Many people assume that the Book of Genesis is a myth, but they have not understood it. It reveals fundamental truths about our world and about the nature of man.

[7] Note: The Garden of Eden is not identifiable today. It was almost certainly swept away in the Flood at the time of Noah. It may have been somewhere in what is now the Middle East, in Mesopotamia, but the fact that we recognize two river names is inconclusive, as the whole geography would have been changed by the Flood.

with bronze and shining, and might indicate that this serpent appeared to shine. This is speculation, but it might have had scales which reflected the sunlight. It was a beautiful creature; and it may have been very attractive to Adam and Eve. The word translated "**cunning**" means 'crafty.' Therefore, despite its beauty, the serpent was crafty.

Revelation 12:9 refers to "**that serpent of old, called the devil and Satan**". The personality behind the serpent was therefore Satan himself. He was cunning and crafty; and he was independent of God.[8]

Who was "**the LORD God**", who had made this serpent? By referring to Genesis chapter 2, we find that the LORD God was the One who had made Adam and given him life (verse 7). He had then given Adam responsibility to cultivate and tend part of the earth: "**Then the LORD God took the man and put him in the garden of Eden to tend and keep it**" (Genesis 2:15). The LORD God was therefore involved in the work of Creation.

In Hebrew "**the LORD God**" is two words, *Jehovah Elohim*. The usual word for "**God**" in Hebrew is *Elohim*. However, "**the LORD God**"—*Jehovah Elohim*—is used here. This is probably a reference specifically to the Son of God— Jesus Christ—the revealed member of the Godhead.[9]

In Genesis 2:16-17, Adam was commanded by the LORD God (Jesus Christ) to eat freely from all of the trees in the Garden except one: "**And the LORD God commanded the man, saying, "Of every tree of the garden you may freely eat; but of the tree of the knowledge of good and evil you shall not eat, for in the day that you eat the fruit of it you shall surely die.""** Adam did not have sin in him at that time, but he did have *freewill*. He could choose either *for* God or *against* God; and it

---

[8] We can learn from various passages of Scripture that Satan was a fallen cherub (a spirit being, and probably an angel of the highest rank—an archangel), who had chosen to act independently of God because of pride. He had led a rebellion against God before this time. We cannot be absolutely certain whether the serpent in the Garden of Eden was a description of Satan, based on his character ("serpent" implies a beguiling, enchanting creature, seeking to attract our attention for treacherous reasons), or a literal physical animal through which Satan spoke. There is strong evidence that it was a literal creature in the Garden through which Satan spoke. Satan's history is outlined in Ezekiel 28:12-19 and Isaiah 14:12-15 and is explained in Basic Bible Study 18, entitled "The Three Falls of Satan." Ezekiel 28:12 confirms that, at first, Satan was full of wisdom and very beautiful.

[9] An explanation of how the Son of God (Jesus Christ) appeared in the Old Testament and why *Jehovah Elohim* may refer to Christ appearing in the Garden of Eden is given in Appendix 3 at the back of this book. Note that *Jehovah* is a transliteration, with vowels added, of the covenant name of God in the Old Testament, which comprised the four Hebrew consonants YHWH. This name may also be rendered as *Yahweh*, and appears in most Bible versions as "LORD" or "GOD" (using capital letters).

was in this matter of the tree of the knowledge of good and evil that his freewill would be tested.

In the last phrase of verse 17, **"you shall surely die"**, the verb 'die' is repeated in the Hebrew for emphasis and could literally be translated, **"dying, you shall die."** Jesus was saying to Adam that the moment he ate of this tree he would die *spiritually*, with the result that he would later die *physically* too. "**For the wages of sin is death**" (Romans 6:23). Spiritual death would mean being separated from God, the source of spiritual life; and physical death would result.

The LORD God then made Eve, who became Adam's wife. They lived in the Garden, naked and with no shame. It seems Jesus used to walk in the Garden, where He talked and communed with Adam and Eve; and they enjoyed unhindered fellowship with Him.

SATAN DECEIVES EVE BY HIS CRAFTINESS

Coming back to Genesis 3, the cunning serpent spoke to Eve: "**And he said to the woman, "Has God indeed said, 'You shall not eat of every tree of the garden'?"**" (verse 1b). It was probably Satan himself or a demon inside the serpent who spoke, perhaps whispering in Eve's ear in the same way that today Satan usually speaks with a whisper in our ear. (That is why we need the helmet of salvation to cover our ears! Our minds need to be protected from Satan's lies by a thorough knowledge of the truth of God's Word.)

The serpent asked Eve, **"Has God indeed said...?"** It is interesting that Satan did not say "LORD God" (*Jehovah Elohim*) but just **"God"** (*Elohim*). It had been the LORD God who had told Adam not to eat from the tree of the knowledge of good and evil. Satan did what religious[10] people always do: by implication, he subtly cut out the blood of Jesus.

Religious people always like to talk about "God", but not about the real Jesus Christ who shed His blood. But if the blood of Jesus Christ is not at the centre of our religion, there is no salvation. Did Buddha or Mohammed or Mary Baker Eddy or any other religious leader ever shed their blood for our sins? No. But the Bible makes clear that "**without**

---

[10] The words 'religious' and 'religion' in these studies are used in the sense of external religiosity. The word 'religion' is derived from the Latin *religio*, thought by most scholars to be derived from *religare*, meaning 'to bind', which implies a system of belief which binds adherents to an external form but which lacks inner reality. "**True and undefiled religion**", however, is a binding to God Himself, with resulting spiritual fruit (see James 1:27).

shedding of blood there is no remission [of sins]" (Hebrews 9:22). Blood is *essential* to our salvation. Other religions cut out the need for the blood of Jesus; they think it is vulgar. But in Old Testament times, in the Tabernacle and the Temple there was blood 'everywhere'; the High Priest regularly used to come out caked in blood from head to toe. The Bible has numerous references to blood, because blood is essential to our salvation.[11]

Sadly, Eve fell into the trap and, in Genesis 3:2-3, she repeated the Satanic error. "**And the woman said to the serpent, "We may eat the fruit of the trees of the garden; but of the fruit of the tree which is in the midst of the garden, God has said, 'You shall not eat it, nor shall you touch it, lest you die.'"**" By saying, **"God has said"**, she had begun to decline into deception, accepting what Satan had said and reasoning it through. (It is no sin to hear something from Satan, but when we take what he says and begin to consider it and agree with it, we are in trouble. We should quickly dismiss what he says.)

Eve not only said, **"God"** (*Elohim*), instead of "*Jehovah Elohim*", but she added **"nor shall you touch it"** to the command Jesus had given Adam in Genesis 2:17. This also was religion: *religion always adds something to the truth and emphasizes outward show rather than inner reality*.[12] To eat the fruit would indeed affect Eve spiritually, but to touch it was just an outward thing. Eve had thus given in to religion not only by cutting out the blood but also by adding **"nor shall you touch it"**.

The serpent then suggested to Eve that what the LORD God had said was not true: "**And the serpent said to the woman, "You will not surely die"**" (Genesis 3:4). In fact, the LORD God had said to Adam, **"in the day that you eat the fruit of it you shall surely die"**—that is, "**dying** [spiritually]**, you shall die** [physically].**"** Satan was suggesting that this

---

[11] Nowhere in the Bible are we told to, "Believe in God the Father and be saved!" (or, "Believe in the Holy Spirit!"), but rather, in Acts 16:31, the Philippian jailer was told, "Believe on the Lord Jesus Christ and you will be saved". This is because Jesus Christ is the only way to the Father, and Jesus is the only member of the Godhead who shed His blood for our sins. The term Jehovah Elohim has the blood of Jesus right at the core. A covenant was almost always made with blood, and Jesus' blood is central to the covenant made between God and man.

[12] Because the Bible says that in the days of Noah people were eating and drinking, marrying and being given in marriage (Matthew 24:38), some religious people say that drinking alcohol is always wrong. However, should the other three of these things be stopped too? That would be absurd! No, rather, the Bible makes clear that those who choose to drink alcohol should do so responsibly, especially if they have responsibilities in the Lord. Total abstinence might have an outer show of spirituality, but the inner reality of the Lord dwelling within us is what matters. Paul told Timothy to drink a little wine (1 Timothy 5:23) and, despite what some may say, it was alcoholic!

THE BARRIER

warning didn't make sense. Eve may well have thought, "God wouldn't want to kill me, would He? He loves me!"

In Genesis 3:5, Satan then played a very clever trick. He insinuated that God was jealous of Eve and was so proud that He did not want anyone else to become just like He was: **"For God knows that in the day you eat of it your eyes will be opened, and you will be like God, knowing good and evil."** This was a terrible blasphemy, and Eve fell straight into the trap.[13]

EVE AND ADAM DISOBEY GOD

"So when the woman saw that the tree was good for food, that it was pleasant to the eyes, and a tree desirable to make one wise..." (Genesis 3:6a). The forbidden tree now became the only tree that Eve wanted to gaze at and eat from, although she had every other type of tree from which she could freely eat. (There is no evidence that the fruit of the forbidden tree was an apple, as is popularly assumed. It was the fact that it was forbidden that was significant.) She also now wanted to eat from the forbidden tree because she thought this tree was **"desirable to make one wise"**. She now wanted above all to be wise, like God, and was no longer satisfied with trusting God. What did she do?

Tragically, **"She took its fruit and ate"** (Genesis 3:6b). She had been deceived by Satan and so she decided to disobey God's command given to Adam. Immediately she was cut off from her relationship with God—that is, she died spiritually.

"She also gave to her husband with her, and he ate" (Genesis 3:6c). When Adam ate of the fruit, he did so deliberately, knowing what the results of his action would be: **"And Adam was not deceived, but the woman being deceived, fell into transgression"** (1 Timothy 2:14). The

---

[13] Note that *Elohim* is translated "God" in the phrase, "you will be like God". This translation is probably correct (see Genesis 3:22), although it could legitimately be translated "gods."

Elohim, the Hebrew word for God, is strictly a plural word, because it ends -im (it is probably the plural form of *Eloah* and is the type of plural indicating more than two). When it is used of the one true God it is generally used with a singular verb. *Elohim* is also used of the gods of the nations, angels or judges etc. (meaning 'god-like ones'), but then it is used with a plural verb. In most cases, the meaning is clear from the context. Here in Genesis 3:5 it is not absolutely clear whether *Elohim* should be translated as "God" or "gods." The latter translation would imply that Satan was tempting Eve to become like he was, with a self-sufficient 'wisdom,' but independent of God.

This rather strange usage of a plural noun for the one true God can readily be understood by a Christian, who believes that God is both one and three in number at the same time. Even in the Old Testament the "Trinity" could be glimpsed.

Bible says that Eve was *deceived* by Satan's craftiness (see 2 Corinthians 11:3) and thus fell into transgression. In contrast, Adam was not deceived; he knowingly chose to sin.

Imagine the scene: Adam was with Eve and saw her eat the fruit and change as she became cut off from God. (She may have lost her clothing of light.[14]) Adam was not yet cut off from God, but was still enjoying glorious fellowship with God. He could therefore choose either God or Eve for fellowship. Deliberately and premeditatedly, he took the fruit for himself, in disobedience to the LORD God's direct command to him; he wanted fellowship with his fallen wife rather than with God. Adam was thus more worthy of blame than Eve.

THE EFFECTS OF THE FALL

Through these actions, commonly known as "The Fall of Man", sin entered the world, and both Adam and Eve became 'fallen' beings. The tragedy of it was that this Fall affected the entire human race, and Adam's one sin led to all the misery experienced by the millions and millions of people in this world.

As we will examine in the next study, what I call the *'old sin nature'* was born in them both at this very time, and this fallen nature is now passed on to all of us, who are Adam's descendants. This means that every person has an irresistible propensity to commit sins. Every child who is born, even before committing a sin, is a sinner by nature, because he or she has an old sin nature.

We can now understand how the bricks in the barrier came about. Sin entered the human race through Adam's one act of disobedience, and all men became sinners (brick one). Being sinners, with an old sin nature, every person inevitably commits sins, which God must punish (brick two). Every person is born spiritually dead—with a human spirit cut off from the life of God and defunct (brick three). Every person is utterly incapable of being accepted by God in view of their character (brick four). Every fallen person is also incapable of pleasing God or becoming

---

[14] There is some evidence in Scripture to suggest that Adam and Eve were clothed in light and glowing radiantly before they fell—in a similar manner as Jesus shone when He was transfigured (see Matthew 17:2 etc.) and His glory was revealed. Psalm 104:2 says that God covers Himself with light as with a garment, and Adam and Eve were made in God's image. Moses' face shone when he talked with God (Exodus 34:29-35), so much so that he used to put a veil over his face when he spoke to the children of Israel. Our resurrection bodies might shine similarly (see Matthew 13:43).

acceptable to Him on the basis of his or her own good works (brick five), as Adam and Eve soon discovered, and as we will see next. Another problem was also introduced: Adam and Eve both began to decay physically, and their eventual physical death became inevitable. This established yet another brick (brick six).

ADAM AND EVE REALIZE THEY ARE NAKED BEFORE GOD

"Then the eyes of both of them were opened, and they knew that they were naked" (Genesis 3:7a). Adam and Eve, who before the Fall had probably been clothed in light, now suddenly saw themselves as they really were and knew that they were naked. Before this time, it had not been necessary for them to know this. God had not wanted them to know this, nor had He wanted them to know the difference between good and evil; He'd only wanted them to know Him and depend on Him. He had wanted them to have fellowship with Him based on trust.

"And they sewed fig leaves together and made themselves coverings" (verse 7b). The word for **"coverings"** (**"aprons"** in the AV) is literally 'loin cloths' or 'girdles,' and the word translated **"sewed"** means 'to bring two things together and join them.' This is the first case of religious "good works." Adam and Eve felt guilt and shame, and were trying to cover their nakedness with leaves and hide from God. Could they? Of course not! But they were content with their efforts. This typifies religion: trying to cover up sin and shame and, by good deeds, trying to *earn* one's own salvation. Religious people believe that good deeds can help them become acceptable to God. But God is absolutely holy and righteous, and *He* says that all such 'good' deeds are as **"filthy rags"** to Him (Isaiah 64:6).

Such an attempt to win God's favour by good works can never succeed. If we could save ourselves, then Jesus Christ would not have had to die. When Jesus said, **"It is finished!"** on the Cross (John 19:30), He was stating that nothing else could be added to the work He had done.

We do not have to *do* anything to gain our salvation; instead, we must, **"Believe on the Lord Jesus Christ, and [we] will be saved"** (Acts 16:31). Our salvation is not dependent on works; rather, it is a *gift* from God. **"For by grace you have been saved through faith, and that not of yourselves; it is the gift of God, not of works, lest anyone should boast"** (Ephesians 2:8-9). *Grace* is the absence of works. We can never earn our salvation. Grace is undeserved: we do nothing and yet God gives to us; it involves no works. However, religion—that is, *legalism*—is opposed to the principle of God's grace; and therefore God hates mere external religion.

Adam and Eve thus made loin cloths in an attempt to cover their sin and nakedness. This was in response to the shame they suddenly experienced when they realized they were naked. But their real problem was that they were cut off from God as a result of their disobedience.

ADAM AND EVE ARE SHOWN GRACE

"And they heard the sound of the LORD God walking in the garden in the cool of the day, and Adam and his wife hid themselves from the presence of the LORD God among the trees of the garden" (Genesis 3:8). Adam and Eve deserved to be abandoned by Jesus and to receive judgment. However, despite what they deserved, they were given grace! Jesus came to them again, walking in physical form in the Garden.

Up to this point, the trees had been a great blessing to them; but now the trees were something to hide behind. Religious people will be in for a terrible shock one day, when they die full of their good deeds. The moment they catch sight of Jesus, they will search for a tree to hide behind to prevent Him from seeing their nakedness. But, there is only one tree we can hide behind—the Cross of Calvary!

Jesus called out to Adam, **"Where are you?"** (Genesis 3:9b). This is grace if ever there was grace. Adam did not speak out to the LORD God, nor did Eve speak out to Him (she had had quite a conversation with the serpent, but had not said a word to Jesus). Instead, *Jesus spoke* to Adam in his fallen state. Adam did not earn this or deserve it. But Jesus loved Adam and Eve and wanted them to realize that they were no longer in fellowship with Him. And that is grace!

"So he (Adam) said, "I heard Your voice in the garden, and I was afraid because I was naked; and I hid myself"" (Genesis 3:10). Adam experienced fear when He heard Jesus' voice. Although he was covered by fig leaves, they had no effect whatsoever. He realized that he was naked when he heard Jesus approaching; it was as if the fig leaves withered up. His covering—his good works—were useless, because Jesus was so righteous. He'd spent time and effort making his loin cloth, but it was to no avail. Adam now knew he would be naked no matter what he might do to try and cover himself.

Even with ten million good deeds, we are still naked before God. Yet, despite our sin, if we come to God trusting in Jesus Christ, we are accepted in heaven, clothed with a white robe, and are made righteous in His sight!

In Genesis 3:11-12, Jesus interviewed Adam: **"Who told you that you were naked? Have you eaten from the tree of which I commanded you that you should not eat?"** (verse 11). Adam had no knowledge of good and evil before this time, yet now he realized he was naked. Jesus was asking Adam how he knew this. **"Then the man said, "The woman whom You gave to be with me, she gave me the fruit of the tree, and I ate""** (verse 12). Instead of admitting his sin, Adam passed the buck to Eve—the first instance of passing the buck! He also indirectly blamed Jesus, for giving Eve to him.

Jesus then interviewed Eve, and she too passed the buck. She blamed the serpent! **"And the LORD God said to the woman, "What is this you have done?" And the woman said, "The serpent deceived me, and I ate""** (Genesis 3:13). Eve at least admitted being deceived.

We commonly pass the buck for our failings, but we should not. We tend to pass the blame to a wife or husband or other family members, or to others in our church or fellowship. If we cannot think of anyone else to blame or no one else will take the blame, then we usually blame God! We have to recognize that if there is something spiritually wrong in our lives, we ourselves are responsible. We must learn that the buck stops with us. No one else should be blamed for obstructing our fellowship with God.

SUMMARY

Genesis 3 is a record of how Adam sinned and, in so doing, introduced sin into the whole human race. Eve was deceived, but Adam sinned knowingly; and, as head of the human race, he was the one who allowed sin to enter mankind. The rest of Genesis 3 will be covered in the next study, which looks at the necessity for the virgin birth of Christ.

In conclusion, here are three passages which confirm the effects of this "Fall of Man." The details will be examined in future studies.

Romans 5:12. **"Therefore, just as through one man sin entered the world, and death through sin, and thus death spread to all men, because all sinned..."** Sin entered the world through the one man Adam; Eve is not mentioned. And because sin entered, the second brick—the penalty of sin—was also introduced. *Death* is the penalty of sin, and so death passed to all men, because all—including all of us—have sinned.

1 Corinthians 15:21-22. **"For since by man came death, by man also came the resurrection of the dead. For as in Adam all die, even so in Christ all shall be made alive."** We are all descended from Adam. Therefore, we are all born spiritually dead, and are all destined to experience physical death. However, as in Adam all die, so in Christ all shall be made alive (which refers to future resurrection).

1 Timothy 2:13-14. **"For Adam was formed first, then Eve. And Adam was not deceived, but the woman being deceived, fell into transgression."** Both Adam and Eve were guilty, but it was Adam who deliberately sinned. An insurmountable barrier between God and man was therefore established by the Fall. We will analyse this barrier in the next few studies, each brick in turn, and see how the answer has been provided to each one. All of the bricks were dealt with forever by the Lord Jesus Christ through His work on the Cross.

NOTES

3. THE VIRGIN BIRTH

In this chapter we shall look again at the condition of fallen man, but this time in greater detail. First, we will see how God designed us to function, by considering Adam before and after he fell. We will then be in a position to understand why Jesus' virgin birth was essential if He was to be a Saviour for mankind.

BODY, SPIRIT AND SOUL [1]

The creation of the first man Adam is described in Genesis chapters 1 and 2. "**And the LORD God formed man (Adam) of the dust of the ground, and breathed into his nostrils the breath of life; and man became a living being**" (Genesis 2:7). The LORD God moulded Adam's body out of the dust of the earth, just as a potter moulds something out of clay. He then breathed the breath (or spirit) of life into Adam's body; this refers to his human spirit being created. Adam thus became a living being, or a "**living soul**" (1 Corinthians 15:45a). He had a body and a human spirit; and the moment his spirit entered his body he became alive—a living soul.

Adam had a body made from the dust of the ground and a spirit which came from God. (*Adam*, meaning 'man' in Hebrew, derives from the word for "**ground**", *adamah,* which means 'red-earth'.) Adam was thus both earthly and heavenly. As a living soul, Adam had an intellect (a mind), emotions and a will. He was alive spiritually and physically.

---

[1] This section has been updated in line with Roger Price's later and more detailed teaching on this subject, in Special Topic Studies STS 101 to 105, entitled "The Healthy Christian". That man's being comprises three distinguishable, yet integrated, parts can be seen in 1 Thessalonians 5:23, Hebrews 4:12, 1 Corinthians 2:14-3:4 for example. The soul comes about when our human spirit enters our body. This can be described in the following way: body + spirit ⇨ soul + body + spirit. The soul and spirit are the invisible part of man.

Note that the human soul, once created, is eternal; it does not cease to exist when the spirit leaves the body at physical death. Because the human spirit of unbelievers is 'dead,' it is hidden within the soul; therefore the Hebrew and Greek words for 'soul' and 'spirit' are sometimes used synonymously. To be alive we must have a spirit, and hence a soul; consequently the words for 'soul' in both Hebrew and Greek also mean 'life.'

God had designed Adam's human spirit to be the 'power-house' which would receive life and power from Himself. That spiritual life was to pass out from Adam's human spirit to fill and empower his soul (his mind, emotions and will) as well as his body. Adam's whole inner being would thus be filled continuously with the life and presence of God, and his body would be a 'temple' of the Holy Spirit.

Like Adam, we who are physically alive have a human body and spirit, and we are living souls. We inherit our bodies from our parents, but our spirit is formed by God (Zechariah 12:1). We too are thus earthly and heavenly. With the body we relate to and experience the physical world, and express ourselves. With the soul we experience ourselves and other people (it includes our self-consciousness, our personality, our emotions, mind and will). We also have a human spirit: that part of us which relates to the spiritual realm. With our spirits we are conscious of God; and through our spirits we relate to, worship and have fellowship with God.[2]

Spiritual death and the Old sin nature

The moment Adam sinned, his human spirit lost contact with the source of its life—God Himself. God communicates with us spiritually (that is through our human spirit), but now God's Spirit was no longer united with Adam's spirit and the Holy Spirit 'withdrew'. Although after the Fall Adam retained his body, and his mind, will and emotions still functioned, he was now empty of God. Adam needed the life of God in his spirit to be able to function effectively, but now he was separated from the source of true life. His spirit, while still there, became inoperative and 'dead'. This is what we call "spiritual death"—the human spirit being 'cut off' or separated from God. ('Death' means the absence of life.)

As power ebbs when a battery fails, so Adam's fallen spirit ceased to give out spiritual life and energy. It was plunged into darkness, having lost contact with God. Adam's soul was also plunged into darkness and discord; and his body became subject to stress, sickness, decay and, eventually, to physical death.

---

[2] "The earth was created for man's body; man's body was created for man's spirit; and, man's spirit was created for God. Man's spirit was designed to be subject to God; man's body was designed to be subject to his spirit; and, the earth was designed to be subject to man's body" (Hugo St. Victor). Body, soul and spirit all affect each other. The soul can be viewed as the 'central' or 'pivotal' part of man, connecting body and spirit. In the soul is our will, by which we choose to live by or reject the influences of our spirit or body, and choose for or against God's will and dependency upon Him.

The LORD God had warned Adam not to eat from the tree of the knowledge of good and evil, saying, **"In the day that you eat the fruit of it you shall surely die"** (more literally, **"...dying, you shall surely die"**), as we saw in Genesis 2:17. Therefore when Adam sinned he immediately died spiritually, with the result that he would eventually die physically.

We saw in the last chapter how, through this one man's disobedience, sin and death entered the world (Romans 5:12) and that **"in Adam, all die"** (1 Corinthians 15:22).[3] Adam's sin therefore brought sin and death to all of us.

However, Adam not only died spiritually at the Fall; something else happened to him at that time in conjunction with spiritual death—what I call the *'old sin nature'* (or the *'sinful nature'* or *'fallen nature'*) began to operate within him. This principle of sin began to affect his whole being,[4] and thus he was now not only dead to communion with God and physically decaying, but also hopelessly in bondage to a sinful lifestyle.

Adam passed this old sin nature on to all his descendants, who in turn passed a sinful nature on to their descendants. Both Cain and Abel were thus born not only spiritually dead, but with an old sin nature too. And we have all inherited this old sin nature from Adam. In fact, every person in this world has such an old sin nature, because every person is ultimately descended from Adam.

The instant we are born, we need saving.[5] Although it has done nothing wrong, even a new-born baby possesses a sinful human nature and a lifeless human spirit. We are thus all born 'sinners' by nature, and that is why we all sin.

---

[3] This verse in context probably refers to physical death but, as we have seen, physical death is a direct result of spiritual death. Adam's disobedience caused both spiritual death and physical death to enter the human race.

[4] Adam's whole being—spirit, soul and body—was affected by the Fall. (This is what is meant by "total depravity".) His body and soul now began to dominate his spirit. His spirit was damaged, and his body became subject to stress and decay. He became self-centred and vulnerable to evil thoughts. He had come to know good and evil, but the principle of sin now at work in him meant he tended to dwell on evil thoughts. His will became fundamentally biased away from God, and he now tended to choose independence from God. His emotions were also affected, and his emotional responses now included fear, anger, sadness, depression.

[5] Though he does not state it here, Roger Price definitely believed that life begins at conception and that the sinful nature is present from conception (Psalm 51:5). It should not, however, be concluded from this that every baby who is stillborn or who dies young is automatically unsaved; there is evidence in Scripture to the contrary (for example, 2 Samuel 12:23).

Adam sinned deliberately, whereas Eve was deceived. Therefore, the old sin nature was passed on to Cain and Abel through Adam, and it is passed on by every father to his children.[6]

If you do not understand that Adam fell, then neither will you understand that *you have an old sin nature*. However, if you are a Christian, you should know it is true, because the old sin nature opposes and rebels against the work of God's Spirit in our lives. God wants to move through His Spirit in our lives and change us, but the old sin nature tends to hold us back all the time and drag us down.

The tragic fall of the whole human race occurred as a result of the events described in Genesis chapter 3, which we saw in the last study. The amazing thing, as we will now see, is that God's answer to this problem of spiritual death and the old sin nature, and indeed to the whole barrier, was also first revealed in exactly the same passage—in Genesis 3.

GRACE AND JUDGMENTS

Genesis 3:11-13 showed us how Jesus questioned Adam and Eve immediately after the Fall. As we saw, they both passed the buck, just as we tend to do. Adam blamed Eve, and then God; Eve then blamed the serpent. However, in verses 14-19, we also see God's grace revealed, because judgment was meted out in the reverse order.

"So the LORD God said to the serpent: "Because you have done this, you are cursed more than all cattle, and more than every beast of the field; on your belly you shall go, and you shall eat dust all the days of your life. (Verse 14.) **And I will put enmity between you and the woman, and between your seed and her Seed. He shall bruise your head, and you shall bruise His heel."** (Verse 15.)

"To the woman He said: "I will greatly multiply your sorrow and your conception; in pain you shall bring forth children; your desire shall be for your husband, and he shall rule over you."" (Verse 16.)

---

[6] *God created man (Adam) "in the image of God" (Genesis 1:27a), "in the likeness of God" (Genesis 5:1b). However, when Adam and Eve had children, the Bible says that, "Adam...begot a son in his own likeness, after his image" (Genesis 5:3). This can be interpreted as referring to Adam passing on his fallen nature, as well as physical and character traits, to his children.*

    This fallen nature is passed on by a father to each of his children. We all have an old sin nature, and we will continue to do so while we are on this earth. However, the good news is that Jesus Christ provided the answer to the old sin nature. We who are believers also receive a new nature, and in our resurrection bodies there will be no sinful nature.

THE VIRGIN BIRTH

"Then to Adam He said, "Because you have heeded the voice of your wife, and have eaten from the tree of which I commanded you, saying, 'You shall not eat from it': Cursed is the ground for your sake; in toil you shall eat from it all the days of your life. Both thorns and thistles it shall bring forth for you, and you shall eat the herb of the field. In the sweat of your face you shall eat bread till you return to the ground, for out of it you were taken; for dust you are, and to dust you shall return."" (Verses 17-19.)

The order of the verses here is very interesting. Note how the serpent was judged first (in verse 14) and *then* the glorious message of salvation was revealed (in verse 15), as we will see below. This was God's answer to the Fall, and it is the first mention of the gospel in the Bible. Only *after* salvation was preached did judgment come on the woman (verse 16) and the man (verses 17-19). This is wonderful; Jesus preached the gospel of salvation to them *before* they were judged.[7] This shows us two things:

1. *Grace always comes before judgment* for mankind. Salvation was preached to Adam and Eve because it applied to them as human beings, and grace was revealed before judgment was pronounced. God *always* gives blessing before cursing, and the gospel *always* comes before judgment. This is an important principle found throughout the Bible: with God there is *always* grace before judgment.[8]

2. Salvation does not apply to animals or fallen angels. There was no salvation for the serpent. But the serpent was representative of Satan. Satan had already rebelled against God before the time of man's Fall, and he would have no second chance.

"So the LORD God said to the serpent: "...On your belly you shall go, and you shall eat dust all the days of your life"" (Genesis 3:14). We saw earlier that this serpent (*nachash* in Hebrew) had probably been a beautiful creature. Undoubtedly, the serpent's body was changed when judgment was pronounced upon it.

---

[7] It is interesting to reflect that Adam and Eve are both almost certainly in heaven today (as explained more fully in the next study.) This is amazing when one considers how religious they had been: they had tried to cover themselves. But the idiocy of this was pointed out to them by Jesus, who showed them that He would shed His blood for their sins. It seems that they believed on the Lord. What a remarkable salvation we have!

[8] This is the main theme of the second series of Basic Bible Studies (BBS 15 to 28). There is judgment with God, but He always shows mercy and gives grace first. "There is therefore now no condemnation (judgment) to those who are in Christ Jesus" (Romans 8:1), that is, for those who believe on Him.

A snake can only move along by moving its spine, because it has no legs. Neither does it have any arms to pick up its prey or dust it off; so a snake has to swallow dust and dirt when it eats its food. This may be evidence of this permanent judgment on the serpent (Isaiah 65:25).

When we consider how Satan was behind the serpent, this judgment was very significant. It pointed to the victory God would one day win over Satan, through His glorious plan of salvation.[9]

Have you ever noticed that most snakes cannot rise very high above the ground? A poisonous snake does not need to—it can bite a man's foot without raising itself, and then the victim's bloodstream will carry the poison throughout the body. On the other hand, a man has a great advantage over a snake because of his upright posture; a snake is therefore quite vulnerable as far as man is concerned. The next verse shows the significance of this.

SALVATION FIRST REVEALED IN GENESIS 3:15

In Genesis 3:15, Jesus went on to declare God's answer to the Fall, and the glorious message of salvation was first revealed. This is the first mention of the gospel in the Bible, and it is vitally important: **"And I will put enmity between you and the woman, and between your seed and her Seed. He shall bruise your head, and you shall bruise His heel"** (Genesis 3:15).

It is important to notice that there is no mention of Adam here; rather, the LORD God said that He would put enmity between the 'seed (offspring) of the serpent' and the 'seed of the *woman.*' To whom was He referring?

We know that Satan was the personality behind the serpent, and so Jesus was saying there would be enmity between 'the seed of *Satan*' and 'the seed of the woman.' The Bible is its own commentary, and to understand who is (or who are) the seed of Satan we need to turn to John chapter 8.

Verses 23 and 24 of John 8 tell us how Jesus spoke to the religious unbelieving Jews, and said, **"You are from beneath; I am from above. You are of this world; I am not of this world. Therefore I said to you that you will die in your sins; for if you do not believe that I am He,**

---

[9] From the point of view of this being a judgment pronounced on Satan, verse 14 suggests that the plot conceived by Satan to destroy mankind, by turning him against God and bringing him under the judgment of God, would come to nothing. Satan would be brought low and would live to regret his foolish scheme for the rest of eternity, and would be afraid of God's ultimate judgment (cf. Micah 7:17).

you will die in your sins." Jesus was giving the gospel to these non-believing Jews.

In John 8:44, He went on to say to them, **"You are of your father the devil, and the desires of your father you want to do. He was a murderer from the beginning, and does not stand in the truth, because there is no truth in him. When he speaks a lie, he speaks from his own resources, for he is a liar and the father of it."** (We need to realize that if we listen to Satan or walk in darkness, we cannot receive any truth. Jesus is the only One to whom we should listen.)

Every person who does not believe on the Lord Jesus Christ is in bondage to this world and to the god of this world, who is Satan. Every single person born in this world who is not a believer is therefore of his or her father the devil.

In contrast, for those of us who are believers, our Father is in heaven and we are included in God's family. Believers are **"children of God"** (see 1 John 3:1, John 1:12 for example) and **"sons of God"** (see Galatians 3:26 for example). This implies that the 'seed of the woman' could refer to all believers.

In John 16:33, Jesus said to His disciples, **"In the world you will have tribulation"**. Also, He said, **"If the world hates you, you know that it hated Me before it hated you...Yet because you are not of the world...therefore the world hates you"** (John 15:18-19). There are thus two distinct camps in the world today: those whose father is Satan and those who have God as their Father in heaven. There is no such thing as a "universal brotherhood of man."

It is not surprising that there is tribulation when we recognize this fundamental enmity between Satan's seed—the unbelievers—and those who are believers. There has to come a point where we are different. The gospel has split families and love affairs apart: **"I (Jesus) did not come to bring peace but a sword"** (Matthew 10:34). The peace that Jesus promised was not 'world peace,' but a peace between man and God. Anyone who believes on the Lord Jesus Christ can have that peace with God. However, he or she will also then be at enmity with the world.[10]

---

[10] The term "world" (kosmos in Greek) in the New Testament refers to more than just the earth. It often means those who are alienated from God and are hostile to the cause of Christ. It also refers to all aspects of the created order that are hostile to God and His purposes, being part of the organized evil which Satan controls and directs (1 John 5:19).

However, 'the seed of the woman' alludes to Jesus Christ Himself. Genesis 3:15b refers to the woman's Seed as "**He**", and it is clear from other parts of Scripture that it has Jesus specifically in mind. We will now examine this in some detail.

THE VIRGIN BIRTH FORETOLD IN GENESIS

The 'Seed of the woman' is Jesus Christ. He was not called the "seed of Adam" or the "seed of the man". It is vital to understand this, because *it pointed to the virgin birth of Jesus Christ.*

There are some people today, including even some Christians, who say the virgin birth of Christ was not important. It is interesting that the first mention of the gospel in the Bible emphasized the virgin birth. Why was it necessary?

As we have seen briefly, all people have inherited an old sin nature from their human fathers, and are thus all slaves to sin. Mohammed, Buddha, Mahatma Ghandi, Mary Baker Eddy, and so on, were all slaves to sin, because they had human fathers. A slave in the ancient world could not possibly buy another slave; that would be ridiculous! It required a *'free-man'*—one who was not a slave—to buy a slave out of bondage. Therefore, using this same analogy, a saviour for mankind had to be someone free from slavery to sin in every way. Only then could he buy freedom for others who were in bondage to sin. Therefore he had to be someone *without a human father.*[11]

Jesus Christ *was* such a man! He was born of Mary, but His Father was God. This is why the *woman's* seed was specifically mentioned in Genesis 3:15 and why Jesus was born from a human woman only. If Jesus had had a *human* father, He would have been born with a sinful nature and a dead human spirit, and thus He would have been a slave to sin like all of us—and salvation would have been impossible. Genesis 3:15 is therefore not only the first statement of the good news of salvation in the Bible, but a clear statement about Christ's virgin birth.

The plan of God is astounding! God had planned all of this before Adam was even created. God knew that Adam, and thus all mankind, would fall; so, in His marvellous plan, the Saviour of mankind was to be born of a virgin! Jesus, the Son of God, had no sinful nature and He was spiritually alive throughout His life up to the Cross. He lived a perfect

---

[11] This subject is dealt with in detail in the next study, where it is called "redemption."

life and, at the Cross, no one—neither Satan, nor any Pharisee or other Jew, nor anyone else—could accuse Him of any sin.

Jesus Christ: God and Man

Jesus was the only human being ever who was not a sinner at birth. And it was because the fallen nature is passed on through the male that Jesus Christ came from the woman only. The virgin birth was therefore absolutely necessary. And remarkably, it was revealed in Genesis some 4000 years before Mary conceived Jesus by the Holy Spirit!

Jesus Christ is therefore unique (that is, the only one). As a man, He is also God. He is unique in the Godhead too, because, as God, He became a man. God the Father and God the Holy Spirit are not man; but Jesus Christ the Son of God is both God and man, perfectly united, forever. He is the union of God and man in one Person, and has in Himself both the nature of God and the nature of man. He is the perfect example of God and man in union and reconciled. This union is a mystery, which is sometimes called the "hypostatic union."

But how could God die on the Cross? The answer is that *God* did not die on the Cross. Jesus Christ did not die in His *divinity*; rather, He died in His *humanity*. How do we know this? It has to be the case, because one of the attributes of God is that He is eternal: He continues forever, with no beginning and no end. So *God* was not dead for three days between the Cross and the resurrection. Rather, Jesus died in His humanity only.

Similarly, God is omnipresent (that is, He is present everywhere). Jesus in His humanity was not omnipresent, but in His divinity He was. God is also omniscient (all-knowing) and omnipotent (all-powerful). In His divinity, Jesus knew everything and could do anything by His power. However, despite being fully God, Jesus assumed the nature of a man, and as a man voluntarily humbled Himself and became as a servant. Whilst dwelling on earth, He chose not to exercise His divine power and knowledge etc., but instead, chose to be completely dependent on and subject to His Father in heaven and the Holy Spirit.[12] He lived on earth as

---

[12] Jesus' total submission to His Father's will is shown, for example, in: John 5:19, 30; 8:28; 14:10. When Jesus, who is the Son of God, chose to leave His glorious position in heaven and to become a man, He chose to live His life on earth on human terms as a bond-servant (Philippians 2:6-8). In His humanity, Jesus voluntarily took on certain limitations, such as in knowledge (see Mark 13:22). However, these limitations did not mean He ceased to be God in any way or that He gave up His authority as God, but rather that He chose to lay aside His right to exercise His divine prerogatives and chose to be dependent on His Father's will for any exercise of His divine abilities.

a man with limitations, His whole being surrendered to God's will: the perfect example of what God intended man to be.

The Virgin Birth foretold in Isaiah

This mystery of God becoming a man was also revealed later and more clearly in the Book of Isaiah, which was written some 700 years before Christ came in the flesh. Isaiah would certainly have studied the Book of Genesis, and from Genesis 3:15 he had probably understood all about the virgin birth of the Messiah.

Isaiah wrote, "**Therefore the Lord Himself will give you a sign: Behold, the virgin shall conceive and bear a Son, and shall call His name Immanuel**" (Isaiah 7:14). This was one of numerous signs given to the Jews to alert them to look out for their Messiah. Other signs included: the throwing down of 30 pieces of silver in the Temple; Jesus' miracles, which were like credentials to say the Messiah was come;[13] the rending of the curtain in the Temple in two when Jesus died; and, many others.

The Hebrew word used in Isaiah 7:14 for "**virgin**" (*almah*) can also be translated 'young woman', and some have used this to cast doubt on the virgin birth. However, unfortunately for these critics, in Matthew 1:23, when Matthew quoted from Isaiah 7:14, the Greek word which he used (*parthenos*) can only mean a 'virgin'. The word for "**sign**" meant 'miracle'. Thus the Jews were to look for a miraculous event, which was that a baby boy would be born to a virgin. One of His titles was to be "**Immanuel**", meaning 'God is with us.'

Isaiah 9:6 confirmed it: "**For unto us a child is born, unto us a Son is given; and the government will be upon His shoulder...**" This is a very important verse, which also spoke to the Jews of the virgin birth of their Messiah. The Hebrew word used for "**child**" is from a word meaning 'to bear,' and pointed to Jesus' humanity—He would be *born* as a baby (requiring a human mother). The word "**Son**" pointed to Jesus' divinity—He would be "**given**" as a Son rather than born—and to the fatherhood of God. Thus, in this verse, the humanity and divinity of the Messiah were revealed, going hand in hand.

---

[13] One miracle for example, was the cleansing of the leper (Matthew 8:1-3, Luke 5:12-15). For the first time, a Jewish leper was cleansed—and he went to the priests, asking them to implement the instructions given in Leviticus 14. Such signs, including this miracle, are discussed in chapter 6.

THE VIRGIN BIRTH   BBS 3

In the future kingdom of God on earth (during the period sometimes known as the '*Millennium*'),[14] which Isaiah described in many places, **"the government will be upon His shoulder"**. Indeed, the Bible says that Jesus **"shall rule them [the nations] with a rod of iron"** (Revelation 2:27, quoting Psalm 2:9; see also Revelation 19:15).

Isaiah 9:6 goes on to say, "**...And His name will be called Wonderful, Counsellor, Mighty God, Everlasting Father, Prince of Peace.**" We will look at these titles in turn:

1. "**Wonderful, Counsellor**". Jesus is indeed a wonderful counsellor.[15] And He promised, shortly before He was about to die on the Cross, that His Father would send *another* Counsellor (or Helper): **"And I will ask the Father, and He will give you another Counsellor, to be with you for ever—the Spirit of truth"** (John 14:16-17a, NIV). It is clear from John 14:26 that this promise referred to the Holy Spirit.

2. "**Mighty God**". Yes, Jesus is God and man. This is a definite statement that He truly is God.

3. "**Everlasting Father**". This is easily misunderstood. An alternative translation is "Father [or Source, Author] of everlasting life". Jesus is the only One to give us eternal life. It comes through Him, and so He is indeed the source and author of it.

4. "**Prince of Peace**". Jesus has made peace between man and God possible, and eventually He will bring world peace when He returns to the earth.

Isaiah described Jesus Christ in many other passages. Isaiah 53 is a chapter about the Messiah, and in verse 9 Isaiah prophesied, "**And they [literally, He] made His grave with the wicked—but with the rich at His death, because He had done no violence, nor was any deceit in His mouth.**" In the first part of this verse, "**the wicked**" refers to the two thieves crucified with Jesus. The word "**death**" in the second part refers

---

[14] This refers to the time, after the Second Coming of Jesus Christ, when Jesus will establish His kingdom on earth. It will be a time of peace and prosperity, and Jesus Himself will reign in Jerusalem as King over the whole earth. Isaiah, as well as many other prophets in the Bible, refer to this time in numerous passages (for example: Isaiah 2:2-4 and 11:6-9; Zechariah 14:8-11, 16-21). This coming kingdom was, and still is, the hope of the Jews. The Millennium is described in Basic Bible Studies BBS 60-61 and in the Special Topic Studies STS 7-10.

[15] Many translations omit the comma between the words, "Wonderful" and "Counsellor", for example, the NASB.

to Jesus' death. The word is plural, and could be translated "deaths", a form of emphasis.

Jesus' Victory on the Cross

We now need to consider how Jesus died on the Cross. Like Adam, Jesus died spiritually and then physically. Adam died spiritually when he ate the forbidden fruit (Genesis 3:6); he then died physically when he was 930 years old (Genesis 5:5), having had many children who inherited a sinful nature from him. When Jesus died on the Cross, He also first died spiritually: His spirit was cut off from fellowship with God. Then, He died physically.

However, there was an important difference between how Adam and Christ died. Adam *chose* to sin and to die spiritually; and he died physically as a consequence. Jesus, however, had sin placed on Him, which caused Him to die spiritually; He then *chose* to die physically.

As we have seen, Jesus was born without an old sin nature and He never sinned. But on the Cross, the sins of the whole world were laid on Him. He **"bore our sins in His own body on the tree"** (1 Peter 2:24a), and was made the sin and trespass offering for mankind. As this happened, God the Father and God the Holy Spirit had to turn away, and Jesus was cut off from God (this is what we have called "spiritual death"). Jesus later screamed, **"My God, My God, why have You forsaken Me?"** (Matthew 27:46b; Mark 15:34b); and the repetition of **"My God"** here could indicate that Jesus was addressing the Father and the Holy Spirit.

After three hours of darkness, Jesus' work on the Cross was complete,[16] and He cried out, **"It is finished!"** (John 19:30a). He then dismissed His spirit and died: **"Father, into your hands I commend my spirit"** (Luke 23:46). He knew that His job was finished,[17] and so He *chose* immediately to die physically. This was 'easy' compared with the

---

[16] It is interesting that for the first three hours, as Jesus hung on the Cross, it was daylight; but then darkness fell over all the land for the next three hours (Matthew 27:45). This may indicate that for the first three hours on the Cross Jesus was like a burnt offering, a pleasing aroma to God (see Ephesians 5:2); then, however, for the next three hours there was utter darkness as He bore our sins and became a sin-offering for us. Alternatively, Jesus may have been the sin-offering for mankind for six hours on the Cross. Christ on the Cross was the final sacrifice to which all the various sacrifices and offerings under the law pointed.

[17] The same principle is true for us who are believers. We will not die until the job appointed for us to do by God is finished. We can rejoice when we hear of a saint dying. We may miss that person, yes; but if he was in fellowship with God, we can be sure he did not die one second before his job on earth was complete.

spiritual death He had just endured. **"So when Jesus had received the sour wine, He said, "It is finished!" And bowing His head, He gave up His spirit"** (John 19:30). There was nothing more to do.

Jesus thus gave up His spirit and died physically. (Death is when the spirit leaves the body.) His soul went to Paradise—the place of rest to which the souls of all believers went in Old Testament times. We know this because Jesus turned to the penitent thief, who was saved on his cross nearby, and said to him, **"...Today you will be with Me in Paradise"** (Luke 23:43). Jesus therefore went down into Hades to the place called Paradise.[18] His body was put into the tomb.

Jesus Christ was cut off and endured spiritual separation from God so that we need never again be cut off from God for even one moment. We can now enjoy fellowship with God every single moment of the day! It is up to us.

Returning to Genesis 3:15, we need to see that it ends with a glorious declaration: **"He shall bruise your head, and you shall bruise His heel."** In Hebrew, the word "**bruise**" is the verb 'to crush' or 'to break.' This verse therefore declared that Jesus Christ, the Seed of the woman, was going to crush the head of Satan; and Satan was going to crush Jesus' heel. Why?

In the same way as a snake injects venom into someone's heel and the venom then spreads and poisons the whole body, Satan injected the poison of sin into the whole human race through Adam; and it spread to every person. But Jesus had no such poison in Him; He was not contaminated by sin. And He was sinless on the Cross. But then the venom of our sin was put on Him and He paid the penalty for it, making it possible for it to be removed from you and me.

---

[18] The Hebrew word *Sheol* (or its Greek equivalent *Hades*, meaning 'not seen') was the name given to the unseen abode of the dead to which all people went when they died before this time. The English word 'Hell' is used in many Bible versions to translate these words, as well as others such as the word *Ge'enna*, which is the Greek form of the Hebrew *Gei-Hinnom* (Valley of Hinnom, the name of the valley outside Jerusalem used for burning rubbish). However, the word 'Hell' is often used inaccurately (for example, to describe the future Lake of Fire) and it is better to understand the original words. Some people wrongly teach that Jesus became a sinner and descended into the place of torment in Hades to which unbelievers go (see Luke 16:23). This is heretical teaching, and should be rejected totally. Jesus completed His work on the Cross and then visited Hades to proclaim His victory and to lead captive dead believers from Paradise to the Father's side in heaven.

More details about these subjects are given in: Special Topic Studies STS 11 to 15, "Victorious Christian Living"; STS 49 and 50, entitled "The Power of God within Us"; and, STS 39, "What happens when a person dies?" which has also been published as a book, entitled "Explaining what happens after death" (Sovereign World).

John 3:14 likens Jesus Christ lifted up on the Cross to the serpent lifted up on Moses' stake (see Numbers 21:4-9).[19] When He was on the Cross, Jesus was made like that serpent. Sin was put on Him, and the Father and the Holy Spirit turned away. He became an offering for our sin. He did not become *sinful* (that is, a sinner by nature), but as a sinless sacrifice He died for us. God viewed Him as being as unclean as we were, and He bore the judgment for our sins. Moses lifted up the serpent on the stake so that all the people could look at it and be saved. In the same way, everyone who looks to Jesus lifted up on the Cross is delivered from the venom of sin and the punishment we all deserved, and is healed, restored and forgiven. This is salvation, and it is brilliant! It was God's brilliant master-plan, first revealed in Genesis 3:15.

Jesus Christ crushed Satan's head through the Cross; and because Satan's head is crushed, he is ultimately finished. When Jesus said, **"It is finished!"**, He had won a tremendous victory. He bore our sins and died, but then He rose from the dead! Satan thought that he had destroyed the Son of God; but at the same time as Satan bruised Jesus' heel, Jesus absolutely crushed Satan's head forever! This came to pass in the most wonderful way, and it was Jesus who scored the triumph for all of us. The triumphant shout must have reverberated all around heaven!

It is a wonderful message: one man, Adam, brought sin and death into the world, but one Man, Jesus Christ, brought salvation and victory over death (see Romans 5:12,19 and 1 Corinthians 15:22).

This is salvation, as first revealed in Genesis 3:15: Jesus Christ crushed the head of Satan forever. The work was completed and Satan was totally defeated. And this was made possible because Jesus was born of a virgin. Without His virgin birth, Jesus' death would have been of no effect.

What Jesus' Victory means to us

1 Peter 2:22-24 describes Jesus: **"'Who committed no sin, nor was guile found in His mouth"; who, when He was reviled, did not revile in return; when He suffered, He did not threaten, but committed Himself to Him who judges righteously; who Himself bore our sins in His own body on the tree, that we, having died to sins, might live for righteousness—by whose stripes you were healed."** The separation between God and man was like a wound that needed healing; and a wound is a division of two parts of your body that need joining together

---

[19] *This passage is studied in chapter 5.*

again. We were apart from God, but "**by [His] stripes [we] were healed**" (verse 24b). We have been brought back together again with God, through Jesus; and the wound has been completely healed.

Adam fell because of a tree. We have been redeemed through a tree: the Cross of Calvary.

1 Peter 2:25 continues, "**For you were like sheep going astray, but have now returned to the Shepherd and Overseer of your souls.**" You were in a 'thornbush,' but one day you heard the gospel and you bleated out, "Jesus, You're the only One who can help me!" Jesus is the good shepherd (John 10:14), and from that day on, the good shepherd and Shepherd of your soul came along and pulled you out of the bush and put you back into the flock. And He has put you there for ever. A good shepherd does not necessarily find pasture for his sheep; the sheep tend to find their own pasture, food and drink. The thing that distinguishes a good shepherd is that a good shepherd *never loses* a sheep, but rather protects his sheep and rescues them if they are trapped or in danger. You might think that you are lost again, but I have got news for you: you are not! We are rescued sheep, and He will never lose us.

"**Therefore, if anyone is in Christ, he is a new creation; old things have passed away; behold, all things have become new**" (see 2 Corinthians 5:17). This is the first verse that helped prove to me that the Bible was true. I knew it was true in my own life.

2 Corinthians 5:18-21 goes on to say that God has *reconciled* us to Himself through Christ's death on the Cross. "**Now all things are of God, who has reconciled us to Himself through Jesus Christ, and has given us the ministry of reconciliation, that is, that God was in Christ reconciling the world to Himself, not imputing their trespasses to them, and has committed to us the word of reconciliation**" (verses 18-19). We now have a "**ministry of reconciliation**", which means a ministry of spreading the gospel. The message we have is that God has reconciled us to Himself through Jesus Christ: "Therefore, be reconciled to God!" And we have to preach the gospel; it is our duty to preach it. "**Therefore we are ambassadors for Christ, as though God were pleading through us: we implore you on Christ's behalf, be reconciled to God. For He made Him who knew no sin to be sin for us, that we might become the righteousness of God in Him**" (verses 20-21).

Verse 21 contains an important principle. There has been an exchange. Jesus bore our sins on the Cross, that we might be given God's own righteousness. We are now righteous—but not because *we* are so great;

rather, we are righteous because *He* is so great! This verse will be referred to many times in this book.

Conclusion

If there had been no virgin birth, then there would be no salvation for us. The virgin birth was essential to our salvation, because it meant Jesus was a free-man, able to rescue us who were enslaved and in bondage to sin and to Satan.

Having glimpsed God's answer to the problem of the barrier, we will now begin to look at the answer in more detail, each brick in turn, and to see how the work of Christ demolished the barrier between man and God forever.

NOTES

4. REDEMPTION

The great barrier that came into existence between God and man at the Fall had God and His character on one side, and us and our character on the other. The barrier, as we have seen, can be visualized as comprising six bricks, each on its own sufficient to cut us off from God.

God knew since before the Creation that He Himself would have to provide the answer. We have already seen a glimpse of the answer God has provided—namely, His plan of salvation through Jesus Christ. We need to understand this salvation. Then we can glory in it and rejoice in wonder that God has been loving enough to provide it for us.

We are now ready to begin dismantling the barrier. The first brick we will deal with is the brick of sin, and we will see in this study how Jesus Christ dealt with this brick through '*redemption*.'

SIN: THE FIRST BRICK IN THE BARRIER

Just as we have visualized the barrier between God and man as comprising six bricks, so the brick of sin may also be divided into several parts:[1]

1. **The old sin nature**

    When Adam fell, he immediately died spiritually and received an 'old sin nature'; and all fathers have passed this 'fallen' or 'sinful nature' on to their children. A newborn baby has an old sin nature, even though it has done no wrong. *Every* member of the human race has such a sinful nature: "**There is no one righteous, no, not one**" (Romans 3:10). We sin because we are sinners by nature; and we

---

[1] Note that the six bricks in the barrier are interrelated, and it is therefore difficult to make an absolute distinction between them, in particular, between the first three bricks (sin, the penalty of sin and spiritual death). In the same way, the three sub-divisions of the sin brick described also overlap, and it is not always easy to apply a scripture to one aspect only. It should be remembered that the problems affecting mankind as a result of the Fall are so far-reaching that the barrier comprising six bricks is merely a way to help comprehend them.

have been sinners from the moment we were conceived. We are all classed as 'sinners' by God.[2]

2. Death reigned following Adam's sin

Adam sinned, and his one sin affected us all. His one offence brought death into the world, and this is proven by the fact that we will all eventually die physically. We are all born "**dead in trespasses and sins**" (Ephesians 2:1, Colossians 2:13). This aspect of the Sin brick is closely related to the fact that everyone is born with a lifeless or 'dead' human spirit, but that subject is important enough to be dealt with separately later, as the third brick in the barrier.

3. Personal sins

We probably cannot remember the first sin we ever committed in our lives. We have all sinned.[3] But just one sin, no matter what it is, is enough to cut us off from God, who is holy.

All three of these aspects of sin affect us. The first two can be traced back to Adam. However, the third is entirely our fault. Any one of these components of the brick of sin would in itself be an insurmountable barrier between us and God; but we are enslaved by *all three* of them!

SLAVERY TO SIN (JOHN 8:30-36)

In John 8:30-36, we find Jesus talking to the Jews about mankind's bondage. There was a crowd around Him listening intently, and, "**As He spoke these words, many believed in Him**" (verse 30). Some wanted to know the truth and were accepting His teaching. They believed in Him. But others were there simply to criticize Him.

"**Then Jesus said to those Jews who believed Him, "If you abide in My word, you are My disciples indeed. And you shall know the truth,**

---

[2] The fact that we all have a 'fallen' or 'sinful nature' is sometimes described as the law or principle of sin at work in us (Romans 7:23, Romans 8:2). Human beings are "all under sin" (Romans 3:9, Galatians 3:22), and all "were made sinners" through Adam's first sin (Romans 5:19). But the good news is that "Christ Jesus came into the world to save sinners" (1 Timothy 1:15), and that "while we were still sinners, Christ died for us" (Romans 5:8).

[3] The Bible makes clear that "all have sinned" (Romans 3:23), whether a Jew or a Gentile (Romans 2:9-12); no one can say they have not committed sins (1 John 1:10). The good news is that "Christ died for our sins" (1 Corinthians 15:3). This is linked to the second brick, which is covered in the next study.

and the truth shall make you free'" (verses 31-32). Jesus was addressing believers, yet He was saying they had a choice as to whether they would abide (that is, stay, remain, continue) in His teaching. We should continue in Jesus' teaching and apply all we learn to our lives. The result will be that we will know the truth and be set free by it. True liberty comes only in this way.

"They answered Him, "We are Abraham's descendants, and have never been in bondage to anyone. How can you say, 'You will be made free'?"' (verse 33). This was the answer of the religious Jews to Jesus' promise, **"The truth shall make you free."** Pride was dominating their lives; they were proud to be descended from Abraham, and thought that this pedigree alone set them above everyone else. As with all proud people, they said foolish things. To say they had never been enslaved was not only untrue, but laughable.

Had not the Jews been slaves in Egypt for 400 years? And what about 70 years of captivity in Babylon under Nebuchadnezzar? More recently, they had been in bondage to Antiochus Epiphanes and, at the very time Jesus was talking to them, the Romans were dominating the whole of Israel! Soldiers were marching about the land, but these religious Jews still proudly stated, **"We...have never been in bondage to anyone"**! They were in fact, at that very moment, in bondage in three ways:

1. Under Roman occupation: there were probably troops in that very street!

2. Under their own religious rules. Theirs was perhaps the most stringent religious system ever, especially in view of the rules laid out in the *Mishna*,[4] which the rabbis and scribes had added to 'expound' and apply the law.

For example, whereas the Old Testament actually said, **"Remember the Sabbath day, to keep it holy...in it you shall do no work"** (Exodus 20:8-10a), the Mishna gave rigid instructions such as these concerning the sabbath day:

(a) if your friend falls over and severs an artery, you must not do anything to help, even if it means you have to watch him die;

(b) if your mule falls into a ditch, you cannot pull it out;

---

[4] The *Mishna* was the Jewish oral law, or Rabbinical tradition, which was finally written down in the 2nd Century AD. The Mishna, together with the *Gemara*, which was a commentary on it and a complement to it, came to form the *Talmud*, the fundamental code for Jewish civil and canon law.

(c) if your mule has a heavy load, you *can* loosen the strap. If the load falls off of its own accord, that is all right; but you must not help it fall off—that would be contrary to the law!

(d) if your wine bottle springs a leak, even if it is the best and most expensive wine you have ever bought, you must not mend the hole.

This was real bondage! But there was another slavery which was worse still.

3. They were *slaves to SIN*. Jesus focused on this, their main bondage, and declared to them, **"Most assuredly, I say to you, whoever commits sin is a slave of sin"** (verse 34). Literally this begins, "Amen, Amen" (*'Amen'* means 'this is true, faithful, sure'). It is important to understand that the word translated **"slave"** did not mean a servant with any sort of dignity, but a slave with no rights at all. Jesus was saying that any person who ever commits any sin whatsoever is a *SLAVE OF SIN*. We are all therefore slaves of sin from birth, because we are all sinners by nature. And the personal sins which we commit are merely proof to us that we are indeed such slaves. As Romans 3:23 says, **"For all have sinned and fall short of the glory of God."** This includes us all; we are *all* slaves.

Jesus now concentrated on this bondage to sin in His conversation with the religious Jews, because it was the most fundamental bondage they were under.

"And a slave does not abide in the house for ever, but a son abides for ever. Therefore if the Son makes you free, you shall be free indeed" (verses 35-36). A slave does not live in the master's house; rather, a slave waits in the house to carry out orders and then leaves after completing all the work. Only the master's family has the right to live in the family house. However, we who have believed on Christ have been made part of God's family, part of God's household! And His house is the Church—God's people. **"For you are all sons of God through faith in Christ Jesus"** (Galatians 3:26). We have been made sons of God through believing on Jesus and, as members of God's family, we can stay in His house forever!

"Therefore if the Son makes you free, you shall be free indeed" (verse 36). Jesus was saying, "*I*, as the Son, *can* set you free from your slavery. I am a *Son*, and I can provide the way of salvation!" Jesus Christ is the only One who can make us free, because He is the only One free from sin Himself. Therefore, He alone is in a position to release slaves.

Sin caused us all to be slaves; and sin, the first large brick in the barrier, affects all human beings—*except Jesus Christ*. Jesus alone was able to provide the way of salvation. And the answer that God has provided to the brick of sin can be expressed in the word '*redemption.*'

REDEMPTION

There are two Greek verbs which are translated as "redeem" in the New Testament:

1. *Lutroō* : this means release by payment of a ransom (*lutron*). A person in bondage or who has been kidnapped can only be released when someone pays the 'ransom price' necessary to set him or her free.

2. *Exagorazō* : this is made up of two Greek words: *ex* or *ek*, which means 'out from' or 'back from,' and *agorazō*, which means 'to buy'. Thus *exagorazō* : means 'to buy back out from.' *Agorazō* specifically alludes to the slave market, which was held in the *agora*—the marketplace (or the Roman *forum* in Latin). Slaves were brought into the middle of the marketplace, shackled and tied up, and probably with their hands manacled to a stick across their shoulders and with their feet manacled to each other, forming long lines. They were waiting for a so-called '*free-man*' to come into the market to buy them. A slave could of course never buy another slave. Rather, it took a *free* citizen to buy a slave. Someone with the status of a free-man could even buy a slave and grant that slave freedom, if the free-man so wished.

Slavery, as we have seen, is a picture that is applicable to every member of the human race. Every person has an old sin nature, and is born dead in sins. In addition, we have all committed personal sins. To set us free, therefore, we need someone who is free from all these aspects of the Sin brick—that is: someone with no old sin nature; someone who is spiritually alive and not dead in sins; and, someone who has committed no personal sins.

JESUS CHRIST: THE ONLY FREE-MAN

The only One who can set us free is Jesus Christ. No other figure central to any of the world's religions can ever set even one person free from sin, because they, like us, were all enslaved to sin. Jesus is the only One ever to have been born free from sin. He had no sinful nature, because of his virgin birth; He was not born dead in sins, because he was not affected by the Fall; and, He committed no personal sins at all throughout His life.

So when Jesus was born, for the first time in history a free-man—a man free from sin—had arrived on the scene. He alone was able to pay the price to buy and set free all those who were slaves of sin. And He paid the redemption price in full when He died on the Cross. In effect He said, "I will buy the lot!" and He bought us out from the slave market of sin. The word *exagorazō* therefore gives us a vivid picture of Christ's work of redemption.

THE SIGNIFICANCE OF BLOOD

When anyone sinned in Old Testament times, he would go to the priest to make a sacrifice, according to the instructions given in the Book of Leviticus. He took with him an animal, usually a young goat or a lamb, which had to be without blemish. The priest took it, tied it up by the brazen altar (the altar of burnt offering) and asked, "What sin has been committed?", in reply to which the sinner confessed his sin. The sinner would then lay his hands on the head of the animal and name the sin. The priest might then ask if other sins had been committed.

However, that was not all. The person then had to slit the throat of the young goat or lamb; and the priest then had to pour out the blood and burn the animal.[5] The animal was perfect and innocent of any sin, yet it had its throat cut and was killed. It was not guilty, yet it died.

Most people at that time lacked access to the Scriptures, and many, especially outside Israel, could not read. Therefore, God had given Israel a 'visual aid' to help illustrate salvation, and the priests and teachers were meant to explain the message to the people. The innocent lamb died because of the sins of the one who came and put his trust in the lamb sacrifice. This demonstrated that a Saviour was necessary. Such a Saviour would be perfect and yet He would die—but not because of His own sins: He would die because of the sins of others.

These Old Testament sacrifices were thus a picture of the Lord Jesus Christ bearing our sins on the Cross and dying for us. The law of Moses demanded that blood had to be shed; but really it was the shedding of *the*

---

[5] The instructions concerning this type of sacrifice are found in Leviticus 4:27-35 and related to the common people when they sinned unintentionally. Leviticus 4 also includes slightly different instructions which applied when a priest, the whole congregation or a ruler had sinned.

blood of Jesus Christ which was pre-figured in the animal sacrifices. Blood *had* to be shed to solve the problem of our sin, and Christ's blood would be shed as the redemption price for mankind. Jesus came to give His life as a ransom (Mark 10:45).

KNOWLEDGE OF REDEMPTION IN THE OLD TESTAMENT

In fact, God showed people the necessity for blood sacrifices throughout the Old Testament. Many Old Testament characters learned about the importance of blood sacrifices, and understood that such sacrifices pointed to the redemptive work of Christ, as we will now see.

Adam and Eve

Going back to Genesis 3, we can see the fundamental error Adam and Eve made. They tried to cover themselves with fig leaves, which represented religious good works. But these leaves *contained no blood*. The Word of God reveals to us this very important principle, which is: **"without shedding of blood there is no remission** [of sins]" (Hebrews 9:22b). Therefore, religious acts can never overcome the problem of sin.

However, the end of the story in Genesis 3 is glorious, and it is possible to infer from it that Adam and Eve were saved: "**Also for Adam and his wife the LORD God made tunics of skin, and clothed them**" (Genesis 3:21). Reading this text carefully shows us that, even as far back as Adam and Eve's first sin, blood had to be shed. Despite their human efforts at covering up their sin, blood had to be spilt.

We can learn from the account that Jesus Himself must have killed an animal and clothed them with its skin. It is extremely important to understand this: Adam and Eve were already clothed, and they did not need new *clothes* to wear. Their fig-leaf loin cloths, which they had made for themselves, were quite adequate in terms of clothing. The skins must therefore have been given to them by Jesus to teach them something.

Imagine the scene: after Jesus had spoken with Adam and Eve and had described the judgments that would affect them as a result of their sin (Genesis 3:9-19), He went out into the Garden of Eden, where all the animals were at peace and where there was no such thing as fear. Jesus Himself must have called one of the innocent animals to Himself. Then, in front of Adam and Eve, He killed it, skinned it, and made the skin into new tunics, which He gave to Adam and Eve to replace the coverings they had made. No blood had ever been shed on the earth before this time. This was therefore an illustration to them, which we can presume

Jesus explained very clearly, that "**without shedding of blood there is no remission** [of sins]" (Hebrews 9:22b).[6]

Adam and Eve evidently accepted these new coverings, and were willing to put on the new coats of skin. This suggests to us that they understood the significance of the blood, and trusted in it. Thus, the blood is mentioned in those skins, and it is on this basis that we can say that Adam and Eve are probably saved and are in heaven today.

Cain and Abel

Cain and Abel learned this important principle: *blood is vital if we and our deeds are to be acceptable to God*. We can read their history in Genesis chapter 4.

Cain was a farmer, a tiller of the field. Abel kept sheep—which must have been to obtain wool or for the purpose of sacrifice, because people were not yet allowed to eat meat. They both worked hard, and both deserved praise from men for their labours.

There was an altar put up at that time, and both Cain and Abel took offerings to present to God on it. However, Abel's offering was accepted while Cain's was not. We need to understand why this was so.

God could not receive Cain's offering because there was *no blood* in it or applied to it. But Abel's offering from his flock *was* accepted by God: blood had been shed.

This shows that all our so-called 'good' deeds are not good in themselves at all, and cannot be accepted by God if no blood is applied. This is because even the best works of fallen man are wholly imperfect to God, who is perfect. But the moment blood is applied—representing salvation—then God can receive our offering.

If we are saved, then God accepts us, and we can then carry out works for God that *are* acceptable to Him. Abel offered his sacrifice to God in faith, on the basis of blood, and it was accepted. (God's acceptance was evidence that he was counted as righteous, as Hebrews 11:4 tells us.) Similarly we who are believers are accepted by God because of the shed blood of Jesus Christ; and on the basis of Jesus' blood our sacrifices or works carried out in faith can be acceptable to God.

---

[6] This is one of many examples of a basic principle being revealed for the first time in Genesis. Genesis is certainly not myth; every detail is important.

Noah

The first thing Noah did after he came out of the ark following the Flood was to build an altar and make a sacrifice to God (see Genesis 8:20). From whom had he learned about sacrifices and the need for blood? This knowledge had almost certainly been passed down by Adam from generation to generation. (There is evidence in Genesis 4 that sacrifices were *regularly* made to God.) Adam learned personally from Jesus about the importance of blood sacrifices, as we have seen, and we can presume that this knowledge was passed down to Enoch, then Methuselah, and then to Noah.

In other words, the message of salvation was being preached right from the time Adam and Eve learnt it. Eventually, one of Eve's descendants, Jesus Christ, would die on the Cross as the Lamb of God—the final sacrifice.

Redemption came through Jesus Christ. And the message of redemption has always been the same. Both Job and David, for example, clearly knew about it.

Job

Job declared, **"I know that my Redeemer lives, and He shall stand at last on the earth; and after my skin is destroyed, this I know, that in my flesh I shall see God"** (Job 19:25-26).

The Book of Job is probably the earliest book in the Bible.[7] Job's declaration was made some 2000 years before Jesus died on the Cross. He believed that his Redeemer—the One who would buy him freedom—was alive even at that time. (If we who live *after* the resurrection say to people that Jesus is alive, they are shocked!) Job clearly believed that he had a Redeemer, who would come and stand on the earth, and that he would see Him in his flesh. This will indeed happen following the Second Coming of Jesus Christ.

Enoch knew about this Second Coming of Christ in power and glory before Job did, as we can learn from the Book of Jude (see Jude 14-15). Enoch possibly passed on the information, through his descendants, to Job. Job clearly knew about the Millennium (that is, the future kingdom

---

[7] The Book of Job was probably written by Moses before the Exodus, during the 40 years that Moses lived in Midian. It describes a wonderful believer who lived in the land of Uz. The Hebrew used is a somewhat obscure dialect with Arabic influence. The Midianites, most of who were probably believers, were descendants of Abraham through his second wife, Keturah (Genesis 25:2); they lived somewhere in the deserts of Arabia. (Arabic was a Southern Semitic language, whereas Hebrew was a Northwestern Semitic language.)

of God) as well, during which Jesus will reign on the earth after His Second Coming. Job knew he was going to receive a resurrection body and that he would see Jesus in it: **"in my flesh I shall see God"**.[8] Christians are thus not the first to know about redemption, the Second Coming, resurrection or the future kingdom of God!

David

In Psalm 34:19-22 (written about 1000 BC), David said, "**Many are the afflictions of the righteous, but the LORD delivers him out of them all. He guards all his bones; not one of them is broken. Evil shall slay the wicked, and those who hate the righteous shall be condemned. The LORD redeems the soul of His servants, and none of those who trust in Him shall be condemned.**" This speaks of the LORD redeeming the soul of His servants. The last verse is a promise for all believers. Those who trust in Him will not be condemned.

THE GOOD NEWS—REDEMPTION THROUGH JESUS CHRIST

Redemption came through Jesus Christ, who died as our Redeemer and bought us out from the slave market of sin. The brick of sin has been completely eradicated, and redemption has replaced it. However, this redemption has to be received.

Jesus died to redeem the whole world, but that does not mean everyone in the world will be saved. All individuals must decide to believe on Jesus Christ for themselves. Jesus described Himself as **"the door of the sheep"** (John 10:7) and as **"the way"** (John 14:6). A door must be walked through to enter a house. In the same way, Jesus provides the way in to salvation, but each person must choose to walk through the door and go in.

Mankind is like a line of slaves, for whom a free-man has arrived and bought their freedom. Some will rejoice and walk free, but some may say they don't want to be free. The people in the world who refuse to accept what Jesus has done for them are doing just that.

Even if some people choose not to believe, Jesus has still paid for their sins in full. He has done enough to set everyone free; but redemption is

---

[8] The Second Coming of Christ and the Millennium are covered in the fourth series of Basic Bible Studies (BBS 43 to 63). In particular, BBS 58 describes "The Second Advent of Jesus Christ" and BBS 60-61 cover "The Millennium." See also footnote 14 in chapter 3.

REDEMPTION

only accrued by those who believe in the salvation God has provided. Through faith in Jesus Christ we receive our redemption.

Peter exhorts us that we should know how we were redeemed: "**Conduct yourselves...knowing that you were not redeemed with corruptible things, like silver and gold, from your aimless conduct received by tradition from your fathers, but with the precious blood of Christ, as of a lamb without blemish and without spot**" (1 Peter 1:17b-19). As we have seen, Jesus died as a perfect sacrifice. He shed His blood for us. And His blood was the redemption price required to set us free from our slavery to sin. Here, Peter was making a little gibe at the religious tradition handed down to many Jews. Such religious people called on their own 'good lives' to gain salvation. They were very devout—they used to visit the Temple and pray seven times a day. But he summarized their religiosity as "**aimless conduct**"!

Ephesians 1:7 says, "**In Him we have redemption through His blood, the forgiveness of sins, according to the riches of His grace.**" This is the good news of the gospel. We were in prison, but Jesus has come and opened the door. To say to someone, "You must live a good life!" is not the good news of redemption. We have been redeemed out of the slave market of sin; Jesus has paid the ransom price and our sins have been forgiven. We can therefore say to any prisoner, "Jesus came to redeem you, and you can walk straight out if you choose to. You think that you are a sinner; so you are, but Jesus has redeemed you!" This truly is good news!

Jesus knew about every sin that had been or ever would be committed, yet He was able to say concerning His work, "**It is finished!**" (John 19:30), when He died on the Cross. The work He had done was enough.

It is important to understand that our redemption is by God's grace alone and does not depend on anything we have done. For example, in World War II, Joachim Von Ribbentrop of Germany caused the deaths of huge numbers of people, especially Jews. Yet it was reported that a few days before his death, a minister told him the gospel and he believed on Christ. If this is true, he is now in heaven with the Lord.

This shows us the nature of grace. Grace is based solely on what God has done for us through the Lord Jesus Christ. Acts 16:31 plainly states the good news: "**Believe on the Lord Jesus Christ, and you will be saved.**" This is the glorious message of the gospel. Nobody is beyond redemption. Christ has paid the redemption price for us all. The first brick in the barrier has gone!

NOTES

5. CHRIST DIED FOR OUR SINS
— ATONEMENT AND EXPIATION

We have so far studied redemption, and seen that Jesus Christ, as a freeman, paid the necessary price and bought us out from our enslavement to sin. In this study we will consider *'atonement.'* We will then see how the second brick in the barrier, the Penalty of Sin, was removed by *'expiation.'* By the end of this study we will have completely removed the top two bricks in the barrier, and there will be nothing left in their place except the Lord Jesus Christ.

ATONEMENT

The work that Jesus Christ accomplished on the Cross[1] to bring about a reconciliation between God and man, is often referred to as "The Atonement". In this section, we will consider Christ's work on the Cross—and learn that Jesus died for the sins of the whole world. Then we will consider the Hebrew word which is often translated 'atone', and see how it was used in relation to Noah's ark.[2]

CHRIST DIED FOR ALL

God is omniscient (all-knowing), and therefore He knew every sin that *you* would ever commit, even before the world was made. He also knew about every sin of every person who would ever live. And He gave His Son Jesus, who died for every sin. Millions of sins, past, present and

---

[1] Scripture plainly reveals how Christ's death on the Cross and the shedding of His blood was the great event of history that dealt with sin and with God's need to judge the sinner. This one righteous act (Romans 5:18) was the climax of Christ's life of obedience (Philippians 2:8; Hebrews 5:8). The birth, life, suffering, death, resurrection, ascension and glorification of the Lord Jesus Christ were all important in God's plan of salvation, but the Cross was central.

[2] The English word 'atonement' signifies a harmonious relationship or that which brings about such a relationship—that is, reconciliation. There are several Hebrew words and several Greek words connected with this idea of atonement and reconciliation, including words translated "propitiation" or "mercy seat" (see chapter 7). The Hebrew word most commonly translated "atone," which means 'to cover,' is discussed in this chapter.

future, were therefore put on the Lord Jesus as He was hanging on the Cross. He died not only for Adam's first sin, but for the sins of every person from the beginning to the very end of time. He died for the sins of the whole world. **"For God so loved the world that He gave His only begotten Son, that whoever believes in Him should not perish but have everlasting life"** (John 3:16).

In 2 Corinthians 5:14b-15, Paul said, **"For the love of Christ constrains us, because we judge thus: that if One died for all, then all died; and He died for all, that those who live should no longer live for themselves, but for Him who died for them and rose again."** The word translated "**because we judge**" means 'having concluded'. Paul had concluded that because Christ died for all, all died (which refers to spiritual death: all people are born dead in sin and 'cut off' from the life of God). The AV says, "**if One died for all, then were all dead**" (and the 'if' clause in Greek indicates that Paul knew that Christ really did die for all). Paul then reaffirms this, and states *why*: so that those who live—who are made alive in Him—should live *for Him*. God has taken care of every single person through the Cross. Everyone had the problem of sin and death; but Christ died for all!

1 Timothy 2:4-6a tells us, "**[God] desires all men to be saved and to come to the knowledge of the truth. For there is one God and one mediator between God and men, the Man Christ Jesus, who gave Himself a ransom for all...**" There is not one person on the earth today whom God does not want to be saved: notice the word "**all**". The Holy Spirit is therefore witnessing to every person, wherever they are, urging them to be saved. God desires all to be saved, for Jesus gave Himself as a ransom for all.

In 1 Timothy 4:10, Paul says, "**For to this end we both labour and suffer reproach, because we trust in the living God, who is the Saviour of all men, especially of those who believe.**" When Jesus died on the Cross, He died to save all men; He was judged for the sins of all. But He is the Saviour especially of those who believe on Him.

Jesus therefore died not only for the sins of believers, but for the sins of unbelievers too. (His work also secured a way of victory over our old sin nature and overcame spiritual death, as will be explained later.) There is not one person, past, present, or future, whose sins were not borne by Jesus on the Cross. Salvation is therefore available to all.

We can therefore say to any person, "No matter how much of a sinner you are, Jesus died for your sins. You can be a free person if only you will believe on Christ!" You can tell your neighbour, "So you think you're so bad? Jesus knew how bad you would be, and He has paid the price for your sins already." That is good news! However, it needs personal faith in Jesus for a person to walk free from slavery. A slave could refuse to walk free, even after a free-man had paid the ransom price and granted him or her freedom.

"And He Himself is the propitiation for our sins, and not for our sins only but also for the whole world" (1 John 2:2). It is a surprise to some people that unbelievers' sins were dealt with by Jesus on the Cross, as well as the sins of believers.

2 Peter 2:1 is an even more surprising verse: **"But there were also false prophets among the people, even as there will be false teachers among you, who will secretly bring in destructive heresies, even denying the Lord who bought them, and bring on themselves swift destruction."** Most heresies in the early days of the Church began with believers who were not walking in fellowship with God. But there were also *false* teachers—that is, those who were never believers—who came in and started spreading false rumours and doctrines.[3] Jesus died for them too; Peter says they were **"denying the Lord who bought them"**. Jesus therefore died to redeem those who were stirring up trouble in the Church. Incredibly, He even died for those who were going to persecute the Church and put many Christians to death.

It is on the basis of verses such as these that the work Jesus accomplished ("The Atonement") can be referred to as *"unlimited."* No one can ever say they have committed a sin that Jesus did not die for, or that their sins are too bad for God to forgive. Jesus died for every sin: past, present and future. And when God planned our salvation, He made it vast enough to encompass our worst sins.

THE GOSPEL MESSAGE

Sin is therefore not the *decisive* issue in salvation any more, because Christ died for our sins. The sins of every person were judged on the Cross and Jesus dealt with them completely, once and for all. The decisive issue now is not your sin, but, **"What do you think about the Christ?"** (Matthew 22:42). As we shall later examine in greater detail, the decisive issue in determining who will be sent to eternal judgment

---

[3] Notice how they "secretly" spread their ideas; this is always how such people do it. They don't do it openly; they won't stand up and say what they believe. Instead, they do things secretly; they go around to a few members of a church, spreading their false ideas gradually.

will not be sins, but whether or not each person ever trusted in the Lord Jesus Christ.[4]

The gospel message is summed up in John 3:18, **"He who believes in Him (Jesus Christ) is not condemned; but he who does not believe is condemned already, because he has not believed in the name of the only begotten Son of God."** Whoever comes under judgment does so because of *not believing* in Christ. Sin is not mentioned.

We are not entitled to go up to people and say, "What a bad life you have lived!" That is not the issue. No matter how bad people's lives are, the issue is whether or not they have believed on the Lord Jesus Christ. The only person who can save them is Jesus, who died for their sins.

In John 3:36 Jesus again gave the same gospel: **"He who believes in the Son has everlasting life; and he who does not believe the Son shall not see life, but the wrath of God abides on him."** Here again, sin is not mentioned.

Therefore, the gospel message we preach must be this: "No matter how bad you have been, Jesus Christ has paid for it all. Believe in Him!" For, as Peter said when he addressed the rulers and elders in Jerusalem, **"There is no other name under heaven given among men by which we must be saved"** (Acts 4:12b).

NOAH'S ARK: A PICTURE OF SALVATION

The Hebrew verb often translated "atone" or "make atonement" in the Old Testament is *kaphar*, meaning 'to cover.' It is helpful to study its use in the account of Noah's ark in Genesis, where we find this latter meaning of it.

(Genesis is sometimes called "The seed-bed of the Bible". Most of the fundamental truths of the Bible are contained in the Book of Genesis in some measure, or can be traced back there.)

The account of Noah's ark is a true story. People who say that the ark could not have contained all the animals must never have realized how big it was! The ark was also a picture of Christ, who is our 'ark.'

---

[4] At the final judgment, it will be the Lamb's Book of Life that will be used to determine everyone's destination (see Revelation 20:11-15). The decisive issue will be whether a person's name is in this Book. The issue will not be sin: "And anyone not found written in the Book of Life was cast out into the lake of fire" (Revelation 20:15). This final judgment, also known as the "Great White Throne" judgment, is explained in BBS 28. It is discussed in chapter 8.

Noah and his family were shut inside the ark during the great Flood, and they were kept safe from the judgment that came upon the whole earth. In the same way, we who are believers are put 'in Christ', and we will be saved from the future judgment that will come upon the earth and heavens through fire (see 2 Peter 3:5-7). Believers are 'in Christ' and are fully identified with Him (see 1 Corinthians 1:30, for example). He is the ark in which we are hidden: **"For you died, and your life is hidden with Christ in God"** (Colossians 3:3). We will be kept safe in Him.

Noah had preached the gospel faithfully to an evil generation for 120 years, but only his family were believers; no one else would listen. After 120 years, God reluctantly decided to flood the whole earth with water.

In Genesis 6:14, God spoke to Noah and said: **"Make yourself an ark of gopher wood; make rooms in the ark, and cover it inside and outside with pitch."** It is fascinating that the word translated **"ark"** in Hebrew meant a chest in which valuable things were kept—a jewel box. This is wonderful, because God was asking Noah to make a jewel box, in which he and his family would be kept safe; they were God's jewels!

The ark had to be a special jewel box: a *floatable* one. Noah was therefore told to cover the wood of the ark with pitch—a waterproof substance, like the thick black volatile liquid (bitumen) that is put on roads today. God thus wanted Noah to build a watertight, floatable jewel box to preserve His own people in.

When God said, **"Cover it inside and outside with pitch"**, the Hebrew noun translated **"pitch"** is *kopher*, and the verb translated **"cover"** is *kaphar*. These two words are closely related. *Kaphar* means 'to cover,' or 'to cover something with pitch,' but it is translated about 70 times in the Old Testament figuratively as "atone" or "make atonement".[5]

Noah thus had to cover (*kaphar*) the ark with pitch, so that he and his family would be protected from the Flood. Noah was safe for the whole duration of the Flood. Similarly, we are safe in Christ for as long as judgment lasts—that is, for all eternity.

---

[5] The word *kopher* not only means 'pitch,' but can also mean 'the price of a life' or 'a ransom.' Another noun, *kippur*, which is from the same root, means 'atonement' (Yom Kippur means the Day of Atonement, for example).

Kapher, a verb related to *kopher*, means 'to cover' (or 'to cover with pitch'), and figuratively means 'to atone,' 'to placate,' 'to appease,' 'to propitiate' or 'to wipe away.' It occurs just more than 100 times in the Old Testament, and is used in connection with the various offerings and the blood that made atonement (Leviticus 17:11). It is also translated as 'appease,' 'cancel,' 'forgive' and 'pardon,' etc.

There were four main reasons why Noah was safe in the ark, and there are parallels we can draw with how we are secure in Christ. Noah was safe because:

1. *God shut him in.* Genesis 7:16 says, "**So those that entered, male and female of all flesh, went in as God had commanded; and the LORD shut him in.**" Noah couldn't shut the door securely, so God did! If Noah had pulled the door shut himself from inside, there would certainly have been some gap, and water could have got in. But we are told that *the* LORD shut the door, and it is reasonable to assume that *He* also pitched it over. In a similar manner, God has shut the door of our salvation. The moment we believed on the Lord Jesus, God placed us 'in Christ' and sealed us in. God has closed the door and pitched it over; and He keeps it closed. We are therefore totally secure forever; *we* cannot lose our salvation. In John 10:28b Jesus confirmed this: **"Neither shall anyone snatch them out of My hand."**

2. *God had designed the ark.* Every stress and strain, and every water pressure the ark would be subjected to, God knew and had planned for. He designed it to withstand them all. In the same way, our salvation has been planned and is stress-proof. God knew every sin, every trial, every pressure and every situation we would ever encounter; and His salvation is big enough to hold us and to take the strain!

3. *The ark was totally covered with pitch.* Noah had to make the joints between the wood in the ark watertight, so that the waters of judgment could not get through to those inside. Our salvation is similarly 'watertight,' and the 'waters of judgment' cannot get through. No one who believes on the Lord Jesus Christ will be judged, because Jesus has already been judged in our place.

4. *God was inside the ark with Noah.* Genesis 7:1 says, "**Then the LORD said to Noah, "Come into the ark, you and all your household, because I have seen that you are righteous before Me in this generation."**" The LORD said, **"Come into the ark,"** not, "Go in," implying He was already in the ark, right inside with them.[6] Jesus Christ is our ark; and He is always 'inside with us' too. We are

---

[6] This is reminiscent of the account of the three young men put into the fiery furnace by Nebuchadnezzar in Daniel chapter 3. In Daniel 3:25, Nebuchadnezzar saw that someone was in the fiery furnace with Shadrach, Meshach and Abed-Nego. "Look!" he (Nebuchadnezzar) answered, "I see four men loose, walking in the midst of the fire; and they are not hurt, and the form of the fourth is like the Son of God." Jesus was right there with them!

in Him, but He also dwells in us. He is right there with us in all the buffetings and trials of life! The ark was in fact more like a 'floating submarine' than a conventional boat; it was really tossed and shaken about in the waters. However, I believe Noah and his family were preoccupied with the LORD, and were not terrified by or even overly concerned about the storms outside. In the same manner, we must keep the reality of Jesus' presence with us constantly in mind. If we are conscious of Him we will be less conscious of our problems.

These were the reasons why Noah was quite safe in the ark. In the same way, we are quite safe in Christ. Jesus has already been judged for our sins, and, as in our legal system, once a penalty has been paid there can be no retrial. As Romans 8:1 says, "**There is therefore now no condemnation to those who are in Christ Jesus**"; and the word here translated "**condemnation**" could equally well have been translated "judgment."

Noah was safe because of his being in the ark, which was covered with pitch. We are safe in Christ. However, our sins have not merely been covered—as people's sins were temporarily covered by the sacrifices made in Old Testament times. Rather, our sins have been *taken away forever* by Jesus, who died for them and then rose from the dead! That is why, although we can learn a lot about what Jesus accomplished by looking at Noah's ark, or the principle of atonement through sacrifices in the Old Testament, the word 'atonement' never actually appears in the New Testament.[7]

We will now look further at Jesus' work on the Cross, and see how He bore our sins, removing them from us and taking the judgment that was due to us.

THE SECOND BRICK: THE PENALTY OF SIN

The second brick in the barrier is the Penalty of Sin. Not only is sin itself a problem, but so are its consequences. Sin carries a penalty which *must* be paid.

Romans 6:23 tells us that "**the wages of sin is death**". Sin earns wages that have to be paid, and the wages is death. It was not enough that sin itself was dealt with on the Cross. The consequence of that sin—namely, death—also had to be taken care of.

---

[7] The English word "atonement" appears once in the New Testament of the AV, in Romans 5:11, but this is a wrong translation; the Greek word used should be rendered "reconciliation".

Jesus Christ paid the penalty of sin for us by dying on the Cross. The English word '*expiation*' is sometimes used to describe this.[8]

Jesus' Cry of dereliction on the Cross

Psalm 22 was written about 1000 years before Christ died, but what Jesus would say on the Cross was revealed to David, who wrote it down. David asked a question: **"My God, My God, why have You forsaken Me? Why are You so far from helping me, and from the words of my groaning?"** (Psalm 22:1). We know from the gospels that, as He hung on the Cross, Jesus cried out loudly the words of the first part of this verse. The Hebrew word translated "**groaning**" (*sheagah*) here literally means 'screaming' or 'roaring'. Therefore, this implies an amazing thing: that Jesus *screamed* on the Cross.

Jesus had been unjustly judged in six trials, all of which had been farcical in terms of justice. The trials had been full of lies, and had been abandoned when witnesses could not agree. Jesus had been punched, slapped and taunted. Isaiah said of Him, "**...Many were appalled at You.... His visage was marred more than any man, and His form more than the sons of men**" (Isaiah 52:14), which suggests Jesus' face became so bruised and puffed up that it was barely recognizable. Yet there is no record that He cried out.

Jesus was then scourged. Usually, the strongest soldiers in the force took a whip with thongs of leather and whipped their victim until there was only just enough life left in him for crucifixion to be possible. The leather had pieces of bone or iron in the tips to cause as many lacerations as possible. They then rubbed salt into the wounds. However, even under scourging, there is no record of Jesus crying out or screaming. "**He was oppressed and He was afflicted, yet He opened not His mouth**" (Isaiah 53:7a).

---

[8] *Expiation* means the making amends for a wrong and the removal of any taint. It is impersonal: one expiates a crime rather than a person. It is not a translation of a particular Greek word in the New Testament; rather, it is used to refer to the wiping out of our sin and its effects. Expiation is the name given to the process whereby the barrier which sin interposed between God and man was broken down.

In contrast, *propitiation* (covered in chapter 7) is personal, and means the turning away of an offended person's anger or wrath. It refers to the process whereby God (the offended One) appeased His righteous anger through the sacrifice of Jesus on the Cross, that He might be gracious to us. It is a translation of the New Testament word *hilasmos*. Both expiation and propitiation were part of Jesus' work on the Cross.

Jesus was then forced to drag His own Cross along to the hill of Calvary, until Simon of Cyrene was compelled to intervene. He was then nailed to it. Yet still we are not told that Jesus screamed. Instead of resisting, He was led as a lamb to the slaughter, and was silent (Isaiah 53:7b).

For six hours on the Cross, Jesus did not cry out, as He repeatedly heaved His body up to breathe, and as His body-weight caused His flesh to tear when He slumped down again. But something of momentous effect clearly happened to Jesus on the Cross (which may have occurred after three hours—for at that moment darkness fell over the whole land). Whatever happened caused Jesus to later cry out with a loud voice. What was it that happened, and why did Jesus scream?

Jesus screamed because *the sins of the whole world were laid on Him*. This is the amazing conclusion: it was OUR SINS that brought forth Jesus' cry. He had endured the pain and everything else in silence; but when sin—the most dreadful thing to afflict man—was laid on Him who had known no sin, a cry of anguish leapt from His lips and He yelled out, **"Eli, Eli, lama sabachthani?" that is, "My God, My God, why have You forsaken Me?"** (Matthew 27:46). In the Gesenius Hebrew-Chaldee Lexicon to the Old Testament, the word *sheagah* is said to mean both the "roaring of a lion", and the "cry of a wretched person, wrung forth by grief."

Why did the other members of the Godhead—the Father and the Holy Spirit—have to turn their back on Jesus as He hung on the Cross? The answer is in verse 3 of Psalm 22: **"But You are holy"**. God is absolutely holy, and so when the sins of the whole world were borne by Jesus on the Cross, God the Father and the Holy Spirit had to withdraw completely.

Jesus' loud cry on the Cross is recorded because it is so important. (It is also found in Mark 15:34, and Luke 23:46 alludes to it.) Screaming is not unusual from a tortured man. But Jesus did not scream when He was tortured. Rather, the Scriptures describe His cry on the Cross to emphasize to us what *sin* did to Him. He cried out only after sin had been laid on Him, and when God the Father and God the Holy Spirit had turned away.

Our sin should therefore never be taken lightly—it caused Jesus Christ to cry out on the Cross. We should always remember this: when Jesus died for all our sins 2000 years ago, He screamed out with all His might.

"Jesus the Nazarene"

On the Cross Jesus became a sin-offering for us (see Isaiah 53:10), and this was demonstrated dramatically by the title that was hung over Him. There is something most interesting that we can learn from John 19:19, and this involves a brief introduction to the significance of certain numbers found in the Bible.

"And He, bearing His cross, went out to a place called The Place of a Skull, which is called in Hebrew, Golgotha, where they crucified Him, and two others with Him, one on either side, and Jesus in the middle. Now Pilate wrote a title and put it on the cross. And the writing was: "JESUS OF NAZARETH, THE KING OF THE JEWS"" (John 19:17-19).

This title, which was hung on the Cross, should literally be translated **"JESUS THE NAZARENE..."** (as it is in the NASB). In most other places in the New Testament, Christ is called "Jesus of Nazareth" or "Jesus Christ the Nazarene"; but His title on the Cross was "Jesus the Nazarene". John's gospel is the only gospel that records this title.

It is well known that the Greeks used the letters of their alphabet to count with; for example: alpha = 1, beta = 2, gamma = 3, and so on. It is therefore possible to evaluate a numerical value for any word or phrase by simply adding up the values of each letter in it. For example, the name Ἰησους (*Iēsous*) in Greek which is translated "Jesus" can be evaluated as: 10 (iota) + 8 (eta) + 200 (sigma) + 70 (omicron) + 400 (upsilon) + 200 (sigma) = 888 in total.[9]

Many numbers have a meaning in the Bible. For example, seven is the number of spiritual perfection or completeness. The number eight, however, is the number of resurrection or new beginnings. The name 'Jesus' thus represents resurrection (repeated three times for emphasis). This is wonderful!

The three Greek words in the title **"JESUS THE NAZARENE"** (ΙΗΣΟΥΣ Ο ΝΑΖΩΡΑΙΟΣ) have the numerical values 888 + 70 + 1239 = 2197 in total. Now 2197 = 13 × 13 × 13; and in the Bible 13 is the number of evil, sin or apostasy. This title nailed above Jesus' head on

---

[9] For a full list of values, see D.F. Hudson's book "Teach yourself New Testament Greek" (Hodder and Stoughton, UK). In the section on numbers, he writes, "Letters were used instead of numbers, and distinguished by accents....But you need not bother about these." This is a pity, because a lot can be learned by looking at the relationship between letters and numbers in the Bible.

Note that in the evaluation of the numerical value of words given here, the Greek character sigma always has the value 200, whereas Hudson ascribes it a value of 6 when it appears at the end of a word. (Roger Price covered the use of numbers in the Bible in some detail in Special Topic Studies STS 98-99, entitled "Numerology".)

the Cross thus points to the fact that Jesus was made sin × sin × sin on the Cross.[10]

We can see how appalling this is when we realize that one other phrase in the New Testament also has the numerical value 2197. It is in Revelation 12:9, which we have referred to previously: "**So the great dragon was cast out, that serpent of old, called the Devil and Satan, who deceives the whole world...**". The phrase "**called the Devil and Satan**" (literally "he who is called Devil and Satan") has the value 2197. All sin originated from Satan, being introduced into the human race through Adam. Jesus actually bore our sins on the Cross, so it is no wonder the title over Him was 13 × 13 × 13.

2 Corinthians 5:21 is a very important verse: "**For He (God) made Him who knew no sin (Jesus) to be sin for us...**". Jesus Christ was the only perfect man who had ever lived, yet God—in His grace and love for us—made Him to be sin for us on the Cross. He did not die because of His own sins, but because *we* were so sinful and evil.

Jesus bore our sins on the Cross, and He was judged for them. In exchange, we are given God's righteousness when we believe on Him: "**...that we might become the righteousness of God in Him**" (verse 21b). God swapped two things: our sin and judgment became His, and we receive the same righteousness as He had.

We will therefore never be judged for our sins, because Jesus, hanging on the Cross, has already been judged for them. Therefore, "**There is now no other name under heaven given among men by which we must be saved**" (Acts 4:12b).[11]

---

[10] Note that there is a numerology cult which tends to take the meaning of numbers in the Bible to the extreme, interpreting the Scriptures mainly according to numerical values. Misapplication of this principle can be a snare and can lead to superstition. For example, Satan has counterfeited this truth in our day, and many people believe that 7 is a lucky number and that 13 is unlucky.

[11] Jesus never became a sinner on the Cross—that is, He never received a sinful human nature, and He never chose to sin. Rather, Jesus bore our sins in His body as He hung on the Cross (1 Peter 2:24). Some people teach that Jesus actually received a sinful nature on the Cross. This idea is heresy. God the Father put our sin on Jesus, causing Him to be cut off from the Godhead in His humanity; but He died as a perfect man on the Cross, sinless and blameless. He was made sin so that we might be made righteous in Him. He was made our sin-offering and, as the sinless One, He died for us who deserved to die. (That is why it is sometimes said, "Jesus died in our place," or that He was our "substitute.")

Jesus Fulfilled the Picture of the Bronze Serpent

The story of Moses' bronze serpent on a pole (Numbers 21:7-9) was fulfilled by Jesus Christ. Jesus explained it to Nicodemus in John chapter 3.

The Israelites at that time had sinned terribly, and God had sent a plague of fiery serpents into their midst. Eventually they came to their senses, because people were dying all around: "**Therefore the people came to Moses, and said, "We have sinned, for we have spoken against the LORD and against you; pray to the LORD that He take away the serpents from us." So Moses prayed for the people**" (Numbers 21:7).

What did God tell Moses to do next? "**Then the LORD said to Moses, "Make a fiery serpent, and set it on a pole; and it shall be that everyone who is bitten, when he looks at it, shall live." So Moses made a bronze serpent, and put it on a pole; and so it was, if a serpent had bitten anyone, when he looked at the bronze serpent, he lived**" (verses 8-9). The word translated "**serpent**" three times in verse 9 is *nachash*—the original name of the serpent (and Satan) in the Garden of Eden. Moses thus made a serpent of bronze and raised it on a pole, and all who looked at it were delivered from the venom of the fiery serpents.

In John 3:14-15 Jesus referred to this: "**And as Moses lifted up the serpent in the wilderness, even so must the Son of Man be lifted up, that whoever believes in Him should not perish but have eternal life.**" (Again, we can see how the Bible is one book, and is its own commentary.) Because of our sin, Jesus, who was sinless, was made like Moses' serpent upon the Cross. The people simply had to look at Moses' serpent on the pole to be delivered from destruction. In the same way today, people just have to look at Jesus lifted up on the Cross and put their trust in Him, and then they will be delivered from eternal judgment. (This is of course precisely what Acts 16:31 and John 3:16 say.) The serpent in Moses' day, although a serpent like those which had brought destruction, was God's means of salvation. Similarly, Jesus was made sin, but became God's way of salvation for all mankind.

Jesus, a "Worm" on the Cross

Returning to Psalm 22, David said in verse 6, "**But I am a worm, and no man; a reproach of men, and despised of the people.**" As we have seen, Psalm 22 foreshadowed Jesus' suffering, and David was foretelling Jesus' words on the Cross. He referred to a "**worm**"—and we can learn some interesting things by looking at the word used.

Several different words are used for "worm" in the Bible; and the word used here in Psalm 22 referred to a special type of worm. This worm was used to produce the dye employed in manufacturing kingly robes. Thousands of them were put into a vat and crushed; and a tap at the bottom was then opened to release a scarlet-coloured fluid, which was the most precious dye found anywhere in the ancient world. Because purple and scarlet have always been difficult colours to produce,[12] kings throughout history have chosen to wear purple or scarlet robes. Such robes were a sign of great riches, because the necessary dye was so expensive.

The lesson for us is this: the Lord Jesus Christ was like a crushed worm on the Cross. And because He was crushed, His blood was shed, which enabled us to be covered in a robe of righteousness—a garment fit for kings. We have now become kings and priests unto God (1 Peter 2:9, Revelation 1:6). His blood was shed to redeem us, and it cost Him His life.

OUR DEBT HAS BEEN PAID AND CANCELLED

Paul, in Colossians 2:13-14, said, "**And you, being dead in your trespasses and the uncircumcision of your flesh, He has made alive together with Him, having forgiven you all trespasses, having wiped out the handwriting of requirements that was against us, which was contrary to us. And He has taken it out of the way, having nailed it to the Cross.**" God has forgiven all our trespasses. The verb translated "**wiped out**" (*exaleiphō*) means 'cancelled out,' 'blotted out,' 'erased' or 'obliterated.' The phrase "**handwriting of requirements**" meant a 'hand-written document,' and was a term used for a signed record or bill of debts—an "IOU" note. (Such a certificate could not be disputed because it was hand-written by the debtor.) God has therefore cancelled all our debts and any record of them through the Cross.[13]

The just penalty for our sin was death; and we were going to pay it when we died. We were due to be separated from God for all eternity. But

---

[12] Only some 140 years ago, when Sir William H. Perkin began analysing the colour purple in a laboratory at Greenford, was a purple dye developed that would not run during washing. He discovered the purple dye "mauve" from coal tar aniline in 1856, leading to the foundation of the aniline dye industry.

[13] Colossians 2:13 also points to God's answer to the old sin nature and the fact that we were born dead in trespasses and sins, which were other aspects of the first brick in the barrier in addition to our personal sins. The penalty of sin has been paid, but God has also provided deliverance from the power of the old sin nature. Although we will always have an old sin nature in this life, we have been made alive together with Christ and have received a new nature 'in Christ', enabling us to live for God now. These aspects of the work Christ accomplished for us are explained more fully in chapters 6 and 9.

Jesus came and died on the Cross for us and paid the penalty we owed. Thus God cancelled our IOU by nailing it to the Cross.

Conclusion

The second brick in the barrier has therefore been eradicated too. Jesus paid the penalty for our sins on the Cross (that is, expiation). He was cut off from fellowship with His Father and the Holy Spirit, and died on the Cross so that we might never be separated from God.

Our salvation was planned before we were even born. God could therefore with confidence write, through Paul, that nothing can ever separate us from the love of God in Christ (Romans 8:35-39). Nothing in our lives, whether circumstances, the devil or anything else, including death, can ever separate us from God's love.

Jesus Christ died on the Cross for us, and we have got something to celebrate! Sin has been dealt with, and the penalty of sin has also been removed. This is good news! Jesus died for the sins of the whole world. Our sins have been forgiven and we will not be judged for any of them.

Jesus said, and He says to everyone today, **"Come unto Me"**! (Matthew 11:28a, AV). By believing on the Lord Jesus Christ we receive eternal salvation, and, having received it, we can never lose it or have it taken away from us.

NOTES

6. WHY MUST WE BE BORN AGAIN?

BRICK THREE: **SPIRITUAL DEATH**

The third brick in the barrier is 'spiritual death.' Every person is born alive physically, but dead spiritually; and this is because of physical birth. We all had a human father, and our sinful nature and spiritual death have been inherited from him.

In Genesis 2:17, the LORD God warned Adam not to eat from the tree of the knowledge of good and evil, saying, **"In the day that you eat the fruit of it you shall surely die"** (or, **"dying, you shall die"**). Notice that He said Adam would die **"in that day"** (AV). Adam *did* eat the fruit, and yet he lived for hundreds of years after that day and died at the age of 930 (see Genesis 5:5). So in what way did Adam die in that day?

To recap, Adam died *spiritually* when he ate the forbidden fruit. Up to that time, Adam's human spirit had been filled with God's life and had been the channel of that life to his soul and body. He had been alive to God. But when Adam sinned, his spirit lost contact with God and became lifeless or 'dead.' Adam also then began to decay physically and to be vulnerable to sickness, and his physical death became inevitable.

THE UNBELIEVER'S PROBLEM — SPIRITUAL DEATH

The Bible says that **"in Adam, all die"** (1 Corinthians 15:22); and this sums up our problem: *the whole human race died spiritually in Adam.* This is evidenced by the fact that we are all destined to die physically.[1]

Watchman Nee expressed it beautifully.[2] He argued that if your great-grandfather had died when a small boy, you would not be here. You would have 'died in him'! Your experience is bound up with his. And not only would *you* have died, but all his descendants would have died in

---

[1] See footnote 3 in chapter 3.

[2] Refer to "The Normal Christian Life" by Watchman Nee, Chapter 2 (various publishers).

him. In the same way, our life comes from Adam, and we were all involved in Adam's sin. By being born 'in Adam' we received from him the result of his sin—that is, the nature of a sinner. The spiritual death of Adam thus meant the spiritual death of the whole human race 'in Adam,' and our physical birth as descendants of Adam inevitably means we were all born in a state of spiritual death.

It is, however, hard to convince most people today that they need a spiritual rebirth. They do not realize they are spiritually dead.

Every unbeliever today has a body, of course, and is a living soul (with intellect, emotions and will). He has an 'old sin nature' which he inherited from Adam, which causes him to commit sins. He also has a human spirit, but it is dead, because it died in Adam. He therefore cannot in any way communicate with God spiritually, because his 'aerial' is not functional, preventing him from receiving anything of a spiritual nature from God. We find this latter problem described in 1 Corinthians chapter 2.

The unbeliever's problem described in 1 Corinthians 2:9-14

This passage describes the unbeliever's problem. It begins, "**But as it is written: "Eye has not seen, nor ear heard, nor have entered into the heart of man the things which God has prepared for those who love Him"**" (verse 9). The eye and ear refer to the body, and the heart refers to the soul. This verse thus tells us that no one can understand what God has prepared for those who love Him by using their natural senses or mind.

"**But God has revealed them to us through His Spirit. For the Spirit searches all things, yes, the deep things of God. For what man knows the things of a man except the spirit of the man which is in him? Even so no one knows the things of God except the Spirit of God**" (verses 10 and 11). Unbelievers are quite unable to take in the things of God, because their human spirits are not functioning, and so they are unable to receive understanding of these things from God. Such information can only be received *spiritually* (that is, through the human spirit, from the Holy Spirit).

"**Now we have received, not the spirit of the world, but the Spirit who is from God, that we might know the things that have been freely given to us by God**" (verse 12). Once we are believers, God *is* able to communicate to us knowledge about the things He has freely given us. We have received the Holy Spirit, who now dwells inside us, and we are able to receive understanding from God through our human spirits which are made alive. We are *spiritually alive*.

"These things we also speak, not in words which man's wisdom teaches but which the Holy Spirit teaches, comparing spiritual things with spiritual" (verse 13). We should talk about the things of God, in spiritual terms. Unbelievers will not be able to understand, and some will think we are mad! But believers should know just what we are talking about.

"But the natural man does not receive the things of the Spirit of God, for they are foolishness to him; nor can he know them, because they are spiritually discerned" (verse 14). The word here for **"natural"** (*psuchikos*) could be translated 'soulish'.[3]

The natural man is one who lives according to his natural life or soul-life. Such a person only receives information in the soul, and so considers the things of the Spirit to be foolishness. Spiritual things can only be *spiritually* discerned; they cannot be discerned by the natural or earthly-minded person. Therefore, all unbelievers are necessarily natural or 'soulish,' because they function in the realm of the soul; their human spirit is dead.

Note that it is also possible for a believer to be soulish. Such a believer only analyses information in his mind. He does not discern it spiritually, and therefore he cannot go on to discover the deep things of God.

We should ask God to reveal to us what He wants us to learn in every situation. Many Christians do not look into what God has done for them and are never thrilled about what the Lord has in store for them, and thus they live at perhaps only 30 per cent of their potential. Having begun in the Spirit, they go on in the flesh (Galatians 3:3). God has things He wants to reveal to us through His Spirit in every situation.

THE WORK OF THE HOLY SPIRIT

How then can any unbeliever ever be saved, because the gospel message is *spiritual* information? How can any unbeliever understand or accept it, since he or she is spiritually dead? It is impossible, or so it seems.

In this we see the wonderful grace and glory of God, because *the Holy Spirit comes alongside and acts in place of the unbeliever's dead spirit!*

---

[3] Psuchikos refers to the one who is animated solely by the natural human life or 'earthly' life which all people share. It comes from psuchē, which means 'soul' or 'soul-life.'

The unbeliever cannot receive the gospel—which is a spiritual message—because his human spirit is lifeless and unable to function. And so the Holy Spirit *by grace* comes to do the work of the human spirit, and starts whispering in his ear. The Spirit comes and preaches the gospel to the unbeliever, convicting him of sin and revealing the truth to him!

It is the purpose and ministry of the Holy Spirit to convict people of their sin and to reveal God's plan of salvation to them (see John 16:8-9); without this ministry, no one would ever be saved. If God were not full of grace and did not love the whole world, then the Holy Spirit would have nothing to do with unbelievers. But God *is* full of grace, and the Holy Spirit comes and bridges the gap while a person is quite unable to receive a spiritual message.

Even today, the Holy Spirit is convicting people of sin and seeking to preach the gospel to every unbeliever on the earth, because it is God's will that everyone should be saved (1 Timothy 2:4). The unbeliever has to choose: "Will I or will I not believe in the Lord Jesus Christ?"

The Word of God plays a very important and powerful role too. When unbelievers hear the Word of God from the Bible, it goes into their mind (that is, their soul). The Holy Spirit can then use it as 'ammunition,' by revealing the truth of this information stored in their soul.

Vast numbers of people have been saved by just reading John's Gospel, for example, or some other part of the Bible. It is important, therefore, to use the Word of God when talking to unbelievers, and not simply to meet their arguments with your intellect.

THE NEW BIRTH: REGENERATION

When unbelievers say, "Yes, I believe," in response to the gospel message that the Holy Spirit is revealing to them, then they are '*born again.*' Their spirit, which was dead, is made alive. This is often called '*regeneration*' or '*new birth.*' The third brick in the barrier—the problem that man is born physically alive but spiritually dead—is solved by *regeneration.*

To live on the earth we have to be born physically into a natural family. Similarly, to live in heaven we have to be born again into a spiritual family—the family of God—which is the Church. Through regeneration our human spirits, which were dead, are made alive; and we immediately enter into a relationship with God.

Jesus' conversation with Nicodemus (John 3)

John 3:1-21 deals with this matter of the new birth. We will look at the passage verse by verse. It recounts Jesus' discussion with a man called Nicodemus.

"There was a man of the Pharisees named Nicodemus, a ruler of the Jews" (verse 1). Nicodemus was a Pharisee. This immediately tells us that he was an extremely religious man. Being a Pharisee meant he would pray at least seven times a day at certain hours, and, being in Jerusalem, he would visit the Temple at least three times a day. As well as this, he would have devoted a great deal of other time and money to his religion and, in fact, spent most of his day in an effort to serve God: talking about God, discussing theology or helping people. The name *Nicodemus* in Greek means 'conqueror of the people.' He was also "**a ruler of the Jews**". He was thus an important teacher of the Jews and someone people would have consulted if they were unsure or confused about something. He would have certainly studied a lot, and his mind (his soul) was therefore very developed; however, he could not receive or understand spiritual things.

"This man came to Jesus by night and said to Him, "Rabbi, we know that You are a teacher come from God..."" (verse 2a). Much is often made of the fact that Nicodemus visited Jesus at night, as if this suggests he was fearful of coming to Jesus or ashamed to do so publicly. However, he may simply have been too busy during the daytime!

He called Jesus, **"Rabbi"**, which meant 'Teacher' or 'Professor', and no more. Although Jesus had evidently impressed him, Nicodemus was not born again. A believer would probably have addressed Jesus as, "Lord," which would have implied, "You are God".[4] Intelligence is in the realm of the soul; and Nicodemus clearly was impressed in his mind—that is, in his soul.

Nicodemus had got it right; Jesus *was* a teacher come from God. He knew God was with Jesus because he had understood the Old Testament: **"Rabbi, we know that You are a teacher come from God; for no one can do these signs that you do unless God is with him"** (verse 2b).

---

[4] In the Septuagint, an ancient Greek translation of the Old Testament, some of the Hebrew names of God (*Jehovah, Adonai*, etc.) were often replaced by the Greek word *Kurios*, which is translated "Lord". Although *Kurios* could simply mean 'Sir,' in a religious context it usually signified God. Thus, if Nicodemus had called Jesus, "*Kurios*," he would have implied, "I know you are divine."

I want to spend some time considering this verse, because a very important principle emerges here.

SIGNS OF THE MESSIAH

God in His grace had revealed many signs to the Jews, in the Old Testament, to help them recognize their Messiah. The miracles Jesus did, and other signs that were fulfilled when He came, were therefore proof to the Jews that He was their Messiah.[5] Many of these signs were revealed in the books of the prophets, such as Isaiah and Zechariah. The Pharisees knew most, if not all, of the Old Testament books off by heart. Among the numerous signs were these, for example:

1. Zechariah foretold the throwing down of thirty pieces of silver in the Temple. "The next time you see this," he was saying, "Your Messiah is with you." This sign was fulfilled by Judas Iscariot (Matthew 27:5-10, Zechariah 11:12).

2. The gift of tongues (other languages) was given as a sign to the Jews to tell them when their Messiah had come. "When you hear the gospel preached in stammering Gentile languages," God was saying, "The Messiah has come" (see Isaiah 28:11 and 1 Corinthians 14: 21-22).

The Messiah's miracles

The miracles that the Messiah would do were distinct signs to help the Jews recognize Him.

"**In that day the deaf shall hear the words of the book and the eyes of the blind shall see out of obscurity and out of darkness. The humble also shall increase their joy in the LORD, and the poor among men shall rejoice in the Holy One of Israel**" (Isaiah 29:18-19).

Isaiah 35:3-6 said, "**Strengthen the weak hands, and make firm the feeble knees. Say to those who are fearful-hearted, "Be strong, do not fear! Behold, your God will come with vengeance, with the recompense of God; He will come and save you..."**" Who was this referring to? It referred to Jesus; He was coming with salvation. "**...Then the eyes of the blind shall be opened, and the ears of the deaf shall be unstopped. Then the lame shall leap like a deer, and the tongue of the**

---

[5] It has been calculated that some 330 Old Testament prophecies were fulfilled specifically by Jesus Christ during His first coming.

dumb sing. For waters shall burst forth in the wilderness, and streams in the desert." Isaiah wrote these things around 700 BC.

All these signs show us God's grace to the Jews. The Old Testament contained enough references to the signs and miracles that the Messiah would fulfil for every Jew, and in fact every Gentile believer too, to know who Jesus was. Unbelievers would have enough evidence to persuade them as well, that they might believe. This was grace: God revealing Himself to men when they did not deserve it.

All the believers should have quickly realized that the Messiah had come. Some of them doubted, however, despite these prophecies, including John the Baptist. John had at one time recognized Jesus, and said, **"Behold! The Lamb of God who takes away the sin of the world"** (John 1:29b). But later, when he was in prison, he doubted whether Jesus really was the Messiah: **"Now it came to pass, when Jesus finished commanding His twelve disciples, that He departed from there to teach and to preach in their cities. And when John had heard in prison about the works of Christ, he sent two of his disciples and said to Him, "Are you the Coming One, or do we look for another?""** (Matthew 11:1-3).

John had heard about the *works* of Christ while he was in prison (we don't know if he had also heard about His *words*). He was confused, so he sent two of his disciples to ask Jesus, "Are you the Messiah, or not?" Jesus' answer to John is very interesting: **"Jesus answered and said to them, "Go and tell John the things which you hear and see: the blind receive their sight and the lame walk; the lepers are cleansed and the deaf hear; the dead are raised up and the poor have the gospel preached to them""** (Matthew 11:4-5).

Jesus' response was to tell John about the miracles He was doing. He did not simply say to John, "Yes," or, "No." Jesus recognized that John knew the Old Testament very well. John would know the answer based on this reply. Jesus' reply was therefore most appropriate: He was answering John—a spiritual man—in spiritual terms.

Jesus' healing of a Jewish leper

Only Jesus could fulfil or obey the Old Testament law. For example, Leviticus 14 was fulfilled for the first time in Jesus' day. Leviticus 13 was known very well by the priests and applied constantly: they used it almost every day to help them recognize leprosy and to know what action to take. "**And the LORD spoke to Moses and Aaron, saying: "When a man has on the skin of his body a swelling, a scab, or a bright spot,** and it becomes on the skin of his body like a leprous sore, then....The priest shall look at him, and pronounce him unclean"'" (Leviticus 13:1-3).

However, the sting came in chapter 14: "**Then the LORD spoke to Moses, saying, "This shall be the law of the leper for the day of his cleansing: He shall be brought to the priest. And the priest shall go out of the camp** [because all the lepers were outside the camp]**, and the priest shall look; and indeed, if the leprosy is healed in the leper, then the priest shall command to take for him who is to be cleansed two living and clean birds, cedar wood, scarlet and hyssop...**"'" (Leviticus 14:1-4).

Leviticus 14 told the priests what to do *when leprosy was healed*. But there is one vital thing for us to realize: leprosy was an incurable condition, and until Jesus' day no Jewish leper had ever been healed. (Naaman who was miraculously healed of leprosy in the Old Testament was a Syrian, as is recorded in 2 Kings chapter 5). So for approximately 1500 years, Leviticus 14 had been learned by the priests, but they had never applied it—until Jesus came!

"**When He (Jesus) had come down from the mountain, great multitudes followed Him. And behold, a leper came and worshipped Him, saying, "Lord, if you are willing, you can make me clean." Then Jesus put out His hand and touched him, saying, "I am willing; be cleansed." And immediately his leprosy was cleansed**" (Matthew 8: 1-3). This man was a believer, as is shown by the fact that first of all he worshipped Jesus.

Most people who read this passage focus on the fact that Jesus was prepared to touch the leper to heal him. Although this was glorious, the real glory is seen in the next verse, which tells us: "**And Jesus said to him, "See that you tell no one; but go your way, show yourself to the priest, and offer the gift that Moses commanded, as a testimony to them"**" (verse 4).

This is extremely interesting. Jesus told the man to go *to the priest*, not to just anyone. This would have been quite a shock to the priest! And all the priests would immediately have known that the Messiah had come.

This was God reaching out in grace to the priests. They knew the Word of God, and this miracle would certainly have been very clear to them indeed. Jesus knew that the Word of God inside those priests could do more than any words of man could, as the Holy Spirit used it and revealed it to them.

WHY MUST WE BE BORN AGAIN?

JESUS TELLS NICODEMUS HE MUST BE BORN AGAIN

Returning to the account in John 3, Jesus then preached the gospel to Nicodemus. Although Nicodemus had correct theology to some extent, the real truth about God is *spiritual*. Jesus did not prolong the intellectual discussion. Instead, He cut right across Nicodemus' thinking.

"Jesus answered and said to him, "Most assuredly, I say to you, unless one is born again, he cannot see the kingdom of God"" (verse 3). Jesus got straight to the point. Again, the words "**Most assuredly**" are literally, "Amen, amen." Nicodemus needed his spirit to be made alive if he was to understand any spiritual truth. Jesus knew that Nicodemus wanted to talk *about* God, but Nicodemus could not receive spiritual information until he was born again. Jesus was not at all impressed with Nicodemus' intellectualism. Nicodemus was soulish. He could only act soulishly; although he did this very well!

"Nicodemus said to Him, "How can a man be born when he is old? Can he enter a second time into his mother's womb and be born?"" (verse 4). Nicodemus was effectively saying, "But that's silly!" He was not able to respond spiritually, so his reply was soulish. Nicodemus knew that Jesus was a teacher, so he was asking Him to explain what He meant.

Jesus gave him more information in verse 5: **"Jesus answered, "Most assuredly, I say to you, unless one is born of water and the Spirit, he cannot enter the kingdom of God.""** It is important to realize that the Greek word for "spirit" and the Greek word used for "wind" throughout John 3 are the same—*pneuma*, which also means 'breath'. (The word for 'spirit' in Hebrew, *ruach*, similarly also means 'wind' or 'breath'.) Also, there is no word for 'the' in front of "Spirit" here. If we translate *pneuma* as 'wind' in this verse, it thus reads, "Unless one is born out from water and wind, he cannot enter the kingdom of God."

Because Nicodemus was a Pharisee, Jesus was giving him an example from Jewish history. Jesus knew that Nicodemus could not take in any spiritual information, so He was not going to talk to him as he would to a believer; instead, He was going to talk to him as to a Jewish unbeliever who knew his history. When Nicodemus heard about water and wind, he would immediately have thought of the Exodus—the birth of the nation of Israel.

We need to look at Exodus 14:21. **"Then Moses stretched out his hand over the sea; and the LORD caused the sea to go back by a strong east wind all that night, and made the sea into dry land, and the waters**

were divided." God sent an east wind that caused the waters of the Red Sea to divide.

Before this event, Israel had been a captive nation, escaping and fleeing from Pharaoh. But, by this miracle of water and wind, Israel became a 'new' nation and escaped to enter the land God was giving them. This was in fact the rebirth of the nation that had been held in slavery by Pharaoh; and this rebirth took place through water and wind. Nicodemus could now see that Jesus was talking about something spiritual; he therefore began to realize that Jesus was talking about a *spiritual rebirth.*

Now let us look at John 3:5 from a different point of view. In the Bible, water is generally used to refer to three main things: the gospel, the word of God, or the Holy Spirit.[6] Jesus was referring to the word of God when He said "**water**" in John 3:5. He could not have meant the Holy Spirit, because He said, "**water <u>and</u> the Spirit**". Jesus was therefore saying that, unless you know about the gospel (and this is by the word of God) and unless you have the Holy Spirit preach it to you, you cannot enter the kingdom of God. The Holy Spirit acts in place of the lifeless human spirit and communicates the things of God. Whoever responds and believes on the Lord Jesus Christ can then enter the kingdom of God.

Jesus continued, "**That which is born of the flesh is flesh, and that which is born of the Spirit is spirit. Do not marvel that I said to you, 'You must be born again'**" (verses 6-7).

We are born physically of the flesh, and our natural bodies are suitable for our lives here on the earth. However, these bodies of ours are quite unsuitable for heaven, because heaven is a spiritual domain. To be fit for heaven, we require a spirit that is alive to God and also a spiritual body. The Israel that was in slavery in Egypt was an entirely different nation

---

[6] First, water is used to refer to the gospel: "Ho! Everyone who thirsts, come to the waters; and you who have no money, come, buy and eat. Yes, come buy wine and milk without money and without price. Why do you spend money for what is not bread, and your wages for what does not satisfy? Listen diligently to me, and eat what is good, and let your soul delight itself in abundance" (Isaiah 55:1-2); "And the Spirit and the bride say, "Come!" And let him who hears say, "Come!" And let him who thirsts come. And whoever desires, let him take the water of life freely" (Revelation 22:17). Of course, spiritual hunger and thirst are often likened to physical hunger and thirst: "Blessed are those who hunger and thirst for righteousness, for they shall be filled" (Matthew 5:6).

Second, water is used to refer to the word of God: "...that He might sanctify and cleanse it (the Church) with the washing of water by the word" (Ephesians 5:26).

Third, water is sometimes used to refer to the Holy Spirit, such as in John 7:37-39. Jesus said, ""He who believes in Me, as the Scripture has said, out of his heart [literally: belly or innermost being] will flow rivers of living water." But this He spoke concerning the Holy Spirit, whom those believing in Him would receive..." (verses 38-39a).

from the Israel which had been released from Egypt; and these contrasting nations typify flesh and spirit respectively. Those of us who have believed the gospel have experienced a spiritual rebirth; and we shall receive a resurrection body, either when we die or when Jesus Christ returns, which will be a spiritual body (1 Corinthians 15:44).

The above verses also highlight the contrast between theology, which can so easily be a mere lifeless activity of the flesh, and the truth, which is a spiritual thing. Christianity is a *relationship* with God through the Lord Jesus Christ, not a religious system.

By this time, Nicodemus' eyes were probably popping out! He simply could not believe what he was hearing.

To demonstrate what He had been saying, Jesus used an illustration about the wind: **"The wind blows where it wishes, and you hear the sound of it, but cannot tell where it comes from and where it goes. So is everyone who is born of the Spirit"** (verse 8). The wind is quite free. You cannot see it but, nevertheless, it is real. The wind can be seen by its effects; sometimes, it even uproots trees. The new birth is just as real and it too has great effects. Jesus was simply saying, "You believe in the wind, don't you?"

Nicodemus, despite being a brilliant man intellectually, simply could not understand: **"Nicodemus answered and said to Him, "How can these things be?""** (verse 9). He just could not take all this in! This is not surprising, since he was not yet born again. But he was going to understand, as we shall see later.

"Jesus answered and said to him, "Are you the teacher of Israel, and do not know these things? Most assuredly, I say to you, We speak what We know and testify what We have seen, and you do not receive Our witness. If I have told you earthly things and you do not believe, how will you believe if I tell you heavenly things?"" (verses 10-12).

In verse 11, Jesus used the term **"We"**. Had the disciples seen and understood these things? No, not really. So who does **"We"** refer to? Jesus meant *Himself and the Holy Spirit*. They were both witnesses to Nicodemus, both challenging him at that very moment! Jesus was providing the word of God and the Holy Spirit was taking it and preaching it to Nicodemus, acting as his spiritual 'aerial' or 'antenna' in place of his lifeless human spirit.

Notice the confidence Jesus had: Jesus knew exactly what He was saying, as did the Holy Spirit. We similarly should be able to speak confidently of what we know. We too should be able to say, "We," because when we are talking to someone about the gospel, the Holy Spirit is adding His own witness. It is again the royal "We"!

Jesus said to Nicodemus, **"If I have spoken to you of earthly things** [that is, the Exodus, the wind, etc.] **and you do not believe, how will you believe if I tell you heavenly things?"** (verse 12). If Nicodemus could not even receive and understand Jesus' earthly teaching in his soul, then how could he possibly receive *spiritual* truth?

"No one has ascended to heaven but He who came down from heaven, that is, the Son of Man who is in heaven" (verse 13). Notice the tenses in this verse; it *is* accurately translated. No human being had ascended to heaven at the time Jesus spoke, although in Old Testament times thousands had been truly saved. But they had gone to Paradise in Hades when they died and not to heaven itself. Jesus similarly went to Paradise when He died.[7] Only *after* His resurrection did He ascend to His Father in heaven.[8] So at the time Jesus spoke this to Nicodemus it was definitely true. Jesus Himself *was* the only man who had ever dwelt in heaven.

However it is not true any more! Now, believers immediately go to heaven when they die—straight into the presence of the Lord (see 2 Corinthians 5:8 for example). There are thus millions of saved souls in heaven today!

Being God manifested in the flesh, Jesus had in fact come down *from* heaven to live as a man on the earth. However, being God, who is omnipresent, Jesus was in heaven all the time—**"the Son of Man who is in heaven"**—in fellowship with the Father and with the Holy Spirit. Jesus Christ was both on the earth and yet also in heaven.[9]

---

[7] See footnote 18 in chapter 3, and explanation in the text above it.

[8] Jesus went straight to the Father when He rose from the dead (John 20:17) and He transferred all the dead believers who were captive in Paradise (a part of Hades) up to heaven. According to Ephesians 4:8-10, "He led captivity captive." Jesus had to be first to go to the Father in heaven, being the firstborn of many (Romans 8:29). For more details about Jesus' resurrection and ascension, and about death, Paradise and heaven, listen to the Special Topic Studies STS 39 by Roger Price, entitled "What happens when a person dies?" or STS 49-50, entitled "The power of God within us". The former study has been published in book form entitled "Explaining what happens after death" (Sovereign World).

[9] There is actually a similarity between this and our status as believers today. Physically we are obviously located on the earth. But we are also in fact indwelt by the Holy Spirit; and so we are spiritually in heaven, in the same sense as Jesus said that He was also in heaven. 1 Corinthians 6:17 says that our spirits are united to Jesus, and Ephesians 2:6 says that we were raised up together with Jesus and made to sit in heavenly places with Him at God's right hand.

Nicodemus hears the Gospel message

John 3:14-21 was Jesus' gospel message to Nicodemus. **"And as Moses lifted up the serpent in the wilderness, even so must the Son of Man be lifted up, that whoever believes in Him should not perish but have eternal life. For God so loved the world that He gave His only begotten Son, that whoever believes in Him should not perish but have everlasting life"** (verses 14-16). When Jesus said, **"whoever"**, He meant, "This includes you, Nicodemus!"

These were the words of Jesus. They are so often quoted today and called "John 3:16." But they were not originally John's words; they were the words of *Jesus* as He talked to Nicodemus—Nicodemus was still sitting there. Many people quote John 3:16 but do not realize it is part of this conversation; there has been no break yet. And Jesus was going to continue.

"For God did not send His Son into the world to condemn the world, but that the world through Him might be saved. He who believes in Him is not condemned; but he who does not believe is condemned already, because he has not believed in the name of the only begotten Son of God" (verses 17-18).

We looked at verse 18 in the previous study in isolation; but it too is part of this conversation. And in fact, Jesus had still not finished. He wasn't going to leave Nicodemus suspended; He was going to give him more of the gospel message.

"And this is the condemnation, that the light has come into the world, and men loved darkness rather than light, because their deeds were evil. For everyone practising evil hates the light and does not come to the light, lest his deeds should be exposed. But he who does the truth comes to the light, that his deeds may be clearly seen, that they have been done in God" (verses 19-21).

Do you see how Jesus put over the gospel message to Nicodemus? He began with the fact that Nicodemus had to be born again. Jesus said to him in effect, "Before you can even think of entering the kingdom of God, Nicodemus, you need to be born again." Nicodemus' spiritual death was a blockage to him, but Jesus told him plainly that the only answer was regeneration.

We can now cross out the third brick of the barrier: Jesus has redeemed us; He died for our sins, and the sins of the whole world; *and* by His Holy Spirit He now provides regeneration, which takes care of our spiritual death in Adam.

NICODEMUS WAS BORN AGAIN

Let us now see what happened to Nicodemus. We can learn from other passages that Nicodemus became a believer; he was honest before the Lord and accepted the fact that he needed to be born again. The message went in! We do not know exactly when he became a believer, but two other passages refer to him. The first is John 7:40-53.

"**Therefore many from the crowd, when they heard this saying, said, "Truly this is the Prophet"** [that is, the Prophet mentioned in Deuteronomy 18:15]**. Others said, "This is the Christ," but some said, "Will the Christ come out of Galilee? Has not the Scripture said that the Christ comes from the seed of David and from the town of Bethlehem, where David was?"'** There were some who knew their Bible and they knew that the Messiah would not come from Galilee but would come from Bethlehem. "**So there was a division among the people because of Him. Now some of them wanted to take Him, but no one laid hands on Him. Then the officers came to the chief priests and Pharisees, who said to them, "Why have you not brought Him?" The officers answered, "No man ever spoke like this Man!" Then the Pharisees answered them, "Are you also deceived? Have any of the rulers or the Pharisees believed in Him? But this crowd that does not know the law is accursed."'**

To paraphrase, the Pharisees were suggesting, "None of us or the rulers have believed in Him; therefore He cannot be the Christ. We would have told you if He was!" But there was one ruler who was very near, and his name was Nicodemus. "**Nicodemus (he who came to Jesus by night, being one of them) said to them, "Does our law judge a man before it hears him and knows what he is doing?" They answered and said to him, "Are you also from Galilee? Search and look, for no prophet has arisen out of Galilee."'**

What a shame it was that the officers, chief priests and Pharisees did not research where Jesus had actually come from, because they would have discovered their error. Jesus *had* in fact been born in Bethlehem, and not in Galilee as they assumed.

The passage ends with, "**And everyone went to his own house**" (verse 53). Perhaps Nicodemus stayed and asked Jesus where precisely He had been born, and at that moment realized Jesus was the Messiah. We just don't know. It may have been during this very conversation that Nicodemus was born again. I think it is a likely guess, although we cannot be sure.

However, by the time of Jesus' death, we know that Nicodemus helped to bury Jesus' body (see John 19:38-42): "**After this, Joseph of Arimathea, being a disciple of Jesus, but secretly, for fear of the Jews, asked Pilate that he might take away the body of Jesus; and Pilate gave him permission. So he came and took the body of Jesus. And Nicodemus, who at first came to Jesus by night, also came, bringing a mixture of myrrh and aloes, about a hundred pounds. Then they took the body of Jesus...**" (verses 38-40a).

Joseph of Arimathea was a disciple of Jesus, and these verses imply that by this time Nicodemus was also. This is thrilling: Nicodemus loved Jesus so much that he helped to bury His body. Nicodemus must have been so excited when he heard about the resurrection! He would suddenly have fully understood Jesus' conversation with him, which he was probably still puzzling over!

Conclusion

The answer to the third brick in the barrier is the new birth—that is, regeneration. Physical birth equips no one for heaven, but being born again does. How are we born again? It is through believing the gospel message. The gospel is spiritual information and so cannot be received by unbelievers who are spiritually dead. But God, in His grace, overcomes this problem by imparting spiritual information via the Holy Spirit.

The moment you believe on the Lord Jesus Christ you are born again. You are indwelt by the Spirit of God and your human spirit is made alive. Immediately you can understand things you have never understood before, and you enter into a relationship with God, who is now your Father. You also begin to experience the reality of Jesus inside you. Thereafter, the Holy Spirit works to reveal the wonderful truth of what God has done, that you might be brought into the glorious liberty of the sons of God.

Finally, we will look at three passages:

"**But as many as received Him, to them He gave the right to become children of God, even to those who believe in His name: who were born, not of blood, nor of the will of the flesh, nor of the will of man, but of God**" (John 1:12-13). The word for "**right**" could also be translated "authority". Those who believe on the Lord Jesus Christ are given the right or authority to be born again into a spiritual family—the family of God. God is your Father after you are born again!

"**But when the kindness and the love of God our Saviour appeared, not by works of righteousness which we have done, but according to His mercy He saved us, through the washing of regeneration and renewing of the Holy Spirit...**" (Titus 3:4-5). This describes our regeneration as a "**washing**", and links it to renewal by the Holy Spirit.[10] We did not earn our salvation, nor did anything in our lives obligate God to give it to us. Rather, He saved us according to His *mercy*.

In 1 Corinthians 15:22, Paul said, "**For as in Adam all die, even so in Christ all shall be made alive.**" We know this is true. We all died in Adam. But this verse testifies to the fact that God has dealt with the results of Adam's disobedience.[11] All will be resurrected, but those who believe on Christ are born again into the family of God and are made spiritually alive.

Notice again the phrase "**in Christ**". How does a person get 'in Christ'? Whenever someone believes the gospel and is born again, the Holy Spirit puts him or her 'in Christ' (see 1 Corinthians 1:30); it is one of the many things that happens to us when we believe. We are joined to Christ, and automatically become full members of the Body of Christ; and all by grace. There is no more condemnation for us at all (Romans 8:1); our life is now hidden with Christ in God (Colossians 3:3).

The gospel is this: "**Believe on the Lord Jesus Christ, and you will be saved**" (Acts 16:31). However, three bricks in the barrier still remain. In the next study we will see how they too have been dealt with.

NOTES

---

[10] The washing could refer to "washing of water by the word" as in Ephesians 5:26. Again, the word of God and the Spirit act hand in hand in the new birth.

[11] See footnote 3 in chapter 3. The resurrection of the dead is discussed in the next chapter.

7. THE BARRIER REMOVED —
PROPITIATION, JUSTIFICATION AND ETERNAL LIFE IN CHRIST

The barrier is now only half its former height, but unfortunately it is still high enough to separate us from God. The last three bricks are the ones we will see demolished in this study: man's incompatibility with the character of God; man's good deeds; and, temporal life. We have spent a lot of time demolishing the first three bricks, and, on that basis, we can now cover the last three more quickly.

Brick Four: THE CHARACTER OF GOD

The Bible reveals several major facets of God's character, such as His sovereignty, His eternal life, His love, holiness, righteousness and justice.[1] Someone who is an unbeliever can never come together with God, because there is a fundamental incompatibility of character between them.

For example, God is absolutely holy and righteous: He shines forth purity and, in Him, there is not even a shadow of sin. If an unbeliever comes into the picture, God's character leads Him to say, "I am sorry, but we are simply not compatible." There can therefore be no meeting between us and God unless God's character can in some way be reconciled with our character, and His opposition to our sin can be satisfied.[2]

Appeasement in other religions

Many religions talk about "appeasing" their god or gods. For example, in Bali, Indonesia, there are people whose god is a volcano; instead of fleeing when it erupts, they go up to it and worship their 'god', because

---

[1] The fifth series of Basic Bible Studies on "The Character of God" (BBS 64 to 77) by Roger Price covers ten major attributes of God's character: the Trinity; God's sovereignty; God's holiness; God's omniscience; God's omnipotence; God's omnipresence; God's eternal nature; God is love; God's immutability; and, God is faithful and true.

[2] We have seen how Jesus paid the penalty for our sins, but our sinfulness contributes to this fourth brick in the barrier as well—another example of how the bricks overlap.

they think he is angry and must be appeased. They think *they* have to do something to earn his goodwill.

Of all the people described in the Old Testament, the Canaanite Baal worshippers were amongst the most degenerate. In fact, there are several chapters in the Bible which warned the Israelites about the Canaanites and about Baal. (The worst king that Israel ever had was Ahab; he was married to a beautiful Canaanite woman called Jezebel, who was a priestess of Baal.)

The worshippers of Baal and Molech (who included the Canaanites and the Ammonites, respectively) used to appease their gods by human sacrifice, and in particular, by the sacrifice of children. They had a statue which had its hands stretched out, and a fire was lit underneath. Children were thrown into the hands and burned alive. An old English word for the place of torment in Hades, Tophet, comes from this terrible form of idol worship: Topheth was an ancient place of human sacrifice near Jerusalem, part of the Valley of Hinnom (see 2 Kings 23:10, Jeremiah 7:31), and the Hebrews used this name for describing eternal 'Hell fire'. Its name possibly derives from a *toph*—the large drum that was beaten during a ceremony of human sacrifice to cover up the cries of the children.

During the 3rd Punic War (shortly after 150 BC), when the Romans were attacking Carthage near the coast of north Africa, the defending army had already been severely diminished; nevertheless, the people of Carthage were found to be slaughtering their young men inside the gates in an effort to appease Baal.

Such attempts at appeasement of the gods is well known. However, we need to realize that our God is never appeased by anything we can do.[3] Sometimes we try, for example by saying, "Oh, Lord, I'll never do that again." But of course God knows us well enough to know that we *will* do it again; and if we were honest, we would admit that we would do it again! Do you see that what we are trying to do is to appease God? We are asking, "God, if I promise to live a better life this week, will you please bless me?" But God cannot be appeased like that.

---

[3] God, who is the one true God, is not capricious or vindictive like many of the pagan 'gods', and He cannot be bribed by gifts or sacrifices from men. He is constant, unchanging and merciful. Nevertheless, He is utterly opposed to sin, and His displeasure and anger at sin itself and all who have committed sin must be averted before He can even look on sinful man.

Propitiation

God is 'appeased' and His anger at sin is averted through one thing only: the death of the Lord Jesus Christ on the Cross. This has satisfied Him once and for all! The message is the same, but this is a different aspect of it: Jesus' death on the Cross appeased God forever, and God said, "That's good enough for Me!"

'*Propitiation*' is the name given to this turning away of God's anger and the satisfying of the just demands of God's character through the Cross. Jesus' sacrifice of Himself ensured that God's holy character was completely vindicated and satisfied, making it possible for Him to show mercy righteously. In exploring propitiation, it will be useful first to look at several references to it in the New Testament.

"And He (Jesus) Himself is the propitiation for our sins, and not for ours only but also for the whole world" (1 John 2:2). We have already seen that Jesus died for the sins of the whole world, but notice the first part of this verse: He is the *propitiation* for our sins.

"In this is love, not that we loved God, but that He loved us and sent His Son to be the propitiation for our sins" (1 John 4:10). God was the author of our salvation. Before time began, He knew we would need saving and He planned to send Jesus as the propitiation for our sins. The Greek word translated "**propitiation**" in both these verses is *hilasmos*.

"(Christ Jesus) whom God set forth to be a propitiation by His blood, through faith, to demonstrate His righteousness, because in His forbearance God had passed over the sins that were previously committed..." (Romans 3:25). This does not mean that everyone will be saved, for verse 26 goes on to say that it is necessary to have faith in Jesus: **"...to demonstrate at the present time His righteousness, that He might be just and the justifier of the one who has faith in Jesus."** We will examine Romans chapter 3 in more detail in the next study. The Greek word for propitiation used in verse 25 is *hilastērion*.

To understand propitiation in more detail and what it meant in the Old Testament, we can look at another use of this same Greek word in a passage in the Book of Hebrews.[4]

---

[4] No one knows who wrote the Book of Hebrews. Some people say it was written by Apollos, or by Nicodemus or Paul. We simply do not know. It doesn't actually matter, because it is the message of the book and not the writer that counts; the Holy Spirit inspired the Book of Hebrews and man does not count at all. All truth is God's truth—it is for this reason that no detailed bibliography is given for these studies; it would have to be extremely long!

Hebrews tells us that many things in the Old Testament pointed to Christ and His work. Hebrews 9:2-5 describes the Ark of the Covenant: "**For a tabernacle was prepared: the first part, in which was the lampstand, the table, and the showbread, which is called the sanctuary; and behind the second veil, the part of the tabernacle which is called the Holiest of All, which had the golden altar of incense and the Ark of the Covenant overlaid on all sides with gold, in which were the golden pot that had the manna, Aaron's rod that budded, and the tablets of the covenant; and above it were the cherubim of glory overshadowing the mercy seat. Of these things we cannot now speak in detail.**" The writer said that this subject of symbols in the Old Testament was so vast that he could not go into detail.

Where is the word *hilastērion*? It is the word translated "**mercy seat**" in verse 5. We will thus learn more about propitiation if we look at the mercy seat and understand what it meant in the life of the people of Israel.

What the Old Testament tells us about Propitiation

The Old Testament tells us how God chose Israel to be His people so that they might preach the gospel to all the world. The message in Israel's charge was this: a Messiah is coming who will take away the sins of the world.

Abraham, who became the first Hebrew,[5] began his life in Ur of the Chaldeans. His family had been idolaters (Joshua 24:2); but Abraham came to understand the gospel. He didn't actually know the Messiah's name, but he believed in Him (John 8:56) and in God's salvation.

The gospel message has always been the same, and people were saved in the Old Testament in exactly the same way as they are now—by believing in God's Messiah, who would come to die for the sins of the people. The only difference then was that the Messiah was to come in the future; today, we believe in Jesus Christ who has already come.

---

[5] The word 'Hebrew' is thought to be derived from a verb meaning 'to pass,' 'to cross over' or 'to go beyond,' and thus means 'one who crossed over' or 'one from the other side.' (It may mean 'son of Eber,' but Eber also comes from the verb 'to pass over.') Abraham crossed over the River Euphrates (Joshua 24:3) and the River Jordan. He was called "Abram the Hebrew" (Genesis 14:13) and his descendants became known as the "Hebrews." They later came to be called the "Israelites" (descendants of Jacob, who was called Israel) or "Jews" (derived from 'Judea'). The peoples of the other nations, that is non-Jews, were known as "Gentiles" (meaning 'nations').

THE BARRIER REMOVED

God chose to illustrate salvation *visually* in Israel, since most people had limited access to the written Scriptures or couldn't read. He gave to the Israelites pictures that would tell them, and the rest of the world, about how He would provide salvation. Everything relating to the Tabernacle (and later, the Temple), the feasts and sabbaths, the priests' garments, the priests' ministries, and all the sacrifices, were pictures relating to the Messiah. They all presented one overall message: God would one day provide a way of salvation.

Every time a lamb was brought, without a blemish, it represented the perfection of Christ; and when that lamb was killed, it represented the death of Jesus on the Cross. All that the people had to do was learn about this future provision of God and put their faith in the salvation God would bring; then they were saved.

The Ark of the Covenant

God gave precise instructions for making all the items relating to the Tabernacle. Each item was significant in representing God's plan of salvation. The Ark was a box made of acacia wood, overlaid with gold; it was beautiful. It was a picture of Christ: the wood spoke of Jesus' humanity and the gold of His divinity. Inside were three things, pointing to man's fundamental rejection of God:

1. The *stone tablets of the covenant* each had the Ten Commandments written on them. The commandments had been given to show Israel that man is a sinner and that he cannot keep God's law and be righteous by himself.[6] They showed that everyone breaks the law and therefore needs a saviour.

2. *Aaron's rod that budded* showed how man rejects God's authority. God chose Aaron as His priest to guide the people, and established His choice when He caused Aaron's rod to bud following a rebellion and murmurings. (This is described in Numbers chapter 17; note that Numbers 17:10 said that Aaron's rod which had budded should be kept as a sign against the rebels.)

3. The *golden pot of manna* represented the fact that people naturally do not accept God's provision, but try to make provision for themselves.

These three things were kept inside the Ark of the Covenant, and were never seen. Because they were hidden inside, they pointed to the grace of God: that our sins and our rebellion are hidden in Christ. The Ark

---

[6] See Romans 3:19-20, 1 Timothy 1:9 and Galatians 3:24, for example.

represented Jesus Christ and His work. Our sins are hidden in Christ, and it is no one's business to look at them.

The mercy seat

The lid over the top of the ark was the "mercy seat," which was a thick slab of gold. It represented propitiation, and pointed to God's character being satisfied. It is described in Exodus 25:

"You shall make a mercy seat of pure gold; two and a half cubits shall be its length and a cubit and a half its width. And you shall make two cherubim of gold; of hammered work you shall make them at the two ends of the mercy seat. Make one cherub at one end, and the other cherub at the other end; you shall make the cherubim at the two ends of it of one piece with the mercy seat. And the cherubim shall stretch out their wings above, covering the mercy seat with their wings, and they shall face one another; the faces of the cherubim shall be towards the mercy seat" (Exodus 25:17-20). Two cherubim were thus over the mercy seat. Their wings probably almost touched above the mercy seat, thus covering it, and their faces were towards each other, looking down at the mercy seat.

Cherubim are always found guarding something in the Bible, and specifically guarding God's holiness in relation to judgment on sin. In Genesis, for example, cherubim were sent by God to guard the Garden of Eden, to prevent Adam and Eve from eating of the tree of life after the Fall (see Genesis 3:24). Here, above the Ark, the cherubim were guardians of the holiness of God at the mercy seat.

"You shall put the mercy seat on top of the ark, and in the ark you shall put the Testimony that I will give you. And there I will meet with you, and I will speak with you from above the mercy seat, from between the two cherubim which are on the ark of the Testimony, of all things which I will give you in commandment to the children of Israel" (Exodus 25:21-22). God was going to come and commune with Israel from above the mercy seat, between the cherubim.

In fact, on one day every year, on the Day of Atonement, the High Priest used to go through the veil and enter the Holy of Holies carrying blood.[7]

---

[7] The High Priest entered the Holy of Holies with the blood of a young bull as a sin offering for himself and for his household, and then with the blood of a young goat as a sin offering for the people. The blood was sprinkled with his finger on the mercy seat and before the mercy seat. A second young goat was not killed but presented alive before the LORD and released as the 'scapegoat,' bearing the sins of all the children of Israel to an uninhabited land. This Day of Atonement is described in Leviticus 16.

THE BARRIER REMOVED

(No one was allowed into the Holy of Holies except the High Priest on this one day.) He took the blood and sprinkled it on the mercy seat; and God was satisfied by it. God's presence then came down on top of the mercy seat and His 'Shekinah' glory[8] would shine there, to show that He was completely satisfied.

The people who were gathered outside the Tabernacle could not see this event, and in fact never saw inside the erected Tabernacle.[9] Rather, they would listen for the sound of the bells on the High Priest's garments. If the noise stopped, it would mean that the High Priest had been slain by God and that God had not accepted the blood. If they heard the bells it meant that God was accepting the blood. (This is a picture of us rejoicing at all times because God is satisfied by the sacrifice of Jesus. We do not need bells on our garments; we have mouths with which to praise God!) The Shekinah glory appearing over the mercy seat therefore reminds us of God's acceptance of the blood of Jesus.

The mercy seat was thus extremely important. It represented the satisfaction of God's character and so it rightly bore the name '*hilastērion*' (propitiation). It represented God saying, "I accept the work of Jesus." Jesus Christ made propitiation[10] for sins and God accepted His work.

Psalm 85:10 gives a lovely description of the work done at the mercy seat: "**Mercy and truth have met together; righteousness and peace have kissed each other.**" As propitiation took place at the mercy seat, God's mercy and truth met. In the same way, God's mercy and truth met and His righteousness and peace came together at the Cross.

The brick of man's incompatibility with God's character has been removed by propitiation. We therefore no longer need to fear the character of God, and think that we will be unable to stand in His presence. God's anger has been averted and He has been satisfied by the shed blood of Jesus. God will therefore be able to say to us, **"Well done,**

---

[8] This is a term derived from the Hebrew word *shakan* meaning 'to rest' or 'to dwell'. It is not found in the Bible itself, but the term was used by the Jews at a later time to express the visible splendour of God's presence, specifically when resting or dwelling between the cherubim above the mercy seat, in the Tabernacle or in Solomon's Temple.

[9] The only time they saw any of these items was when the Tabernacle was dismantled and the camp moved on. Special families had to dismantle it all and transport it. The people would then be told by the priests and Levites what the items were for and what they represented.

[10] Another closely associated Greek word *hilaskomai* is used twice in the New Testament, being translated as "make propitiation" in Hebrews 2:17, and as "be merciful" in Luke 18:13.

good and faithful servant.... Enter into the joy of your lord" (Matthew 25:21,23), and we will not be ashamed.[11]

Brick Five: MAN'S GOOD DEEDS

Most people would say that there is good and there is evil, and would recognize that there is some difference and conflict between the two. But here we are considering a clash between *two types of goodness*. The Bible makes clear that there is *God's* goodness and there are *man's* own attempts at goodness; and the latter cannot match up to God's goodness in any way.

We may think that certain qualities we observe in other people or certain of their deeds are 'good.' However, *God* does not necessarily call these same things good. Many atheists, for example, do a lot of charitable deeds that we might call good. However, the critical question is not whether the good that we—or someone else—may do is acceptable in the eyes of other people, or even ourselves, but rather whether it is acceptable to God.[12]

This is the problem: all of man's best deeds do not even begin to approach God's standard of goodness. It is not whether you get on with *me* that counts, but rather how you get on with *God*. "**For all have sinned and fall short of the glory of God**" (Romans 3:23). We might be able to match up to a man's glory and obtain favour with men, but we can never match up to God's glory. We all fade in comparison with God in every way. Isaiah 64:6 tells us that, "**we are all like an unclean thing, and all our righteousnesses are like filthy rags.**" In fact, this verse implies that the harder we work to try and impress God with our good deeds, the more filthy rags we accumulate, and therefore the bigger the

---

[11] In context, these words will be spoken by Jesus to believers who have carried out good works in faith and in obedience to God. These verses are dealt with in detail in Basic Bible Study BBS 23, entitled "Palaces or Mud Huts?" which covers the judgment of believers' works.

[12] In fact, many unbelievers live lives that are ostensibly 'better' than those of believers. In some ways, this should not surprise us, since when an unbeliever is saved, he or she suddenly acquires some terrible new enemies: the world, the flesh and the devil. As a new Christian, you suddenly are completely at odds with the things the world represents. Immediately the flesh starts causing trouble and you have problem after problem. The devil becomes your arch enemy and he hates you. Many believers consequently have a much more difficult time than unbelievers. Also, as a Christian, you can no longer hide the bad elements of your character so easily, because, as the Holy Spirit begins to work deeply in you, He makes sure that the hidden areas are dealt with. It is hard for a Christian to live a life that the world will call blameless or a shining example, but as the indwelling Holy Spirit gains control, it is not long before the glory of God shines forth, and the transcendent power is seen to be of Him!

obstacle there is between us and God! Therefore, not only do our sins cut us off from God, but our filthy good deeds do too. Any attempts we may make to reconcile ourselves to God or gain favour with God make the problem worse. There is nothing therefore that *we* can do about it. We are all helpless.

IMPUTATION

As we have seen before, Peter said in Acts 4:12, **"Nor is there salvation in any other [than Jesus Christ], for there is no other name under heaven given among men by which we must be saved."** It is not your good deeds, but faith in the Lord Jesus Christ that will ensure your acceptance by God.

To understand how the problem of our good deeds not matching up to God's goodness has been solved, it is useful to consider our goodness versus God's in terms of our 'account' before God. The problem we face has been solved by a 'transaction' that is often called *"imputation"*. The English word 'impute' means 'to ascribe to another person'.[13]

In accounting there are debits and credits. I have drawn out two accountancy balance sheets, one for Jesus and one for us.

Jesus' balance sheet looks good: He had no old sin nature and He never committed any sins; therefore on the debit side He has nothing. On the credit side He has absolute righteousness, because He is completely holy, good, and just.

Our balance sheet, on the other hand, looks bad. On the debit side we have our old sin nature and our personal sins. Our sins originate from our old sin nature, but they become a second item on the debit side of our account. In addition, as we have seen, our good deeds actually count *against* us; therefore they also go on the *debit* side, not on the credit side. On the credit side we have nothing.

---

[13] To impute thus means to endue or clothe someone with a virtue not intrinsically his own. The English word 'impute' occurs rarely in most New Testament translations, but other words are used, such as 'reckon' or 'count,' to convey the same idea. These words are used to translate the Greek verb *logizomai*, which means 'to reckon,' 'to calculate,' 'to count,' 'to consider' or 'to suppose.' In the context of accounting, *logizomai* can mean making an entry on the credit or debit side of an account.

The Greek word *ellogeo*, which occurs twice in the New Testament (Romans 5:13, Philemon 18), is translated "impute" in some versions. It was a commercial or accounting term, meaning 'to charge to someone's account,' that is, 'to make an entry on the debit side.'

JESUS	
DEBIT	CREDIT
0	
0	absolute righteousness
0	

ME	
DEBIT	CREDIT
old sin nature	
personal sins	0
'filthy' good deeds	

To have fellowship with God we need a righteousness equal to God's. Our disastrous account therefore must be changed to make it like Jesus' account. How could this be done?

The answer is given in 2 Corinthians 5:21, which we have studied before: **"For He (God the Father) made Him who knew no sin (Jesus) to be sin for us, that we might become the righteousness of God in Him (Jesus)."** This is a very important verse, and it explains God's wonderful solution.

God's solution was simple but remarkable. God the Father took our debits and He put them on Jesus Christ, who paid the penalty for them on the Cross. Jesus died for our sins and paid our debt (which as we learned before was expiation); and our old sin nature and good deeds were dealt with too. We therefore have no more debits; and neither has Jesus, because He paid the debt.

However, to have fellowship with God we still need a righteousness equal to the absolute righteousness of God. God solved this impossibility by *imputing* (or *reckoning*) His absolute righteousness to our account, **"...that we might become the righteousness of God in Him."**

Notice that we become righteous **"in Him"**, that is, 'in Christ'. At the moment of salvation, we are put in Christ and absolute righteousness becomes ours *in Him*—God's own righteousness is imputed to us. We do not earn it or deserve it, and we do not gain it through our good deeds. Therefore, we can say, "Lord, *I* am a sinner. But thank you, Lord, that Your righteousness is given to me!"

Therefore, we who are believers can now have fellowship with God! Imputation solves the whole problem as far as God is concerned. He dealt with our sins, but He also gave us His righteousness. We have ended up not only without sin, as far as our account with God is concerned, but we now have the righteousness of God in Christ! God could only meet us on equal terms, and He gave us grace, grace, grace! This righteousness comes through faith in the Lord Jesus. If you believe on the Lord you receive this righteousness *in Him*. It has nothing to do with your works.[14]

It is important, however, to understand that all believers should produce good works. As we learn to live and walk according to the Holy Spirit who now indwells us, He will produce fruit in us. Thus, 'good works' in a believer's life are those produced through the working of the Holy Spirit in us, as we walk by faith and live by the Spirit. These good works are then the outworking of the life of Christ in us and *are* pleasing to God. They are no longer the works of the flesh, and are no longer like filthy rags to God.[15]

JUSTIFICATION BY FAITH

Righteousness therefore comes by *faith*, not by works. Israel made a great mistake about this. "**What shall we say then? That Gentiles, who did not pursue righteousness, have attained to righteousness, even the righteousness of faith; but Israel, pursuing the law of righteousness, has not attained to the law of righteousness. Why? Because they did not seek it by faith, but as it were, by the works of the law. For they stumbled at that stumbling stone**" (Romans 9:30-32). Those who tried to work to become righteous failed; but those who believed on the Lord Jesus Christ received God's righteousness *by faith*.

In Old Testament times, it wasn't only Israelites who were saved; many Gentiles were saved too.[16] Some Gentiles were saved when Jewish

---

[14] Believing is an act of the will, which involves the whole person, not just the intellect or emotions. It is a definite act in which one chooses to trust Christ for salvation and to receive Him by faith.

[15] Works of the flesh are those that originate from the old sin nature of the natural man; they are always like filthy rags to God. However, good works are those that have their origin in Jesus Christ, and are carried out in obedience to God and in the power of the Holy Spirit by faith, with dependence on God. Such works are pleasing and acceptable to God. We should seek to do such good works—not to try to earn anything from God, but rather to please God who is now our Father, in fulfilment of His plans for us (see Ephesians 2:10).

[16] Melchizedek, a Jebusite, is but one example. He ministered one day to Abraham, and it is clear he was a believer (see Genesis 14:18-20). Rahab is another example (see Joshua chapter 2, Hebrews 11:31).

believers preached the gospel to them, but others were saved when God revealed Himself by other means.

The Gentiles knew they could not keep the law and, in general, did not even try. Similarly, at the time Paul wrote, the Gentiles were not seeking after righteousness, but they were laying hold of it by putting their faith in Christ. (In fact, the religious Jews often made things difficult for the Gentiles by trying to burden them with the law.)

In the Old Testament it was the same as now—righteousness was reckoned on the basis of faith. Abraham is a good example, who **"believed in the LORD, and He accounted it to him for righteousness"** (Genesis 15:6). Abraham was saved by faith in just the same way as we are: his faith was reckoned to him for righteousness. Righteousness was imputed to him; and in the same way, righteousness is imputed to us. (We will examine Paul's discussion of this in Romans 4:1-8 in the next study.)

The religious Jews thought that by keeping the law they would become righteous; and Paul called this principle their "**law of righteousness**". They used not only to try to obey the law, but to pray seven times a day and to keep numerous other rituals.[17]

The translation of Romans 9:31 could be amended to read, "But Israel, pursuing a law of righteousness, did not arrive at a law of righteousness." They were pursuing a pattern of behaviour associated with righteousness, but they did not arrive at a successful pattern which could produce righteousness. They tried to keep the law and, therefore, because God's righteousness comes by faith and not by man's good deeds, they did not obtain His righteousness.

The religious Jews thus missed righteousness and stumbled over Jesus. Paul quoted Isaiah in Romans 9:33, "**As it is written: "Behold, I lay in Zion a stumbling stone and rock of offence, and whoever believes on Him will not be put to shame"**" (quoted from Isaiah 8:14 and Isaiah 28:16). The religious Jews could never be made righteous by trying to keep the law. They had stumbled over Jesus on this very issue of faith versus good works; and they thus crashed into the brick of man's good deeds.

---

[17] In Philippians 3:6 Paul spoke of "the righteousness which is in the law", according to which he was blameless. But God can only be satisfied by His own righteousness.

"**Knowing that a man is not justified by the works of the law but by faith in Jesus Christ, even we have believed in Christ Jesus, that we might be justified by faith in Christ and not by the works of the law; for by the works of the law no flesh shall be justified**" (Galatians 2:16). This verse uses the word "**justified**", which means 'vindicated.' In the New Testament it specifically means to be declared righteous and treated as righteous by God.[18] Trying to keep the law will not succeed. Even if we kept the whole law (which is impossible in view of the old sin nature), it would not be good enough. The righteousness of God comes by faith in Jesus Christ.

Not one of us could ever expect to keep the whole law, not even the first great commandment, "**You shall love the LORD your God with all your heart, with all your soul, and with all your might**" (Deuteronomy 6:5, Matthew 22:37-38). Each of us has surely failed in this; and so we have to go 'beyond' law by faith in the Lord Jesus. Jesus *did* keep the whole of the law given in the Old Testament; and He has always loved His Father completely. We who believe are now holy because He is holy. God's righteousness has been *imputed* to us, and that is grace!

No one can ever be justified based on works of the law, but we have been justified by putting our faith in Christ. "**Therefore, having been justified by faith, we have peace with God through our Lord Jesus Christ**" (Romans 5:1). We have been given the righteousness of God in Christ, and so we are justified in His sight! There is therefore no need for us to be ashamed. We have peace with God.

The brick of man's good deeds has thus been dealt with by imputation and by justification. There is now only one more brick left.

---

[18] Note that the two families of English words 'just,' 'justice,' 'justified' etc. and 'righteous,' 'righteousness' etc. are alternative translations of Hebrew and Greek words derived from common roots. For example, the Greek word *dikaiosunē* can be translated 'justice' or 'righteousness'.

The Hebrew words translated 'righteous' or 'just' carried the idea of being 'straight' or 'upright' in one's relationships with God and man.

Righteousness thus implies conformity to God's law, but is really summed up by loving God with all of one's being and loving one's neighbour as oneself. There is no distinction between the claims of love and righteousness in Scripture. Righteousness thus relates to our right-standing with God, but it must be outlived and demonstrated by how we treat others.

'Justification' (to be accepted as righteous) was part of the process of judgment under the law (see Deuteronomy 25:1): the righteous were those acquitted by the judge, and righteousness was the standing of those so acquitted. But justification had not only a legal meaning. It also had a civil meaning, namely, restoration to a position as heir and entitlement to receive and keep an inheritance.

Brick Six: TEMPORAL LIFE[19]

When God created Adam and Eve to inhabit the earth, He designed them to have fellowship with Him and to glorify Him forever in their human bodies. As physical and spiritual beings they enjoyed unhindered fellowship with the Lord until it was suddenly broken because of sin. The result was spiritual separation from God; but they also received the sentence of physical death upon their bodies. Without God's plan of salvation, physical death threatened to be their permanent state.

We have all inherited 'temporal life' from Adam and Eve. None of us is naturally going to live forever, because we all come under the same sentence of death and so must all die physically (unless the Lord Jesus returns first). This is the sixth and final brick in our barrier between God and man.

We have already seen how the new birth overcomes spiritual death. Believers are made spiritually alive when they are born again: **"And you He made alive, who were dead in trespasses and sins....For by grace you have been saved through faith..."** (Ephesians 2:1,8). Just as spiritual death is undone through new life in Christ, physical death is undone through the provision of a resurrection body. These are God's provision for us to have fellowship with Him forever, according to His original design.

Eternal Life in Christ

God is eternal and unchanging. He has always existed, and He lives forever. In fact, He inhabits eternity (Isaiah 57:15).[20]

Without *eternal* life we cannot have fellowship with God forever. It is therefore essential to God's plan that we receive *eternal* life. **"And this is eternal life, that they may know You, the only true God, and Jesus Christ whom You have sent"** (John 17:3).

---

[19] This section has been expanded compared with the audio tape of BBS 7, to complete the logic. Brief details have been included about Jesus' victory over death, which made it possible for us to receive new 'resurrection' bodies in the future.

[20] God is the eternal One. He told Moses that He should be known by the name "I AM THAT I AM" or simply "I AM" (Exodus 3:13-14). Time to God is always present. He is not bound by time as we are; rather, He created time. He can review the whole of time in an instant, for He dwells outside of its constraints. Eternity is not simply endless time; rather, eternity is the uncreated realm in which God Himself exists.

The moment we were born again, and the Holy Spirit put us 'in Christ,' we entered in to all that was in Jesus Christ already, and we received everything that He has. 2 Corinthians 5:21 tells us how we received God's own righteousness in Christ: "**...that we might become the righteousness of God in Him**". However, we have entered into much more besides!

"**And this is the testimony: that God has given us eternal life, and this life is in His Son. He who has the Son has life; he who does not have the Son of God does not have life**" (1 John 5:11-12). There is *eternal* life in the Lord Jesus Christ—who is God. We have been put 'in Christ' and, therefore, we have received eternal life in Him. This is thrilling. God's brilliant plan has taken care of every eventuality! Our temporal life now means nothing, because we are in Christ. Our temporal life is utterly "**hidden with Christ in God**" (Colossians 3:3).

Christ is now seated in heaven at God's right hand. If we are believers, we are therefore seated with Him in heavenly places in reality at this very moment, although we still have to live on the earth for a short while longer. Christ is our witness in heaven; He intercedes for us there as our advocate. But we are now witnesses and ambassadors for Jesus on the earth. He represents us there; but we represent Him here on the earth.

We need to understand how to live in these two realms. We must learn to walk by faith and not by sight (2 Corinthians 5:7), because, although we are living *in* the world, we are truly seated with Christ in heaven right now and are not *of* the world (John 17:15-18).

The moment we die, however, we will become united with Christ completely. Spiritually, we are already joined to the Lord (1 Corinthians 6:17) and already live in heaven, and so when we die our spiritual life simply continues unaffected. Believers will go straight into the presence of the Lord when they die, and physical death will be the gateway through which they pass to be with Him, which is far better than continuing to live in this fallen world (Philippians 1:23). Physical death is therefore no longer a barrier to fellowship with God, but is rather the entrance to a life in which we can enjoy fellowship with Him face to face (1 Corinthians 13:12), and in which we will be freed from our old sin nature.

With such joy in prospect, we no longer need to fear death. Jesus Christ came in the flesh so that, "**through death He might destroy him who had the power of death, that is, the devil, and release those who through fear of death were all their lifetime subject to bondage**" (Hebrews 2:14b-15).

Jesus said to Martha, just before He raised Lazarus from the dead, **"I am the resurrection and the life. He who believes in Me, even though he dies, he shall live. And whoever lives and believes in Me shall never die…"** (John 11:25-26).

The amazing gift of eternal life has been made available to everyone: **"For God so loved the world that He gave His only begotten Son, that whoever believes in Him should not perish but have everlasting life"** (John 3:16). If we have believed in Him, our position is now *in Christ*, and by virtue of this glorious position we have received eternal life. **"The gift of God is eternal life in Christ Jesus our Lord"** (Romans 6:23).

ALL SHALL BE MADE ALIVE

The whole of mankind died spiritually in Adam at the Fall, and became subject to physical decay, sickness and death. When Jesus died on the Cross, like Adam He died spiritually and then physically. Three days after Jesus' work on the Cross was completed, God raised Him from the dead! Death could not possibly hold Him (Acts 2:24) and so He had to leave its domain. God raised Him up and His body was transformed into a glorious resurrection body, which will never experience decay. He overcame death—both spiritual and physical death—once and for all. **"Christ, having been raised from the dead, dies no more. Death no longer has dominion over Him"** (Romans 6:9b).

In 1 Corinthians chapter 15, Paul proclaims Jesus' victory over death. Because Jesus conquered death, all people will be made physically alive in Christ, who is **"the last Adam"** (verse 45b): **"For since by man came death, by Man also came the resurrection of the dead. For as in Adam all die, even so in Christ all shall be made alive. But each one in his own order…"** (1 Corinthians 15:21-23a). Clearly, there will be a future resurrection of every person (see also John 5:28-29).[21]

The resurrection body that the believer will receive will be a **"spiritual body"** (1 Corinthians 15:44b). It is the same body that is raised up, but in

---

[21] Future resurrection, which will take place in various stages, is discussed in Special Topic Study 124 entitled "The Resurrection of the Dead". Jesus was the first-fruits, the first-born from the dead: the first person to be permanently resurrected. (Others were temporarily raised out of death before this time, such as Lazarus in John 11, etc.) All true believers at the time of Christ's return will then be resurrected; and, finally, all who still remain in the grave will be resurrected at the end of the Millennium (see Revelation 20:13).

the process of resurrection significant changes will take place (see 1 Corinthians 15:42-49).

Our resurrection bodies will be incorruptible: free from sickness, decay and not subject to death. Our present bodies are bodies of humiliation (Philippians 3:21), being affected by sin: they are limited, weak, frail and ageing, and are subject to physical needs. However, our resurrection bodies will be raised in power and free from such limitations. Our present bodies are natural (or 'soulish') for, since the Fall, our bodies and soul tend to dominate our human spirits. However, our resurrection bodies will be "spiritual" bodies, in which we can fully glorify God and show forth forever the spiritual life we have received in Christ. These bodies will never be a burden to us, and will be similar to Christ's glorious body.

The last brick in the barrier, our temporal life, has therefore been completely removed and dealt with by our position in Christ, in whom we have eternal life and the promise of future resurrection.

THE BARRIER HAS GONE

The work of Jesus Christ on the Cross was so perfect and complete that He dealt with every aspect of the barrier between God and man. All the bricks in the barrier have been eradicated, but every person must believe on the Lord Jesus Christ to be saved. Christ alone now stands between God and man. He Himself is in effect the only remaining 'barrier.'

Jesus said, **"I am the way, the truth, and the life. No one comes to the Father except through Me"** (John 14:6). Jesus is the only way by which a person can come to God. If someone rejects Jesus, salvation is impossible.

In Genesis, Jacob had a vision of a ladder from earth to heaven: **"Then he (Jacob) dreamed, and behold, a ladder was set up on the earth, and its top reached to heaven; and there the angels of God were ascending and descending on it"** (Genesis 28:12). In John 1:51, Jesus said to Nathanael, **"Most assuredly, I say to you, hereafter you shall see heaven open, and the angels of God ascending and descending upon the Son of Man."** *Jesus* was the ladder Jacob saw; Jesus is the only way to God—the ladder between us and heaven.

Reconciliation

The removal of the barrier is what the apostle Paul called **"reconciliation"** (Romans 5:11). There was a barrier, but it has been demolished: God has reconciled man to Himself through Jesus Christ:

"**Now all things are of God, who has reconciled us to Himself through Jesus Christ, and has given us the ministry of reconciliation**" (2 Corinthians 5:18). We now have the ministry of reconciliation—a ministry of conveying the gospel message.

The gospel includes the following glorious truths that we have learnt about our salvation. Jesus Christ died to deliver us from our slavery to sin. He paid the penalty for all our sins on the Cross when He shed His blood and died for us. By believing in Him we can be born again—that is, made spiritually alive. God was wholly satisfied by Jesus' sacrifice of Himself on the Cross. We therefore do not have to work to earn our salvation, for righteousness comes only through faith in the Lord Jesus Christ. Any of us can have eternal life in Christ if we will believe on Him, and then we will live with Him forever.

God demonstrated His love towards us by sending His Son to die for us while we were sinners. Jesus died for us, but then God raised Him up from the dead! Through the act of believing on Him we are given His life, so that even now we might have fellowship with God *and* have power to live in a new way: "**...Just as Christ was raised from the dead by the glory of the Father, even so we also should walk in newness of life**" (Romans 6:4b). Eternal life is available to every one of us, not only to make us fit for heaven after we die, but to empower us to live for God now in a manner pleasing to Him.

This is the gospel message. It is the message that Jesus came to proclaim, and it is the message that we now have the great privilege of being able to pass on to all mankind. Jesus is alive because He knocked down the barrier, and He is now seated in heaven with God the Father to represent every person who believes on Him.

NOTES

8. THE UNFORGIVABLE SIN

We are now in a wonderfully happy position, having learned that God has completely removed the barrier between Himself and man through what Jesus Christ accomplished on the Cross. God has now entrusted us with this wonderful message: He has reconciled us to Himself through His Son. We have a message to give all people: "Jesus died for you and paid the penalty for your sins!"

The chasm that existed between God and man has been bridged. There is one bridge across—the precious Lord Jesus Christ; and therefore the gospel can be summed up in the words of Paul and Silas in Acts 16:31, **"Believe on the Lord Jesus Christ, and you will be saved"**.

My prayer about this whole course of Bible studies is that they will enable us to witness unashamedly and far more effectively than ever before. We have something to shout about—something wonderful to praise God about—a glorious message for this very needy world.

We now need to address an issue which causes concern or confusion for some Christians. In the gospels we find Jesus making several references to what is sometimes called the "unforgivable sin". Many Christians do not understand what it is and wonder at times whether they have committed it. Before we look at this issue in detail, it will help us to take one final look at the barrier to rehearse some of the important principles of salvation we have already glimpsed. This will enable us to understand the unforgivable sin and what Jesus taught about it.

FAITH VERSUS WORKS

In Romans 3:20 to 4:8 Paul discusses the difference between salvation through faith and the principle of the law in the Old Testament. Many Christians are confused about the law. We therefore need to examine why the law was given.

It is important to note first that the law in the Old Testament was only given to Israel; and it was given for three main reasons:

1. The law proved that all people are sinners

In James 2:10 we find a very shocking statement: that if we break just one part of the law, then we are guilty of having broken it all.

If we looked down a list of sins such as those found in the Ten Commandments, most of us would find a few commands that we think we have broken at some time. Most of us would say, "I haven't committed murder," although when *Jesus* talked about the law, He said that whoever is even *angry* with his brother without a cause shall be in danger of judgment (see Matthew 5:21-22). The apostle John wrote, **"Whoever hates his brother is a murderer"** (1 John 3:15). But leaving these slightly disturbing statements aside, most of us would still insist that we measure up quite well in relation to the law.

James' statement should bring us to a full stop: **"For whoever shall keep the whole law, and yet stumble in one point, he is guilty of all"** (James 2:10). If we honestly consider the first great commandment, **"You shall love the LORD your God with all your heart, with all your soul, and with all your might"** (Deuteronomy 6:5), we quickly realize that we have not kept it. We are therefore guilty of breaking the whole law.

The religious Jews were totally wrong in their view of the law: they thought that salvation came by keeping it. However, the law was there because *it could not be kept*. We all stand condemned by it. They misunderstood it completely.

On this basis, we can understand Romans 3:20a, **"Therefore by the deeds of the law no flesh will be justified in His sight..."** By keeping the law you cannot become righteous before God. As Paul continued: **"...for by the law is the knowledge of sin."** Thus, the law was given to prove to us that we are sinners.

2. The law was a shadow of Christ

The law pointed to Christ. As the Book of Hebrews shows clearly, all the items relating to the Old Testament law (the feasts and holy days, the sacrifices, the Tabernacle, the priests' garments, and so on) pointed to Jesus and to different aspects of His work (see Hebrews 10:1). They pointed to the fact that God provides the answer to sin. For example, every innocent lamb that had its throat cut was a witness to those Jews who were watching that God would one day send *His* Messiah, to die for His people and take away their sins.

"But now the righteousness of God apart from the law is revealed, being witnessed by the Law and the Prophets..." (Romans 3:21). The law and other parts of the Old Testament Scriptures pointed to the fact that righteousness comes not from keeping the law[1] but from God, through faith in the Lord Jesus Christ: "**...even the righteousness of God which is through faith in Jesus Christ to all and on all who believe**" (Romans 3:22a). All who believe receive God's righteousness through faith.

3. The law provided a basic set of rules to give peace in Israel

God wanted Israel to have peace and order within its society, so that the gospel could be proclaimed to the whole world. God's purpose was that, in being separated unto Himself, Israel might be blessed and might point all nations to the one true and living God who was in her midst.[2]

We can see from Romans 3 just how wrong the religious Jews were. No sooner had the law been given than religion came in. Some people immediately began saying that to be saved you had to keep all the commandments. They also said that the lamb itself could actually take away your sins if you kept the law. But it could not! Religious people turned the law completely on its head. It was supposed to indicate to the people, "Believe in the salvation *God* will provide. Believe in the Messiah who is to come, whom *God* will send!"

The righteousness of God is through faith in Jesus Christ; and it is given to the one who believes. This is imputation, as we saw in the last study. Notice that in verse 22a Paul said this righteousness is "**to all**"; however, it is only "**on all who believe.**" The *message* of the gospel is thus "**to all**" (Greek *eis*), but the *results* of the gospel are only "**on all**" (Greek *epi*) who believe. Righteousness is imputed as a result of faith in Christ only on those who believe, although it is available to everyone.

"**For there is no difference; for all have sinned and fall short of the glory of God...**" (verses 22b-23). There were some people who knew the law, and some who did not. Some thought that they were good; others knew that they were not. However, *all* had sinned. Paul was saying that there was no difference between them in God's eyes. All stand before God as sinners.

---

[1] The word translated "apart from" in verse 21 means 'separate from,' 'independent of,' 'without any intervention, participation or co-operation from.'

[2] We are told now to pray for our governments (1 Timothy 2:1-4), so that we might have peace and order. Again, the reason given is that we might live godly lives, because God desires all men to be saved.

"**Being justified freely by His grace through the redemption that is in Christ Jesus...**" (verse 24). We are justified *freely* by God's grace. Grace is undeserved. We cannot earn righteousness and we do not deserve it, but God declares us to be righteous in Christ! Religion (that is, legalism), in contrast, is anti-grace. Religion says that we have to *do* something to obtain anything from God. It drives us, saying, "Go and earn it," "Go and get it," "Go and do it!"

Paul continued: "**Whom God set forth to be a propitiation by His blood, through faith, to demonstrate His righteousness, because in His forbearance God had passed over the sins that were previously committed, to demonstrate at the present time His righteousness, that He might be just and the justifier of the one who has faith in Jesus**" (verses 25-26).

Verse 25 mentions propitiation which, as we have seen, refers to how Jesus' sacrifice of Himself satisfied God's character, as foreshadowed in the mercy seat in the Old Testament. Verse 26 says that *God* is our justifier: it is God who has declared us to be righteous. *He* is the justifier, and not us. And through the Cross God has demonstrated His righteousness.[3]

In these verses, imputation, justification, redemption and propitiation all come together. By now, these terms should make sense to us.

BOASTING AND THE LAW OF FAITH

In verse 27 of Romans 3, Paul began by asking, "**Where is boasting then?**" If salvation was by works, then we could boast about what we had done to gain it. But there can be no boasting, because salvation does not come through works at all. It is only by grace.

When it comes to the issue of salvation, we are all equally bankrupt. Everyone needs Jesus; our salvation depends on Him alone. This is a most wonderful message. If only Christians would grasp this truth thoroughly, they would stop boasting about how spiritual they think they

---

[3] *God had to provide salvation in a way consistent with His own character, that is, in a just way. We all deserved death and, until the time of the Cross, God had patiently overlooked the outstanding penalty for man's sin. God wanted to be merciful and bring salvation. And in the Cross, God was entirely just in making Jesus a sacrifice and justifying those who put their trust in Him.*

are! If anyone is saved, it is because of grace. If anyone is spiritual, it is because of grace. If anyone has a ministry, it is because of grace alone.[4]

"Where then is boasting? It is excluded. By what law? Of works? No, but by the law of faith. Therefore we conclude that a man is justified by faith apart from the deeds of the law" (verses 27-28). According to the law of works (that is, according to the false principle that we can gain our salvation by works) boasting would be fine; in fact, it would increase our reason for boasting. However, by the law or principle of faith, boasting is excluded. We are justified by faith alone, and our works are irrelevant. Boasting is therefore excluded.

At that time, there were Jews in the Body of Christ who were saying to the Gentiles, "It's not good enough only to believe on the Lord Jesus; you also have to keep the law." They were telling the early Gentile Christians that they had to keep the sabbath, give tithes, and be circumcised, etc. (The religious Jews even had rules such as, "A ladder can only be moved four paces on the sabbath"!) This was all wrong! We do not have to keep the law to be saved, because *Jesus* kept it all, and then He died as the perfect sacrifice once and for all time. Paul had to write this letter to the Christians in Rome to bring a correct understanding and orderliness to what they believed. He wrote, **"Therefore we conclude that a man is justified by faith apart from the deeds of the law."**

The *whole* law is therefore excluded: we do not have to keep the law to be saved. We died to the law in Christ, and should now live and serve God in a new way, according to the principle of the Spirit (Romans 7:4-6).

We saw earlier that there were three main purposes of the Old Testament law, and Jesus fulfilled each of these purposes, because:

1. He died for the sins of the whole world;
2. He was the Messiah to whom the law pointed; and,
3. He brought peace by His death.

"Or is He the God of the Jews only? Is He not also the God of the Gentiles? Yes, of the Gentiles also, since there is one God who will justify the circumcised by faith and the uncircumcised through faith" (verses 29-30).

---

[4] People we consider to be 'great' ministers are sometimes disappointing when we meet them face to face. We should remember that their ministry is by grace. Sadly from time to time we may hear about a 'great' minister who died because of alcoholism, or who committed some terrible sin. While this is sometimes difficult to understand, God's gifting is by grace alone, and God may continue to work through His children, despite their failings.

The work Jesus Christ accomplished was for the Jew *and* the Gentile. The law was only given to the Jews, and therefore many of them assumed, "For Gentiles to have salvation, they must obey everything the Jews obey." Paul was saying in these verses, "No! God is not only the God of the Jews; He is the God of the Gentiles too!" God justifies both Jew and Gentile on the same basis—*according to faith*. This is wonderful news for those of us who are Gentiles.

If you are a Gentile believer, you can be proud that God is truly your Father. I am just as proud as any Jew that He is my God! We are in the 'commonwealth of heaven,' comprising Jews and Gentiles, of which God is the one ruler. The law was only given to Israel, and yet both Jew and Gentile are justified by faith alone. Both are thus on the same level when it comes to salvation.[5]

"Do we then make void the law through faith? Certainly not! On the contrary, we establish the law" (verse 31). Faith does not make the law void, but, on the contrary, it establishes the law. How can this be so?

If we have faith in Jesus Christ, we acknowledge that we are sinners and that we are unable to keep the law. We also recognize that Jesus came to die for the sins of the world, and we recognize Him as the long-awaited Saviour. Thus, by believing, we establish the law, because we prove that the law was correct and agree with God's reasons for giving it.

It is important to remember that Romans chapter 4 followed on without a pause from Romans 3:31. The chapter divisions were added much later. Paul's choice of Abraham as an illustration was an important part of his argument.

The example of Abraham

"What then shall we say that Abraham our father has found according to the flesh? For if Abraham was justified by works, he has something of which to boast, but not before God" (Romans 4:1-2). The Jews were very proud of their father Abraham. *Supposing* Abraham was in fact justified by works, then he would have had something to boast about before men. That is true. But not before God! All his good works would still have been like filthy rags *to God*. Even if we have a

---

[5] Note that all believers are put "in Christ", who was the Seed of Abraham (see Galatians 3) and hence a Jew. As Jesus said in John 4:22, "salvation is of the Jews." Although both Jew and Gentile are justified through faith, Paul argued in Romans 3:1-2 that the Jews had significant advantage, chiefly because God had entrusted them with His oracles, namely the Old Testament Scriptures. (Today, however, many Gentiles have access to the Scriptures—the New Testament as well as the Old Testament.)

million good deeds to present to God, He looks at them and they are a million filthy rags to Him. It is no wonder salvation has to be through faith!

"For what does the Scripture say? "Abraham believed God, and it was accounted to him for righteousness"" (verse 3). The Jews knew the Old Testament very well. Paul was quoting Genesis 15:6, which says, **"And he (Abraham) believed in the LORD, and He accounted it to him for righteousness."** The words **"accounted it to him"** refer to imputation. When Abraham believed in the LORD, this became righteousness reckoned in his account, in just the same way as we believe and have righteousness reckoned to us. It was the same 4000 years ago! (And **"the LORD"** in the Hebrew is probably a reference to the Lord Jesus. The Lord Jesus Christ *is* God.)

There are many people who are not born-again believers who think that by going to church on Sunday they are actually reaching God. They will be in for a terrible shock. There are many people who think that if they try to live a good life, that will be sufficient. It is not true!

The example of David

Paul then immediately gave King David as a further example of someone who had discovered how righteousness is reckoned.

"Now to him who works, the wages are not counted as grace but as debt. But to him who does not work but believes on Him who justifies the ungodly, his faith is accounted for righteousness, just as David also describes the blessedness of the man to whom God imputes righteousness apart from works" (Romans 4:4-6). A worker receives his wages because he has worked. The one who works *deserves* wages, and they are counted as a debt. If you do not work and yet still get paid, then that is *grace*. There is a crucial difference.

A believer experiences faith reckoned to him as righteousness; and it is not because of works but grace! When you believe, you have done nothing to earn righteousness, but nonetheless it is *given* to you; this is grace. The Bible says, **"Believe on the Lord Jesus Christ and you will be saved"** (Acts 16:31), and that is the end of the matter.

King David, who lived around 1000 BC, thus knew the principle of salvation too. He knew that salvation was by grace apart from works, even in his day, and was able to write: **"Blessed are those whose lawless deeds are forgiven, and whose sins are covered; blessed is the man to whom the LORD shall not impute sin"** (Romans 4:7-8, quoting Psalm 32:1-2). David knew that God would in no way impute sin to his account.

FAITH, NOT SIN, IS THE DECISIVE ISSUE IN SALVATION

Salvation is by grace alone and not by works. Jesus now stands in the gap between God and man. He is like a door. To enter a room, you have to choose to go through the door. If you do not go through the door, you cannot enter the room, no matter how hard you try.

Jesus Christ is a wide open door between man and God, and the decisive issue in salvation is whether or not we choose to trust in Him. We do not gain salvation by trying to live a sinless life. (After we have been saved, we *must* aim to live a life free from sin for the glory of God, but not to try to earn or repay our salvation; there is an important difference.)

In Matthew 7:13-14 Jesus said, **"Enter by the narrow gate; for wide is the gate and broad is the way that leads to destruction, and there are many who go in by it. Because narrow is the gate and difficult is the way which leads to life, and there are few who find it."** The gateway to heaven is as narrow as one man: it is through the Lord Jesus Christ, and He is the *only* way in. The gateway to destruction is extremely wide. It includes everything and everyone else, such as living a good life, trying your best, or any other religion. The wide gate leads to separation from God forever. Jesus is the only One who died for the sins of the whole world, and He is the narrow gate which leads to life. **"I am the way, the truth, and the life. No one comes to the Father except through Me"** (John 14:6).

Sin is not the *decisive* issue in salvation. When Jesus died for the sins of the whole world, He dealt with the issue of sin and its penalty completely and forever. As we have seen, Jesus died even for the sins of those who choose never to believe in Him. But this does not mean they will go to heaven. Although Jesus dealt with sin and the penalty of sin for everyone, and was the propitiation for our sins, unbelievers still need God's solution to all the other bricks in the barrier. And Jesus is the only way through.

"He who believes in Him is not condemned; but he who does not believe is condemned already, because he has not believed in the name of the only begotten Son of God" (John 3:18). In some ways this is a clearer gospel message than is found in the better known verse, John 3:16. If you do not believe, you stand condemned already. You may have lived a wonderful life full of 'good' deeds, yet, according to Jesus' words, you still stand condemned before God—*because you have not believed on Him, the Son of God*. However, if you have believed on the Lord Jesus you are not condemned.

John 3:36 says the same: **"He who believes in the Son has everlasting life; and he who does not believe the Son shall not see life, but the**

wrath of God abides on him." As we saw in the last chapter, it is *eternal* life that we are given. It is the very life of God and this life is everlasting—it goes on for ever and ever.

The first part of this verse is an unconditional promise: **"He who believes in the Son has everlasting life"**. This implies that we cannot lose the eternal life we are given, as we will discuss in more detail in the next three chapters. Again, sin is not mentioned as being the issue determining who will have life; rather, the issue determining this, as well as who will receive judgment, is whether or not we have faith in Jesus Christ the Son of God.

This is why the gospel message is so simple in Acts 16:31. The Philippian jailer wanted to be saved and asked Paul and Silas, **"Sirs, what must I do to be saved?"** (Acts 16:30b). They replied, **"Believe on the Lord Jesus Christ, and you will be saved"**, and they added nothing else. They did not give him five other steps to follow too!

We can easily hinder the gospel message from going forth if we are not careful, by complicating it or by making it virtually incomprehensible in some other way. It is important always to present the gospel simply. We should explain that salvation for every person depends on Jesus Christ and His work on the Cross, rather than a person's 'good' works. Also, salvation is not hampered by the degree of a person's sin. There should be repentance, but the crucial thing is for each person to believe on the Lord Jesus Christ and be saved.

SIN WILL NOT BE THE DECISIVE ISSUE ON THE DAY OF JUDGMENT

Revelation 20:10-15 deals with the Day of Judgment.[6] It describes the final judgment of people before God's great white throne, which will take place in the future. It is interesting to note that the word 'sin' does not appear anywhere in the passage.

These events take place at the end of the Millennium (see Revelation 20:7). The passage begins: **"And the devil, who deceived them, was cast into the lake of fire and brimstone where the beast and the false prophet are. And they will be tormented day and night for ever and ever. Then I saw a great white throne and Him who sat on it, from**

---

[6] The Book of Revelation is not as difficult to understand as many people imagine. The word translated "Revelation" actually means 'disclosure' or 'uncovering,' that is, the revealing of what was previously hidden. Jesus gave it as a sermon. It is sermons about the Book of Revelation that are often more difficult to understand!

whose face the earth and the heaven fled away. And there was found no place for them" (Revelation 20:10-11).[7]

Having described the judgment of the devil, these verses go on to describe the judgment of unbelievers. The unbelievers appear before God, who is sitting on a great white throne. White is the colour of righteousness in the Bible; and God is absolutely righteous. Heaven and earth have to flee away from the face of God. (A new heaven and a new earth appear later, following the judgment, in Revelation 21:1.)

"**And I saw the dead, small and great, standing before God...**" (verse 12a). The "**small and great**" refer to those who were small or great in the sight of men: the great are the presidents, the prime ministers, the leaders, the kings; the small are the tramps and the outcasts, or those who were never recognized as important by the societies in which they lived. They all stand there, equal before God.

"**And books were opened. And another book was opened, which is the Book of Life. And the dead were judged according to their works, by the things which were written in the books**" (verse 12b). This is an awesome event. I imagine a scene of tables with huge books on them. Every single book is opened; and all these unbelievers are lined up in front, hoping to gain salvation.

The dead are judged according to their works. Sin is not mentioned; but, instead, the Lord looks at the *works* of the unbelievers, recorded in the books, presumably to see if any of them are righteous. But the *works* (Greek *ergon*) of these unbelievers were carried out in their own strength, and the books only prove their need of salvation. It is as though God, in His grace, 'double-checks' the books to see if any of those standing before Him have enough 'good' deeds to qualify for salvation, but the test fails in every case. Only believers have God's imputed righteousness. These unbelievers stand there in vain with their piles of filthy rags.

"**The sea gave up the dead who were in it, and Death and Hades delivered up the dead who were in them. And they were judged, each one according to his works. Then Death and Hades were cast into the**

---

[7] Revelation 20 is a prophetic passage. The beast and the false prophet will live during a future period which is often called "the Tribulation". At the end of this Tribulation period they are cast into the lake of fire (Revelation 20:3). The devil is also locked up, but only for 1000 years. At the end of this 1000 year period (or 'Millennium') he is let out for a season (verse 7) to deceive the nations of the world. God then destroys the world's armies (verse 9) and the devil is put into the lake of fire for ever (verse 10). All these events and characters are explained in detail in the fourth series of Basic Bible Studies (BBS 43 to 63). The Great White Throne judgment is covered specifically in BBS 28.

lake of fire. This is the second death. And anyone not found written in the Book of Life was cast into the lake of fire" (verses 13-15). The unbelievers had been in Hades until this time, but they have now been resurrected. (The believers are in heaven at this time, where they are with the Lord.)[8]

The unbelievers are judged according to their works; and Death and Hades are then cast into the lake of fire. Some people say as part of their gospel message, "You will go to Hell forever!" But this is not strictly true. No one will go to 'Hell' forever; Hades is going to be cast into "**the lake of fire**".[9] This *lake of fire* is in fact the final place of judgment. It is called "**the second death**", and it follows this final resurrection and judgment at the end of the Millennium.

Notice how verse 12b said, "**And books were opened. And another book was opened, which is the Book of Life.**" As well as all the books containing a record of works, the Book of Life is opened as well.

Verse 15 is the important verse: "**And anyone not found written in the Book of Life was cast into the lake of fire.**" The deciding factor at this time will not be your works or your sins, but whether your name is in the Book of Life. The dead are judged according to their works, but they are cast into the lake of fire because their names are *not* written in the Book of Life. If their names were written in the Book of Life, they would escape the lake of fire.

How do you know whether your name is in the Book of Life? On that day, the names of all those who believed on Jesus Christ will have their names written in the Book of Life. It records the names of all the believers there have ever been in the whole world: those who have received the life of Christ. And their names will remain in the Book of Life for ever and ever.[10]

---

[8] Those who are believers are with Jesus at this time, having appeared before the Judgment Seat of Christ (when their works were judged) and having then lived and reigned with Him for 1000 years. These people standing before God's great white throne are the unbelievers, most of who have just been resurrected. The judgment of believers' works is covered in BBS 23, and the Millennium in BBS 60-61.

The "sea" in verse 13 may refer to 'the Abyss,' the place where fallen angels had been chained up. This would imply that fallen angels will be judged at the same time as unbelievers.

[9] See footnote 18 in chapter 3 for an explanation of the terms 'Hades' and 'Hell'.

[10] See Revelation 3:5, which is discussed at the end of chapter 11. The Book of Life is sometimes called "The Lamb's Book of Life," referring to Jesus, the Lamb of God who was slain (Revelation 13:8). The Book of Life is also referred to in several other places in the Book of Revelation, and in Philippians 4:3. It is also alluded to in Luke 10:20 and in Hebrews 12:23.

Whoever believes on Christ receives eternal life (John 3:15-16, John 3:36). **"He who believes in Him is not condemned; but he who does not believe is condemned already..."** (John 3:18). Jesus died for the sins of the whole world, and He simply demands that a person says, "Yes," to Him to be saved. We are able to declare this not on the basis of what we feel or what we think, but on the basis of the Word of God.

THE UNFORGIVABLE SIN

With this essential background, we are now in a position to understand the so-called "unforgivable sin". Many believers have been troubled by this. Early in my Christian life, I thought I had committed it *several* times! What sin is it?

It is clear that the unforgivable sin is not suicide; it is not some sexual sin; nor is it calling your brother a fool, or any other such sin. How do we know this? We can be certain of it, because in 1 John 1:7, John said, **"But if we walk in the light as He is in the light, we have fellowship with one another, and the blood of Jesus Christ His Son cleanses us from all sin"** (literally, **"every sin"**). This verse does not say, "every sin *except one*" can be cleansed, but *every* sin.

The Old Testament confirms this: **"Come now, and let us reason together,"** says the LORD. **"Though your sins are like scarlet, they shall be as white as snow; though they are red like crimson, they shall be as wool"** (Isaiah 1:18). This is grace—God choosing to reason with us. (One African translation says, "...as white as coconut kernel," because the people have never seen snow!) Notice that all sins are included; no exception is made. In Isaiah 43:25 God says, **"I, even I, am He who blots out your transgressions for My own sake; and I will not remember your sins."** Again, no specific sin is excluded.

We therefore cannot 'commit' a sin that God will not forgive. So what then is the "unforgivable sin"? The unforgivable sin must be *a sin that Jesus could not and did not die for*. And the only sin that Jesus could not and did not die for, as we have seen, is rejection of Himself and His work on the Cross. If someone rejects the Lord Jesus Christ, there is no other way to be saved; this must therefore be the only unforgivable sin. (If you reject life-saving medicine when you are on your death-bed, then death is inevitable; it is not the doctor's fault.) As we saw in John 3:18, **"...he who does not believe is condemned already"**.

There are several passages which make reference to this so-called "unforgivable sin". In Mark chapter 3 Jesus described it as "blasphemy against the Holy Spirit," and stated that all sins would be forgiven except this blasphemy:

"**And the scribes who came down from Jerusalem said, "He has Beelzebub," and, "By the ruler of the demons he casts out demons." So He called them to Him and said to them in parables: "How can Satan cast out Satan? If a kingdom is divided against itself, that kingdom cannot stand. And if a house is divided against itself, that house cannot stand. And if Satan has risen up against himself, and is divided, he cannot stand, but has an end. No one can enter a strong man's house and plunder his goods, unless he first binds the strong man, and then he will plunder his house. Assuredly, I say to you, all sins will be forgiven the sons of men, and whatever blasphemies they may utter; but he who blasphemes against the Holy Spirit never has forgiveness, but is subject to eternal condemnation"**—because they said, **"He has an unclean spirit"**" (Mark 3:22-30).

Note that in verse 28 Jesus said, **"All sins will be forgiven the sons of men..."** However, this does not mean we should take sin lightly. We should be uncompromising about confessing our sins, because our sins affect our fellowship with God. "**If we confess our sins, He is faithful and just to forgive us our sins and to cleanse us from all unrighteousness**" (1 John 1:9). This important subject will be dealt with later, in chapter 12.

BLASPHEMY AGAINST THE HOLY SPIRIT

We now need to consider the questions: how can a person blaspheme the Holy Spirit, and why is the so-called "unforgivable sin" described as "blasphemy against the Holy Spirit"?[11]

Jesus Christ, being God, has all the attributes of God. He is thus omnipotent. When Jesus became a man, He made Himself of no reputation and took on the form of a slave (see Philippians 2:7). Jesus chose not to independently exercise His own power, which was His because He was God, but chose to live humbly as a man in dependency upon His Father in heaven. His public ministry, which commenced at His baptism, was carried out by the power of the Holy Spirit (Acts 10:38). He *could* have made use of His own divine

---

[11] When someone is baptized or filled with the Holy Spirit, Satan often comes and suggests to that person, "This is not from God," causing him or her to doubt whether what has been received is from the Holy Spirit. Such doubting is not blasphemy against the Holy Spirit. Nor is it blasphemy against the Holy Spirit if someone mistakenly considers that a genuine miracle or gift of speaking in tongues is from the Devil.

power at any time, but He chose to rely on the power of the Holy Spirit working through Him according to His Father's will.

As we saw in chapter 6, Jesus performed many miracles and signs to prove that He was the Messiah, so that the people might believe in Him. By rejecting the ministry of Jesus, people were rejecting Him as their Messiah. The religious leaders in Mark 3 knew very well from the Book of Isaiah and other Old Testament scriptures that the Messiah would perform many such miracles and specific signs. By saying that Jesus' miracles were performed by the power of Satan rather than by the power of the Holy Spirit, they were blaspheming against the Holy Spirit in order to justify their rejection of Jesus.

The miracles *proved* that Jesus was their Messiah in front of their eyes; and furthermore, the Holy Spirit was witnessing this fact within them too. Nevertheless, they insisted on attributing Jesus' works to Satan. They thus blasphemed against the Holy Spirit and were effectively calling Him a liar. It all amounted to the same thing: these scribes were choosing to reject Jesus Christ as their Lord and Messiah despite the evidence in front of them.

Therefore Jesus said to them in Mark 3:29, **"He who blasphemes against the Holy Spirit never has forgiveness, but is subject to eternal condemnation"**. The AV translates this last phrase, **"is in danger of eternal damnation"**, and it means 'liable to' or 'under the sentence of' eternal condemnation. It is important to notice that Jesus only suggested they were **"in danger"** of eternal condemnation, because the Holy Spirit would continue to convict them of this sin again and again, and they would have further opportunity to believe on Him as their Messiah and be saved.

John 16:8-11 defines the main ministry of the Holy Spirit today, and includes a clear statement about the unforgivable sin. Jesus defined the Holy Spirit's ministry as threefold: **"And when He has come, He will convict the world of sin, and of righteousness, and of judgment: of sin, because they do not believe in Me; of righteousness, because I go to My Father and you see Me no more; of judgment, because the ruler of this world is judged."**

Jesus was talking about the ministry the Holy Spirit would carry out on earth after He had risen from the dead and been glorified. (The Holy Spirit was still *in* Jesus at that time and working in other ways, of course.) Note that the sin the Holy Spirit convicts the world of is not that people have lived such awful lives, or that they continue to commit certain sins again and again. Rather, it is described in verse 9: **"...of sin, because they do not believe in Me"**. This defines the unforgivable sin.

The only *unforgivable* sin that any member of the human race can commit is never to believe on the Lord Jesus Christ during his or her lifetime. And this verse tells us that this is the very sin of which the Holy Spirit has come to convict the world. This is the unforgivable sin, and the crucial scripture in understanding it is thus John 16:9. It is the "**sin**" (singular) which the Holy Spirit convicts of; note that Jesus did not say "sin<u>s</u>."

Conclusion

There is salvation through no other person except Jesus, the Son of God. **"Nor is there salvation in any other, for there is no other name under heaven given among men by which we must be saved"** (Acts 4:12). The gospel message is, **"Believe on the Lord Jesus Christ, and you will be saved"** (Acts 16:31), *plus nothing else*. This is the message that the Holy Spirit is spreading throughout the world—through us. We can tell any person that if he or she does not ever believe in the Lord Jesus Christ, then this is the unforgivable sin. There is no other way to be saved. **"He who believes in Him is not condemned; but he who does not believe is condemned already..."** (John 3:18).

If you die having rejected the Lord Jesus, you will be beyond salvation, and there can be no forgiveness for you at all. The good news, however, is that if you have believed on Jesus Christ, even if you at first rejected Him, you can never commit the unforgivable sin.

No believer should ever be attacked, depressed or fooled into thinking that he or she has committed the unforgivable sin. It is impossible, because it is a contradiction. If you are a believer, then, by definition, you have not committed the unforgivable sin. Conversely, if you are an unbeliever, you are in danger, because you are committing the sin of rejection of the Lord Jesus Christ, which He Himself said was unforgivable. Therefore, **"Believe on the Lord Jesus Christ, and you will be saved"**!

NOTES

9. OUR MOTIVATION TO HOLINESS
— ETERNAL SECURITY (PART 1)

Having laid a firm foundation in our understanding of salvation, we can now take a deeper look at the wonderful glories of our salvation. In this study we will begin to examine the issue of "eternal security". It is a much misunderstood subject, and can be given wrong emphasis. It is one of those subjects that can get people 'hot under the collar,' because it involves this crucial question:

Q. Is it possible for a person who has truly believed on the Lord Jesus Christ, and who has been truly born again, to lose his or her salvation and end up in the lake of fire forever and ever, in absolute separation from God?

On a personal level, the question could be posed as follows: is it possible for me and my brothers and sisters in my church or fellowship not to spend eternity together? People usually ask this question if they have met someone who says they once were a Christian, but who now seems to reject Jesus, or is now living a sinful or worldly life and does not seem to care very much about it. (Of course, it is possible that such a person was never in fact born again. However, that is not the issue we are looking at here. We are asking whether those who are *truly* born again can ever lose their salvation.)

This subject is so important that we will look at it in three parts, in this and the following two chapters:

Part 1: introduction, stressing the importance of holiness.

Part 2: scriptural evidence supporting the view that once you are saved you are secure forever and can never lose your salvation.

Part 3: responses to the case put against eternal security.

I think that I should make it clear at the outset that I *do* believe in eternal security. However, it is important to stress right at the beginning that once you are a born-again believer, God desires and expects holiness and fruit from your life.

THE PURPOSE OF THE CHRISTIAN LIFE

The Bible makes it clear that the purpose of the Christian life is that we should become like Jesus, being continuously conformed to His image, and glorify Him forever.

"Therefore be followers of God as dear children. And walk in love, as Christ also has loved us and given Himself for us, an offering and a sacrifice to God for a sweet-smelling aroma" (Ephesians 5:1-2). This means we are to follow Christ's example and should show forth Christ's love and holiness.[1]

Paul expressed it another way in Galatians chapter 1. **"But when it pleased God, who separated me from my mother's womb and called me through His grace, to reveal His Son in me..."** (Galatians 1:15-16a). Note the words "**in me**." The Bible is a 'book of prepositions'; they are all vital. Paul said, "**in me**," not, "to me." God's purpose is to reveal Christ in us. This is the essence of Christianity.

We are not Christians primarily for the purpose of having a club, or handing out tracts, or doing any other such activity. In fact, "Christ in me" is the best kind of evangelism. People should meet Christ when they meet us. All God's dealings with us, including our problems, sufferings and trials, are for the purpose of making us more like Jesus. God wants to reveal a mystery, "**...which is Christ in you, the hope of glory**" (Colossians 1:27). Christ's own righteousness has got to be seen *in me*. God has called every Christian to a walk of holiness and righteousness, that we might show forth His righteous life on this earth.

A.J. Gordon put it like this: "A true Christian walk is the reproducing in our lives of the righteousness that is already ours in Christ." As we have seen in earlier studies, we have been given the positive righteousness of God; we were not just made neutral when our sins were forgiven. God gave us His own righteousness, so that we could have fellowship with Him on that basis. Christ Himself *is* our righteousness (1 Corinthians 1:30). When we come to the Father, we actually go into His presence with the same righteousness as Jesus. **"For He made Him who knew no sin to be sin for us, that we might become the righteousness of God in Him"** (2 Corinthians 5:21). So when we get to heaven we will meet God on the same terms of righteousness. We won't have to cower away. But

---

[1] Note that the kindred words 'holy,' 'sanctify,' 'saint' etc. are alternative translations of words derived from common roots in Hebrew and Greek, which relate to being 'set apart'. To be holy or sanctified thus means to be set apart unto God (for a holy purpose) and therefore also set apart from sin and the world (from what is unholy).

God's aim is to reveal that same righteousness in us now, as we live our lives on earth. Therefore I want it to be true of me now; and that is the aim of the Holy Spirit in me.

It is important for us to remember this as we go on to look at eternal security; it will save us from extremism. Some people say that it does not matter how we live now, because righteousness is a gift of God. That view is absolutely wrong.

CALVINISTS AND ARMINIANS

There are two principal viewpoints on the question of eternal security, the Calvinist and the Arminian. However, if you say, "I am a Calvinist," or, "I am an Arminian," people unfortunately tend to associate you not only with the truths held by these groups, but with their extremism as well.

The Calvinist view is named after John Calvin (1509-1564). Calvinists believe in eternal security, generally speaking. They believe that God foreknew every believer (that is, knew beforehand—even before the foundation of the world) and that, because of this, He called and chose each one. Thus believers are chosen by God, and so will be saved. It is God who has done all the work as far as salvation is concerned. He chose believers in the past, and therefore they will be saved in the future. A problem with this view is that it tends to leave out the present. In the extreme, it can lead to the conclusion that it does not matter how a person lives now, and there have been extremists within this camp who have lived lives of great immorality.

Arminians, in contrast, concentrate much more on the present. They are named after Jacobus Arminius (1560-1609). They believe that God has indeed called and chosen us, but that this calling is only *operative* if we believe every day. This leads to the conclusion that if I live a holy life today, I am all right, but if I do not believe or if I sin tomorrow, I am in danger. Some believers who are Arminian become legalistic, and try to keep long lists of rules. In the extreme, they try to keep the law of Moses to ensure they will not lose their salvation. Many rigidly keep the sabbath, for example. Some are more in bondage to law than most Jews ever were!

I do not like to ally myself totally with either one of these camps, because that would mean I would be classed with the extremist views. I consider it important to adopt a firmly balanced and biblical viewpoint on the whole subject, rather than to adhere rigidly to a theological system.

It is true that God has foreknown us. It is also true that we have been chosen and called, and that, because of this 'election,' we will be saved. We see this in Romans 8:29-30: "**For whom He foreknew, He also predestined to be conformed to the image of His Son, that He might be the first-born among many brethren**" (verse 29). Thus, because God foreknew us, we are "predestined" to be conformed to the image of Jesus in the future. The fact that we are predestined means that we really will get there: "**...that He (Jesus) might be the first-born among many brethren.**" One day we definitely will be just like Jesus! He is the first-born, and we are going to be like Him.

Paul continued, "**Moreover whom He predestined, these He also called; whom He called, these He also justified; and whom He justified, these He also glorified**" (verse 30). This is a continuum. If we are foreknown, then we are definitely going to be glorified. God does not begin a work without bringing it to completion. Calvinists are correct in this. They are also quite correct in saying that we have been promised eternal salvation, and that our unrighteous standing before God has been dealt with by justification. All of this is true.

THE INTERCESSION OF JESUS

However, the Bible also concentrates on the present. There is a commitment we must make in the present that Calvinists sometimes neglect. Jesus is alive today and the Bible tells us that He intercedes on our behalf before God every day: "**And there were many priests, because they were prevented by death from continuing. But He (Jesus Christ), because He continues for ever, has an unchangeable priesthood. Therefore, he is also able to save to the uttermost those who come to God through Him, since He ever lives to make intercession for them**" (Hebrews 7:23-25).

I need an intercessor until the end of time, and because Christ will live for ever and be faithful, I will be all right! Israel always needed a High Priest to represent the nation before God. We have a High Priest who represents us continually, and He is Jesus. Our names have been on the lips of Jesus today!

My eternal security and my salvation therefore depend not only on what God did for me in the past, but on the fact that Christ has been interceding for me today and every day. There is therefore a *present* aspect of my salvation. If on any day Jesus failed to intercede for me, I would lose my salvation. The Greek word translated "**to the uttermost**" (*panteles*) means 'completely,' 'utterly,' or 'finally'; it can also mean 'everlastingly'—that is, forever, and the context here suggests this: Jesus has saved us completely and everlastingly!

This present aspect of our salvation means that God expects something of us today. He does not overlook our sin today simply because Jesus died on the Cross 2000 years ago. No! *Every sin is still loathsome to God*.

We need to realize that today our sins affect Jesus, and provoke a reaction in heaven, because He has to intercede for us as a result of the sins for which He died. If we only consider the past, then we have not understood the present intercession of Jesus. If we sin, Christ has to say to the Father, "I suffered and died for that sin." Jesus therefore has to have our sin and therefore His suffering brought before Him again. This is why the Holy Spirit, through the Word of God and through His presence inside us, continually appeals to us, "Will you live a life that is holy before God?" We should not think our sins are nothing: they are of *tremendous* significance—because Jesus paid the full price for them when God's judgment descended on Him on the Cross. Although we may be eternally secure, God desires and expects holiness from us every day.

"**And do not grieve the Holy Spirit of God, by whom you were sealed for the day of redemption**" (Ephesians 4:30). We need to understand this. The Holy Spirit loves Jesus deeply, and sin in our lives causes the Holy Spirit who dwells inside us to be grieved, because His Beloved in heaven has to intercede on behalf of our sin. He therefore constantly makes a call to holiness within us.

THE BASIS OF OUR ETERNAL SECURITY

The eternal security of our salvation is thus based on two equally important things:

1. the work and calling of God in the past; and,
2. the fact that Christ ever lives to make intercession for us.

If we understand these *two* aspects, it will keep us exactly on course in our Christian lives, and keep us from extremism. We will then not be too lenient, considering that sin does not matter. Nor will we try to live under law, because our *love* for Jesus and our gratitude to Him will lead us on towards holiness.

Some Arminian preachers believe that the threat of a lost salvation is what will motivate their flocks to live holy lives. They consider it wrong to preach about grace too much, because they believe it encourages laziness and deters Christians from seeking holiness in their lives. This is completely misguided! In contrast, the Bible indicates that it is knowledge of the grace and love of God and of the fact that Jesus intercedes for us that, far from producing sin, will provoke Christians to live holy lives. The threat of lost salvation does not lead to holiness, but rather to despair.

Instead of simply judging this for ourselves, we need to check this in the Scriptures, and look at passages that call us or inspire us to holiness. We need to see if they contain a threat of lost salvation.

Our Motivation to Holiness

We will see clearly from the following examples that it is on the basis of *grace* that God appeals to us to live holy lives.

"For the grace of God that brings salvation has appeared to all men, teaching us that, denying ungodliness and worldly lusts, we should live soberly, righteously, and godly in the present age, looking for the blessed hope and glorious appearing of our great God and Saviour Jesus Christ" (Titus 2:11-13).

The *grace of God* teaches us to live godly lives. The Bible teacher Dr M.R. De Haan explained it like this: "If you think that grace encourages sin, then you don't understand grace." It is grace that calls us to holiness; and an understanding of God's grace, demonstrated in what Jesus did on the Cross, is the greatest possible incentive to personal holiness.

"For by grace you have been saved through faith, and that not of yourselves; it is the gift of God, not of works, lest anyone should boast. For we are his workmanship, created in Christ Jesus for good works, which God prepared beforehand that we should walk in them" (Ephesians 2:8-10). It is the revelation that we are saved by grace and that we are God's workmanship that will cause us to walk in the good works God desires for us.

Romans chapter 6 includes one of Paul's strongest exhortations to believers to live holy lives. Was it based on a threat?

"Likewise you also, reckon yourselves to be dead indeed to sin, but alive to God in Christ Jesus our Lord. Therefore do not let sin reign in your mortal body, that you should obey it in its lusts. And do not present your members as instruments of unrighteousness to sin, but present yourselves to God as being alive from the dead, and your members as instruments of righteousness to God. For sin shall not

have dominion over you, for you are not under law but under grace" (Romans 6:11-14). Paul was saying, "Don't sin, because you died to sin. You are alive in Christ! You are not under the law any more!" The word "Therefore..." at the start of verse 12 refers to what Paul had just said. Paul's reasoning in Romans 6:1-10 had been that we have been baptized into Christ and were therefore baptized into His death. We therefore died to sin with Christ, were buried with Him through baptism into death, and now have been raised into a new life to live for God. Because we are no longer dead but alive, we have been freed from sin's dominion and should surely live for God.[2]

Paul asks in verse 15, **"What then? Shall we sin because we are not under law but under grace? Certainly not!"** Various translations answer the question with, "God forbid!" or, "Never!" or, "Perish the thought!" Why should we not sin? It is because we are alive in Christ and we are now under grace! We should make a positive response to positive truth, not a negative response to a negative command.

These are just three passages so far. In fact, there is no verse in the New Testament in which an appeal for holiness is linked with a threat that we might lose our salvation. We will now look at some very practical passages, which contain instructions on how to live holy lives and how to avoid certain sins.

1 Corinthians 6:15-20 says, **"Do you not know that your bodies are members of Christ? Shall I then take the members of Christ and make them members of a prostitute? Certainly not! Or do you not know that he who is joined to a prostitute is one body with her? For "The two," He says, "shall become one flesh." But he who is joined to the Lord is one spirit with Him. Flee sexual immorality. Every sin that a man does is outside the body, but he who commits sexual immorality sins against his own body. Or do you not know that your body is the temple of the Holy Spirit who is in you, whom you have from God, and you are not your own? For you were bought at a price; therefore glorify God in your body and in your spirit, which are God's."**

Paul repeats the question, **"Do you not know?"** several times. He did not say, "If you have a sexual relationship with a prostitute you will lose your

---

[2] Romans 6:1-14 thus explains our salvation from the power of the old sin nature. This is the practical solution to one aspect of the first brick in the barrier. Deliverance from the power of sin is through Jesus Christ (Romans 7:25) as we walk according to a new principle of life—by the Spirit. Victory stems from an attitude of faith, and dependency on the indwelling Spirit.

salvation." (In fact, Corinth was the one place he probably could have made such a threat, if it were true!) Instead he said to them, "You are members of Christ. Are you then going to join your members to a prostitute, knowing this, and knowing that the Holy Spirit dwells in you?"

Ephesians chapter 4 begins, "**I, therefore, the prisoner of the Lord, beseech you to lead a life worthy of the calling with which you were called...**" Paul said, "**therefore**", because he was appealing to the believers in Ephesus on the basis of what he had already said in chapters 1 to 3 about all that has been done for us in Christ.

Had Paul given them a lecture on how they would lose their salvation if they didn't live holy lives? Not at all. In chapter 1 Paul had described how: we have been chosen (verse 4); we have been predestined (verse 5); we have been redeemed (verse 7); we have been given an inheritance (verse 11); and, we have been sealed with the Holy Spirit (verse 13). These are all positive truths. In chapter 2 he described how: we have been raised up and seated with Christ in heavenly places (verse 6); we are now fellow citizens with the saints and members of God's household (verse 19); and, we are being built together to be a habitation for God through the Spirit (verse 22). In chapter 3, Paul prayed that the believers might "**know the love of Christ which passes knowledge**" (verse 19).

He immediately continued, "**Now unto Him who is able to do exceeding abundantly above all that we ask or think, according to the power that works in us, to Him be glory in the church by Christ Jesus throughout all ages, world without end. Amen. I, therefore, the prisoner of the Lord, beseech you to lead a life worthy of the calling with which you were called...**" (Ephesians 3:20-4:1). Paul's appeal for a worthy life in chapter 4 verse 1 thus follows straight on. Clearly, it is based on truth about what God has done for us in Christ, and is not made on the basis of any threat or fear.

In 1 Thessalonians 2:10-12 Paul described the manner in which he had taught the believers in Thessalonica: "**You are witnesses, and God also, how devoutly and justly and blamelessly we behaved ourselves among you who believe; as you know how we exhorted, and comforted, and charged every one of you, as a father does his own children, that you would live a life worthy of God who calls you into His own kingdom and glory.**" Paul had come to them like a father approaching his own children. Any father who threatens his children with exclusion from the family in order to gain their obedience has lost the battle for their obedience before he begins.

The tendency to use a threat of lost salvation to appeal to Christians to live holy lives is often used by Arminians. Jay Adams, a Christian pastoral counsellor from the USA, has estimated that the large majority of Christians who have nervous breakdowns or mental illness are of Arminian persuasion. Many such believers feel a sense of hopelessness: that they are not good enough to be accepted by God.

For two years I was depressed and condemned because of the sin which so easily beset me. Despite having believed on Christ, I considered that my sins put me in grave danger of 'Hell fire'. Did this mean that my life revolved around Christ? No! Rather, I was sinning more and more and, in my depression, became preoccupied with my sins and my failure. It was only when someone whispered in my ear, "You are kept by the power of God!" that I began to have a revelation of Jesus and His love. I began to fall in love again with Jesus, and I could begin to leave my sin behind!

We need to look at just a few more verses on this theme. There are many others.

Colossians 3:1 says, "**If then you were raised with Christ, seek those things which are above, where Christ is, sitting at the right hand of God.**" The Greek tells us that Paul assumed the 'if' clause to be a fact, and so the verse could be translated, "*Since* therefore you were raised with Christ...". Paul's appeal was again based on positive truth.

Paul continued, "**Set your mind on things above, not on things on the earth. For you died, and your life is hidden with Christ in God. When Christ who is our life appears, then you also will appear with Him in glory. Therefore put to death your members which are on the earth: fornication, uncleanness, passion, evil desire, and covetousness, which is idolatry**" (verses 2-5). There is no statement saying, "If you continue and remain faithful..."; Paul simply said that, when Christ appears, we *will* appear with Him in glory too. We *are* going to be like Him. This truth should spur us on to put to death such sins, to which we have already died in Christ.

2 Corinthians 6:14-18 is a call to believers not to be yoked together with non-Christians (for example, in marriage). Paul does not threaten them; he reasons with them. "**Do not be unequally yoked together with unbelievers. For what fellowship has righteousness with lawlessness? And what communion has light with darkness? And what accord has Christ with Belial? Or what part has a believer with an unbeliever? And what agreement has the temple of God with idols? For you are the temple of the living God....Therefore, "Come out from among them and be separate, says the Lord..."**'" (verses 14-16a...17a).

The apostle John used the same approach. John appeals to us to prepare ourselves for Christ's return and to live pure lives. His appeal is based on us recognizing that we are God's children and on our hope of what we shall be like when Christ returns: "**Behold what manner of love the Father has bestowed on us, that we should be called children of God! Therefore the world does not know us, because it did not know Him. Beloved, now we are children of God; and it has not yet been revealed what we shall be, but we know that when He is revealed, we shall be like Him, for we shall see Him as He is. And everyone who has this hope in him purifies himself, just as He is pure**" (1 John 3:13).

We could go on and on and see many more verses like these. But it is clear already: God does not use fear or outward things to spur us on to holiness. Rather, it is the truth inside us that will cause a response in our hearts. We respond to God's grace and love. Only when we see all that God has done for us in Christ, and when we realize that Christ is interceding for us every day, will we come to comprehend our present responsibility to live lives of holiness.

HOLINESS REQUIRES A NEW NATURE

There are some people who claim that they once were Christians but that now they no longer are. However, many such people were never in fact born again. Some people just give mental assent when they hear the gospel message, and say, "I think Christianity is a good moral system," for example.

We have got to beware. Some people may be able to live a so-called "Christian" life in terms of outward behaviour and morality for a short time, but their nature has not been changed inside. They may study the beatitudes in the Bible (see Matthew 5:3-12), for example, or they may study the life of Christ and try to live like He did; but they are trying to change the outside without the inside being changed. Only a new nature inside us can possibly produce true holiness on the outside.

Jesus said that the Pharisees were like **"whitewashed tombs which indeed appear beautiful outwardly, but inside are full of dead men's bones and all uncleanness"** (Matthew 23:27); they looked super on the outside, but their outward appearance of holiness was a sham, which could not possibly last. Trying to do good cannot be successful without the life of Christ inside.

In the early days of the Church, the genuine believers were plagued with such people. Within a few decades of Christ's death and resurrection, all sorts of groups with weird ideas had started emerging within the churches. They had learned about Christ, but they had never been born again. They came into the churches, leading people astray. The message of some was, "Try to be good!", but they tried to be 'good' *by themselves*. Others brought in more sinister heresies. In chapter 2 of his second epistle, Peter described such false teachers.

"But there were also false prophets among the people, even as there will be false teachers among you, who will secretly bring in destructive heresies, even denying the Lord who bought them, and bring on themselves swift destruction ...But these, like natural brute beasts made to be caught and destroyed, speak evil of the things they do not understand, and will utterly perish in their own corruption....These are wells without water, clouds carried by a tempest, to whom the gloom of darkness is reserved for ever" (2 Peter 2:1,12,17).

The whole chapter describes these false teachers who had infiltrated the Church and yet were not born again. They were still slaves of sin: **"While they promise them liberty, they themselves are slaves of corruption"** (verse 19). They would inevitably produce sins, no matter how hard they tried outwardly to cover up their corrupt nature.

"For if, after they have escaped the pollutions of the world through the knowledge of the Lord and Saviour Jesus Christ, they are again entangled in them and overcome, the latter end is worse for them than the beginning. For it would have been better for them not to have known the way of righteousness, than having known it, to turn from the holy commandment delivered to them" (verse 20-21). These false teachers might have been taught about Christ, but they did not have the Holy Spirit dwelling inside them and they would not be able to keep up the pretence of a holy life for long. Such people are worse-off at the end when they revert to their sinful ways. They tend to end up more hard-hearted and more evil than before.

I have certainly found this to be the case today: those who only know about Christ in their heads and who think they are Christians are harder to penetrate with the truth of the gospel than those who know they are wretched sinners.

Verse 22 is Peter's terrible conclusion: **"But it has happened to them according to the true proverb: "A dog returns to his own vomit," and, "a sow, having washed, to her wallowing in the mire.""** After a dog is sick, it is not long before it goes back and starts sniffing the vomit and starts eating it again. Why? *Because it is a dog!* Similarly, a pig is always a pig, and it will always love filth, even if it has just been washed clean on the outside.

A pig can be washed, perfumed, taught to walk on two legs or dressed like a man, but it is still a pig. An Archbishop of Canterbury was once asked about apes and men by a biologist. The biologist said, "There's not much difference between the two, because, if you were to take a human baby and put him in a chimp family, he'd grow up like a chimpanzee." The Archbishop stood up to answer, and said, "It is perfectly true that, if you take a human baby and put him among the apes, he will grow up like an ape. *But*, if you take a baby chimpanzee and put it among humans, it can *never* grow up to be anything but a chimpanzee!"

In the same way, it is important to understand the difference between someone who is just moralistic and a real Christian. That is the point we need to grasp. With the people described in 2 Peter 2, there was only change on the *outside*.

However, it is different for those who are born again: Christians have a new nature *inside*. The Holy Spirit indwells us and we have become partakers of the divine nature. We are in Christ and Christ is in us. The "new man" inside is created for righteousness and genuine good works. And, whether we believe in eternal security or not, the Holy Spirit inside us wants us to live lives of holiness and purity in utter dedication to God.

Summary

We have looked at the issue of our motivation to holiness before we go on to study specific verses about eternal security, because the major objection put to those who believe in eternal security relates to this. Opponents of eternal security often wrongly imagine that if you *do* believe in it you must inevitably conclude that you can live as you want. You cannot! And soon we will see the reason why you cannot do so in practice: God is a very good father, who disciplines His children well— and He is committed to disciplining those who *are* His children.

To emphasize the point again: God desires holiness. And we who love Christ should seek for Him to be revealed in us in all His fullness, all of His power, and all of His holiness.

10. OUR SECURITY IN CHRIST
— ETERNAL SECURITY (PART 2)

We have seen how it is essential to have a correct balance in our view of salvation, and that we should not only emphasize aspects of the past but also of the present. First came God's foreknowledge, our calling and God's work in the past. Now we are upheld by Christ's constant intercession for us in the present. An imbalanced view of either of these two aspects can lead to complacency on the one hand, or to legalism and despair on the other.

We saw in the previous study how it is the grace, gifts and calling of God that inspire us to live holy lives. Worldliness in the Church has *not* been caused by the preaching of eternal security. Oh, that eternal security *had* been taught! Rather, there has been great misunderstanding and a lack of sound teaching on the *grace* of God and the principles of grace. I believe it is this lack that has led to worldliness within the Body of Christ. It is certainly the truth about God's grace, together with the knowledge that all my sins have to be represented before God personally by Jesus, that have led me to desire greater holiness in my own life.

In this study we are going to look at some of the principles underlying belief in eternal security—that is, the view that once we have been truly born again, we remain secure in our salvation forever. I have counted more than 90 passages of Scripture which support this view. We obviously cannot look at every such verse, but we can do justice to the subject by splitting it up into topics and looking at several passages under each one.

TWO VIEWS OF SALVATION

Some people say that man's work can help him earn salvation, whereas others say salvation is entirely God's work. Both of these views have logical implications.

If salvation can be earned or deserved in any way, based on what we do, then there is the possibility that we might fail and lose it again. This is what those who subscribe to a 'social gospel' (that is, a gospel of good works) tend to believe. They think salvation is gained by doing good works, and so we must be careful how we behave lest we fail to live up to the necessary standard.

If, however, like the majority of Christians, you believe that salvation is entirely the work of God and not of man, and that it is given to us as a gift, then there can only be one possible way in which we might lose salvation, after having received it—and that is if *God* fails. This is of course an amazing blasphemy.

What does the Bible say?

Paul made it clear that our salvation is indeed a *gift* of God. "**For by grace you have been saved through faith, and that not of yourselves; it is the gift of God, not of works, lest anyone should boast. For we are His workmanship, created in Christ Jesus for good works, which God prepared beforehand that we should walk in them**" (Ephesians 2:8-10).

The word translated "**grace**" means *undeserved* favour. We did not earn or deserve our salvation in any way. The phrase "**not of yourselves**" tells us salvation did not originate from us. Instead, it is a "**gift**"; and the terminology implies it is a *free* gift—salvation is something God has *freely given* us. And it is "**the gift of God**", which means 'belonging to God.' *God* is therefore the source of our salvation, and as verse 9 explains, *God* deserves all the glory. We were His enemies, yet he reconciled us to Himself. If I had had any part in earning my salvation whatsoever, then I would share some of the glory and I could boast; but I cannot.

Verse 10 emphasizes this: "**For we are His workmanship**". God is the One who has created us in Christ, just like a potter creates a pot.

I love the story Willy Burton told about the lady who had a picture on her wall, entitled "Rock of Ages." It depicted a stormy sea, and in the midst of the raging water was a rock, in the shape of a cross. A woman dressed in white was clinging to the rock from the sea, trying to get a firm hold on it. The lady who owned the picture thought that salvation was like that; she thought that salvation meant hanging on to Jesus with all your might, trying not to be caught away. However, one day as she was looking at the picture, God spoke to her through two scriptures.

The first scripture was 1 Peter 1:5, "**[We] who are kept by the power of God through faith for salvation ready to be revealed in the last time**". She thought to herself, "We may be kept by the power of God, but it says, "**through faith**"; so doesn't it depend on my faith?"

Then God spoke to her again through a second scripture. She read Hebrews 12:2, "**...looking unto Jesus, the author and finisher of our faith, who for the joy that was set before Him endured the cross, despising the shame, and has sat down at the right hand of the throne of God.**" She realized that it is Jesus who is the author *and finisher* of our faith. It is He who perfects our faith! She then knew that the painting was completely wrong and so she destroyed it. She realized that we are not in the sea, clinging by our fingertips on to Jesus the Rock. No! We are '20 miles inland'—safe and secure!

In this study we will see *why* we are in fact '20 miles inland,' and what the results should be in our lives. We will identify four basic, logical principles, and look at each in turn. If someone believes that we can lose our salvation, then he or she needs to answer these points.

FOUR PRINCIPLES

These four principles are foundations of our salvation. They are thus also foundational to the security of our salvation.

Principle 1: God's omniscience

The Bible teaches us that God knows everything—past, present and future. The word 'omniscient,' which is often used to describe this facet of God's character, means 'all-knowing.' God therefore knew all about us before He chose us in Christ and before He even created the world: "**...just as He (God) chose us in Him (Christ) before the foundation of the world, that we should be holy and without blame before Him in love**" (Ephesians 1:4). God knew everything about us back then. He knew every day and every detail of our lives. He knew every problem. He knew all about our sins and our failings.

Imagine designing a plan when you've got full information at your fingertips! It was *with such knowledge* that God designed our salvation. He did it with the very worst sinner in mind. The apostle Paul considered himself to be the "**chief**" of sinners (1 Timothy 1:15). And God designed salvation with Paul in mind, but also with me (I'm sure I run a very close second) and with you in mind.

Jesus told a parable about a man who began to build a tower and then could not finish it. He said that the man was mocked (see Luke 14:28-30). This man made a mistake because he did not know how many bricks he would need for the house and, having partly built it, found he had run out of materials and money. In other words, this man was not omniscient. If God had designed our salvation and then later discovered that one person's sins were worse than He had imagined and planned for, then that would make God a fool. This is nonsense. Jesus died for the sins of the whole world and no one's sins can catch God unawares.

2 Timothy 2:13 says, "**If we are faithless, He remains faithful; He cannot deny Himself.**" This verse deals with the particular sin of our unfaithfulness toward God. It tells us that our faithlessness does not affect the faithfulness of God. Of course it doesn't! God cannot be caught out by the number or severity of my sins. How ridiculous that would be! Do we really think that we can shock God? It should be a great comfort to us that God knows all about us, and that He can manage! Our salvation was planned and given to us by God even while He knew every sin we would ever commit.

Some people believe that a person can be saved for a few years and then do something so terrible (that God knew about anyway!) that he or she will suddenly lose salvation and be cast into the lake of fire forever. But it is important to realize that at the moment of salvation, many changes take place in us, which are described throughout the New Testament.[1]

For example, when we were born again, the Holy Spirit baptized us into the Body of Christ, and we became members of the Body of Christ. We were put 'in Christ' and became fully identified with Christ; His past became our past, and we therefore died on the Cross with Him. We were raised with Him to new life. We were filled with the Holy Spirit. The Holy Spirit came and indwelt us. We were made to sit at the right hand of God, and so on. All these things and many others happened to us at the moment of salvation. The list goes on and on.

God did all this for us when we could not even understand it. Would God do all this knowing that a few years later we would commit some sin and lose our salvation, and thus need all these changes reversed? This would seem absurd. In fact, the Bible never mentions any of these changes being reversed in anybody. I would have to be amputated from the Body of Christ, kicked out of the heavenlies, and so on. If this were true, the Body of Christ would be covered in amputations, where people had been saved, made members of the Body, and then removed again. Such ridiculous statements are the logical implications of the belief that we can lose our salvation. Set against God's omniscience, they are nonsense.

---

[1] The changes that happen to us when we are born again are grouped into a list under 37 headings in Basic Bible Study 102.

I personally believe that if it were in *my* hands to throw away my salvation later, God would never have given it to me and then left me to live on earth. I consider that the love of God for us is so great that if any of us could lose our salvation and be separated from Him forever, then He would have killed us at the point of salvation and taken us home to be with Him immediately. The fact we *are* here suggests that God is quite confident that we cannot do anything to lose our salvation! That we are still alive and are expected to be ambassadors for Christ is therefore actually an indication of our total security.

I consider that our salvation is 'devil-proof' and 'world-proof.' In the last study we looked at Romans 8:29-30. Now we will go on to look at the next few verses, namely Romans 8:31-39. "**What then shall we say to these things? If God is for us, who can be against us? He who did not spare His own Son, but delivered Him up for us all, how shall He not with Him also freely give us all things? Who shall bring a charge against God's elect? It is God who justifies. Who is he who condemns? It is Christ who died, and furthermore is also risen, who is even at the right hand of God, who also makes intercession for us. Who shall separate us from the love of Christ? Shall tribulation, or distress, or persecution, or famine, or nakedness, or peril, or sword? As it is written: "For Your sake we are killed all day long; we are accounted as sheep for the slaughter." Yet in all these things we are more than conquerors through Him who loved us. For I am persuaded that neither death nor life, nor angels nor principalities nor powers, nor things present nor things to come, nor height nor depth, nor any other created thing, shall be able to separate us from the love of God which is in Christ Jesus our Lord.**"

These verses argue that we cannot be separated from the love of God. Nothing in the list can separate us from the love of God; and the list includes, "**neither death nor life**". This should reassure us that *nothing* in our lives can ever cut us off from our relationship with God— including our sins. Nothing in our lives is capable of doing it, because God has decreed that we are going to be conformed to the image of Jesus, as the verses before these stated (Romans 8:29-30).

There is a wonderful passage in the Old Testament in Isaiah 46:9-10 which speaks of God's omniscience: "**Remember the former things of old, for I am God, and there is no other; I am God, and there is none like Me, declaring the end from the beginning, and from ancient times things that are not yet done, saying, "My counsel shall stand, and I will do all my pleasure."**'" God knows the end of everything; that is omniscience. Standing at the beginning, He declares what the end is going to be. God's counsel always stands and He does what He chooses and determines to do. He has looked at me and said, "You're going to be saved; you are going to be conformed to the likeness of Jesus." Our salvation is a gift of God's grace, according to His sovereign will. This brings us to the second principle.

PRINCIPLE 2: THE NATURE OF A GIFT FROM GOD

What is a gift from God like? Salvation is a gift from God (as we saw above in Ephesians 2:8-10), so if we know what a gift from God is like, we will learn more about our salvation.

Romans 6:23 says, "**For the wages of sin is death, but the gift of God is eternal life in Christ Jesus our Lord.**" A wage is earned, but a gift is something we are given. These things are contrasted. A gift is never earned or given as a payment or reward for something; for then it would no longer be a gift. The Greek word used for gift in this verse (*charisma*) actually means a *free* gift, and emphasizes that the gift of eternal life is given because of God's *grace* (*charis*) to us.[2] The wages of sin is death: if you sin, you are going to die. You earn it and deserve it. And you will get what you deserve, unless you believe on the Lord Jesus Christ and receive salvation; "**but the gift of God is eternal life in Christ Jesus our Lord**"!

Eternal life is therefore a gift, but what is the *nature* of that gift? The nature of a gift from God is described in Romans 11:29, which says, "**For the gifts and the calling of God are irrevocable.**" The gift of salvation is therefore irrevocable, and the calling of God we have received is irrevocable. What does this mean?

The Greek word translated "**irrevocable**" is *ametamelētos*, meaning 'not regretted,' which comes from the verb *metamelomai* (the prefix *a-* makes it negative). *Metamelomai* means 'to care for or be concerned with afterwards,' signifying 'to regret,' 'to feel sorry,' or 'to relent.' It can mean 'to weep in repentance,' but it does not mean true repentance (which involves changing one's mind);[3] rather, it refers to remorse or being upset. Judas Iscariot had this type of remorse after he had betrayed Jesus (Matthew 27:3). Judas clearly did not change his mind about Christ and become a believer, although he did bitterly regret what he'd done.

---

[2] The word *charis* also suggests 'that which gives pleasure or delight.' *Charisma* means 'that which is given freely with no expectation of return.'

[3] True repentance is a different Greek word altogether, *metanoeō*, which means literally 'to change one's mind.' This word is discussed in chapter 12.

Ametamelētos thus means 'not regretted,' signifying 'without regret or change of purpose.' In relation to the gifts and calling of God, this means that God does not take back or cancel His free gifts and calling. Some translations say "irreversible" or "without repentance" (AV); but "irrevocable" probably best conveys the sense here. The gifts and the calling of God will not be revoked or withdrawn. Not one person exists who could ever say to God, "I'm going to reverse the gifts and calling You have given me." God is not going to be sorry that we received the gift of salvation and His calling (and, incidentally, neither will we be sorry).

If we could lose our salvation, it would suggest not only that God is not omniscient, but that God is not omnipotent. If there was something we could do to lose our salvation, it would imply that we could manage to revoke what God has declared irrevocable: in other words, that God's plan was not big enough or that He was unable to fulfil it.

In Romans chapters 9 to 11, Paul contends that Israel has *not* lost the calling and gifts from God that it received in Abraham's day. The argument is that because Israel has not lost *its* calling and gifts, then neither can we lose ours. Israel was chosen by God to be His special nation and was given the Promised Land as its inheritance, and Israel will continue to be God's chosen nation forever.[4]

There is an interesting section in Genesis 3, which, when we understand it, seems to confirm that salvation is forever and ever. After Adam had fallen and was expelled by God from the Garden of Eden, God set cherubim to guard the tree of life: "**So He (the LORD God) drove out the man; and He placed cherubim at the east of the garden of Eden, and a flaming sword which turned every way, to guard the way to the tree of life**" (Genesis 3:24).

Why was this necessary? The answer is given in verse 22: "**...lest he (Adam) put out his hand and take also from the tree of life, and eat, and live for ever.**" If Adam had eaten of the tree of life he would have lived forever. God wanted to prevent Adam from being condemned to live forever in his fallen state. Were it possible for Adam to lose eternal life, surely God would not have needed to guard the tree of life?

---

[4] Christians should never have doubted that Israel would eventually come back into its Promised Land. This came about in 1948. However, before 1948 there were very few Christians who believed that Israel would ever exist as a national entity again and come back to the Land. Most did not understand the nature of a gift from God or God's unchanging faithfulness to Israel.

Principle 3: The work of the Father, Son and Holy Spirit in our salvation

As we saw earlier, to say that we can lose our salvation is to attribute failure to God. Such a view implies that God the Father, Son or Holy Spirit must have failed in some aspect of the work they planned to accomplish for man. A consideration of the work of each member of the Godhead will quickly dispel any such notion.

The work of the Father

Ephesians 1:3-7 tells us some glorious things the Father did for us: **"Blessed be the God and Father of our Lord Jesus Christ, who has blessed us with every spiritual blessing in the heavenly places in Christ, just as He chose us in Him before the foundation of the world, that we should be holy and without blame before Him in love, having predestined us to adoption as sons by Jesus Christ to Himself, according to the good pleasure of His will, to the praise of the glory of His grace, by which He has made us accepted in the Beloved. In Him we have redemption through His blood, the forgiveness of sins, according to the riches of His grace..."**

God the Father planned our salvation. If the Father's plan was flawed—if He got it wrong like economic planners so often do today—then certainly we have no hope at all, and the lake of fire is coming to every person. But He is omniscient, and He has not failed! He chose us in Christ before the foundation of the world, that we should be holy before Him. This is what He did for us in the past—before we came on the scene to mess things up! Our blessings in Christ are therefore based on the Father's plan. His work is thus the basis of everything.

When we read "**by which**" in verse 6, it is referring to God's grace. The Father, in grace, did all these things for us before we were ever born. And in His foreknowledge, there is no room for misplaced grace. By grace, the Father has predestined us to adoption as sons,[5] and has given us redemption and forgiveness of sins in Christ.

---

[5] The word *huiothesia* translated "*adoption as sons*" literally means 'the placing of a son' (*huios* means 'son'). It does not simply refer to the believer being born into the family of God (which is 'regeneration'), but rather to the believer being given the status and privileges of sonship, and full rights of inheritance (Galatians 4:1-5). Adoption as sons may have been linked with maturity in the ancient world, and those verses referring to our adoption as sons could imply we are predestined to reach maturity. Whether the word *huiothesia* implies this or not, as believers we are made sons of God with an inheritance and are indeed predestined to be conformed to the image of Jesus Christ (Romans 8:29). When He is revealed, we shall be like Him (1 John 3:2).

In Philippians 1:6 Paul expressed his assurance: "**...being confident of this very thing, that He who has begun a good work in you will complete it until the day of Jesus Christ.**" We are kept by God the Father. If we believe that we might lose our salvation, then we are saying that God may not be able to keep us. Are we greater or more omniscient than God? No! For Paul, the fact that God had begun was evidence enough that He would complete the job He planned to do, all the while keeping us safe and making us more and more like Jesus.[6]

The work of the Son

(i) *Jesus died for every sin*

As we have seen before, Jesus died for the sins of every person—past, present and future. He thus died for all of *my* sins, each one of which was foreknown by God. If even one sin was not dealt with when Jesus died, then we are all in grave danger. But the truth is that no sin can now affect God's plan, because His plan has already taken into account that Jesus died for the sins of the whole world.

(ii) *Jesus our Advocate*

Another part of Jesus' work, as discussed in the previous chapter, is His intercessory work as our advocate. It is described in 1 John 2:1. John said, "**My little children, these things I write to you, that you may not sin. And if anyone sins, we have an advocate with the Father, Jesus Christ the righteous.**"

What is an advocate? In Greek the word is *paraklētos*, which literally means 'one called alongside.' A *paraklētos* was a defence lawyer in the ancient world. (The word may also be translated 'comforter' or 'helper'.)

This is an amazing thing! Jesus is our "**advocate with the Father**" today. *Jesus does not turn His back if we sin*; rather, He rushes to our side—because He is our advocate! The word translated "**with**" is the Greek word *pros*, which usually means 'to' or 'towards'.[7] This suggests that, if we sin, Jesus has to turn towards the face of the Father on our behalf.

---

[6] The "day of Jesus Christ" here probably refers to the rapture of the Church, when Christ will return and Christians will be taken up to be with Him forever, meeting Him in the clouds (see 1 Thessalonians 4:13-17).

[7] The main meaning of *pros* is 'to' or 'towards'. It can be translated 'with', although it never completely loses its meaning of direction towards. In this context *pros* expresses Jesus turning towards the Father in order to plead for us; in other contexts it emphasizes that He is ever with or before God the Father (as in John 1:1 and 1 John 1:2), that is, in His presence or 'face to face' with Him.

Jesus says to the Father, "Yes, I know he is guilty; but I paid for that sin on the Cross!" As our Advocate, Jesus thus presents His work on the Cross as the answer to every sin we commit. Note that John said, "**if anyone sins**," Jesus is our advocate. John was referring to sin in a moment of time, not habitual sin, and his assumption was that we might sin.[8]

(iii) *Jesus is both Judge and Advocate*

How clever God is! The Father has chosen Jesus to be our judge (see John 5:22 and 27). But Jesus is also our defence lawyer by our side! Therefore, both the judge and the defence lawyer in this courtroom are Jesus; and so both are *for us*! "**If God is for us, who can be against us?**" (Romans 8:31b). This court is rather 'biased' in our favour! We will be all right, therefore; Jesus is alongside us in court. He will never have to say to the Father that He lost a case. If we believe we might lose our salvation, then we are saying that Jesus, despite being both judge *and* advocate, may still lose our case![9]

When we get to heaven, there will be great rejoicing. "**He (Jesus) shall see the travail of His soul and be satisfied**" (Isaiah 53:11a). Jesus won't be surprised or relieved when we reach heaven. Rather, He knows we will make it and He is waiting for us with eager anticipation!

The work of the Father and the Son together

The work of the Father and the Son always go hand in hand, as is shown by the following two passages.

In John 6:37-40 Jesus said, "**All that the Father gives Me will come to Me, and the one who comes to Me I will by no means cast out. For I have come down from heaven, not to do My own will, but the will of Him who sent Me. This is the will of the Father who sent Me, that of**

---

[8] This verse gives us the right balance. John wrote this to deal with both those who were wilfully sinning after becoming believers, and those who thought they were holier than others. John dealt with both groups in one verse!

Note that John said he was writing so that we might not sin. This tells us that we do not have to sin. If we are devoted to God and filled with the Holy Spirit every moment of the day, then we won't sin. Although we still have our old sin nature, its power over us will be neutralized by our walking in the Spirit. (The translations "destroyed" in the AV, or "done away with" in the RAV and NKJV, in Romans 6:6 are inaccurate; the Greek word means 'neutralized,' 'made powerless,' or 'rendered inoperative' as it says in the margin of the NKJV.) However, we are weak and so at times will fail and sin.

[9] Being the perfect Man who gave Himself as a sacrifice for sins, Jesus has been appointed as Judge. In Revelation chapter 5, which gives a picture of the Church in heaven, Jesus is presented as "a Lamb as though it had been slain" (verse 6). Jesus still bears the marks of His sufferings. He is the Judge; yet it is on the basis of His work on the Cross that we are acquitted!

all He has given Me I should lose nothing, but should raise it up at the last day. And this is the will of Him who sent Me, that everyone who sees the Son and believes in Him may have everlasting life; and I will raise him up at the last day."

The Father, in grace, gives men to Jesus and puts them into His safekeeping. In accordance with the Father's will, Jesus is responsible not to lose any who are given to Him. If Jesus fails, then we are lost. Will Jesus fail in this? Of course not! He always does the Father's will impeccably. When Jesus died on the Cross, He had carried out His Father's will perfectly. He has not changed, and that is why our salvation is perfect and will surely be completed in the day when He shall raise us up into our eternal inheritance.

In John 10 Jesus described Himself as **"the good shepherd"** (John 10:11). Now a good shepherd is one who does not lose any sheep. A bad shepherd is one who loses sheep. In John 10:27-30 Jesus said, **"My sheep hear My voice, and I know them, and they follow Me. And I give them eternal life, and they shall <u>never</u> perish; neither shall <u>anyone</u> snatch them out of My hand. My Father, who has given them to Me, is greater than all; and <u>no one</u> is able to snatch them out of My Father's hand. I and My Father are one."**[10] In the phrase, **"they shall never perish"**, the Greek is very emphatic. It is a double negative; and it could be translated, "they shall never ever perish".

The work of the Holy Spirit

In the first chapter of his letter to the Ephesians, as Paul recounts the blessings of salvation, he rounds off by describing the guarantee: **"In Him you also trusted, after you heard the word of truth, the gospel of your salvation; in whom also, having believed, you were sealed with the Holy Spirit of promise, who is the guarantee of our inheritance until the redemption of the purchased possession, to the praise of His glory"** (Ephesians 1:13-14). We were sealed with the Holy Spirit *at the*

---

[10] The word translated "anyone" (*tis*) in verse 28 literally means 'any'. 'Anyone' or 'any man' is often a perfectly acceptable translation, but such a rendering is not complete enough in this verse, because it leaves the possibility that the devil or his demons could snatch us away from the hand of Jesus. The verse literally tells us that, 'no-one at all—no man, not the devil, nor anyone else' can snatch us away from the hand of Jesus. Similarly, the word translated "no one" (*oudeis*) in verse 29 suggests 'no man, or demon, or anyone or anything else.' And even if His hand was found to be insufficient, Jesus continued, "My Father...is greater than all; and no one is able to snatch them out of My Father's hand." Are we bigger or more powerful than God? No! We therefore can never do anything to escape from the hand of Jesus or the hand of God the Father!

moment of salvation. This is implied in the Greek, and confirmed by other passages of Scripture.

We need to understand what a seal was in the ancient world, because a seal was important and had several very definite characteristics.

1. First, a seal was put on a *completed business transaction*. This verse therefore implies that our salvation is a finished transaction; we have been bought once and for all.

2. Second, a seal was a sign of *ownership*. We now belong to God; and the Holy Spirit in us is God's mark of ownership.

3. Third, a seal meant *complete security*, as can be seen from the following two passages.

   In Esther 8:8, King Ahasuerus said to Esther and Mordecai, **"You yourselves write a decree for the Jews, as you please, in the king's name, and seal it with the king's signet ring; for a letter which is written in the king's name and sealed with the king's signet ring no one can revoke."** A document used to have hot wax put on it, and the king's ring was pressed into it to leave an imprint. This seal meant the decree could not be reversed by anyone else.

   In the Book of Daniel we find that King Darius the Mede put his seal on the lion's den. No one could open it and take Daniel out until the king did so personally. **"Then a stone was brought and laid on the mouth of the den, and the king sealed it with his own signet ring and with the signets of his lords, that the purpose concerning Daniel might not be changed"** (Daniel 6:17).

The fact that we have the Holy Spirit in us means that we are sealed as the property of the King of Kings. A king's seal could never be reversed; therefore the King of King's seal can certainly never be reversed!

The Greek word for "**guarantee**" (*arrabōn*) in Ephesians 1:14 (translated "**earnest**" in the AV) was the word for a 'down-payment' or 'guarantee of future payment.' It meant a first payment towards ultimate ownership, and so constituted a promise that what had been purchased would ultimately be redeemed in full: "**until the redemption of the purchased possession**". It was also the word used for an 'engagement ring.' (*Arrabōna* is still the Greek word for an engagement ring today.) In the ancient world, if you became engaged, then you were as good as married; a bill of divorce was needed to break off the engagement. The *arrabōn* was thus given as a token that the husband would indeed soon marry his wife. In the same way, the Holy Spirit has been given to us as a guarantee that we belong to Jesus forever as His bride—and He, who is faithful, will never break off the relationship.

Peter tells us that God has "**begotten us again....to an inheritance incorruptible and undefiled and that does not fade away, reserved in heaven for you**" (1 Peter 1:3-4). An inheritance awaits us, and the Holy Spirit is our guarantee and first down-payment. He is not apart from us as something we might lose, but dwells inside us as God's inner seal.

The Holy Spirit does several other things for us when we become Christians. He baptizes us into the Body of Christ (1 Corinthians 12:13). He is the other "**Helper**" (this is the Greek word *paraklētos* again—one called alongside), whom Jesus promised to send after He had departed (see John 14:26 and John 16:7). He rushes to our side when we need Him, and helps us in our weakness. When we do not know how to pray, He comes and intercedes for us, interpreting our prayers to the Father (see Romans 8:26).

Finally, we will look at two verses which overlap with the next section. The first describes the Holy Spirit's role in our new birth: "**...He (God) saved us, through the washing of regeneration and renewing of the Holy Spirit**" (Titus 3:5). Every Christian has been born twice: into a natural family and into a spiritual family. We all had a natural father of course; but we now have a spiritual father too—and it is the Holy Spirit who has accomplished this.

1 Peter 1:23 says we "**have been born again, not of corruptible seed but incorruptible, through the word of God which lives and abides for ever.**" We were born again by the Holy Spirit (John 3:5), of incorruptible seed, through the word of God. This incorruptible seed makes us sons of God, and therefore our relationship with the Father is also totally incorruptible. We are sons of God by the work of the Holy Spirit. If He has failed, then I am not a son of God. If He has succeeded, then I am indeed a son of God forever.

PRINCIPLE 4: THE FAMILY OR KINDRED RELATIONSHIP

God became our Father in heaven when we were born again. We were born into His family: "**For you are all sons of God through faith in Christ Jesus**" (Galatians 3:26).

I may not like my natural father, but there is nothing I can do to alter the fact that I am his son. I might change my appearance or my nationality; I can run away and even deny who my father is; but my father will still be my father and I will still be his child. When we come into a kindred relationship with our heavenly Father, there is similarly nothing we can do to escape. For various reasons we might deny that God is our Father; but He will still be faithful to us. We might behave in ways not befitting our heavenly citizenship, and might deny our nationality by saying we no longer belong to the 'commonwealth of heaven'; but God will still be our Father, and we will still be His sons. Whatever we say or do, we will still belong to the great and marvellous family of God.

Conclusion

We have seen four principles on which our salvation, and hence our eternal security, is based: God's omniscience; the nature of a gift from God; the work of the Father, Son and Holy Spirit in our salvation; and, our family or kindred relationship with God. In conclusion, let us look at four more bold statements of the eternal nature of our salvation.

"Most assuredly, I say to you, he who hears My word and believes in Him who sent Me has everlasting life, and shall not come into judgment, but has passed from death into life" (John 5:24).

"But God demonstrates His own love towards us, in that while we were still sinners, Christ died for us. Much more then, having now been justified by His blood, we shall be saved from wrath through Him. For if when we were enemies we were reconciled to God through the death of His Son, much more, having been reconciled, we shall be saved by His life. And not only that, but we also rejoice in God through our Lord Jesus Christ, through whom we have now received the reconciliation" (Romans 5:8-11).

"These things I have written to you who believe in the name of the Son of God, that you may know that you have eternal life, and that you may continue to believe in the name of the Son of God" (1 John 5:13). John said, **"that you may know that you have eternal life"**. He did not say, "That you may know today, but think that you may lose it tomorrow"! John wanted us to have assurance of our salvation.

"Now to Him who is able to keep you from stumbling, and to present you faultless before the presence of His glory with exceeding joy, to God our Saviour, who alone is wise, be glory and majesty, dominion and power, both now and for ever. Amen" (Jude 24-25).

In the next study we will look at the other side of the coin, and discuss verses which seem to contradict these clear principles of eternal security.

11. RESPONSES TO THE CASE AGAINST
— ETERNAL SECURITY (PART 3)

In Part 1 of our study on eternal security we saw how the Bible calls us to live holy lives. We saw how God's grace *leads* us and *inspires* us to holiness; God does not threaten us. In Part 2, we studied some of the scriptures that establish four principles underlying eternal security. We saw, by reference to Scripture as well as by logic, that in fact every believer *is* secure in his or her salvation.

Part 3 is perhaps the most interesting of the studies, because there are many Christians who think that the believer stands in danger of losing salvation—in other words, they deny the fact of eternal security. In this study, we will look at some of those verses which these Christians quote as evidence that we can lose our salvation. Again, it is helpful to look at these verses under various topics, because most scriptures not covered specifically fall naturally into one or other of them.

It is important to realize that only one of the camps concerning this question of eternal security can be correct. We either are eternally secure or we are not. Therefore, one of the camps must be misinterpreting the Bible.[1]

In the previous chapter, most of the scriptures which suggested that we *are* eternally secure were without another interpretation. For example, Jesus said, **"They [my sheep] shall never perish"** (John 10:28), and this cannot be interpreted to mean anything other than what it says; there is no conditional phrase following to say that this is only true under certain conditions. We even saw that the Greek has a double negative. Jesus went on to say in the same passage, **"Neither shall anyone snatch them out of My hand"** (verse 28). He then said, **"My Father, who has given them to Me, is greater than all; and no one is able to snatch them out**

---

[1] Being God's Word, the Bible is without contradiction. Those people who say that the Bible is "full" of contradictions often have not studied it or know only a little about it. A little knowledge is a dangerous thing, and a Christian with a little knowledge is someone quite vulnerable; such a person can easily be misled on every count. We need to study and come to understand the Word of God, and the principles it reveals.

of My Father's hand" (verse 29). We have Jesus' hand and God the Father's hand holding us!

We also saw that all believers have been, among many other things, **"sealed with the Holy Spirit of promise...until the redemption of the purchased possession..."** (Ephesians 1:13-14). Notice that Paul did not say that we have been sealed until we sin terribly or until we turn away from God. The day of redemption is when Jesus comes again.

Romans 8:31-39 was also clear: "**[nothing] shall be able to separate us from the love of God which is in Christ Jesus our Lord.**" This passage lists certain things: tribulation, persecution, life, death, angels, and so on. It indicates that *nothing at all* can separate us from the love of God, either now or in the future.

There were many other such verses. Assuming these verses are correct, and that we are indeed eternally secure, then the verses thrown up against this viewpoint must be either misinterpreted or misapplied. We will see in this study that this is the case.

ERRORS MADE IN INTERPRETING THE BIBLE

In general, there are two major types of error made in interpreting a verse of the Bible (which of course overlap): either, the verse or passage is misapplied, that is, it actually has another subject in view altogether; or, the verse is taken out of context, so that its meaning is distorted.

In the case of eternal security, people often quote a scripture that is not about salvation at all, and try to use it to prove that we can lose our salvation. For example, people make reference to Paul saying we can "fall from grace," and they take this to mean that we can lose our salvation. They quote Galatians 5:4, "**You have become estranged from Christ, you who attempt to be justified by law; you have fallen from grace.**"

It is therefore quite true that it is possible to "fall from grace," but this verse is not talking about losing salvation at all! Beware, because the phrase that is quoted is the last part of the verse, and the verse comes at the end of a passage which is about how to live the Christian life. The phrase "**fallen from grace**" is therefore being quoted out of its context.

What was the context? False teachers had come into the midst of the Galatian churches, teaching the people that they had to fulfil the Jewish law to be saved (by being circumcised, for example). The Christians were being brought into bondage by these teachers. One of the reasons why

Paul was writing this letter to the Galatian churches was to tell the Christians how worthless such teaching was. In Galatians 3:1 Paul said to them, "**O foolish Galatians! Who has bewitched you that you should not obey the truth...?**", and in Galatians 5:1 he said, "**Stand fast therefore in the liberty by which Christ has made us free, and do not be entangled again with a yoke of bondage.**"

The argument of Paul in Galatians 5:1-4 was that, if they became circumcised, then they would be obliged to keep the whole law: "**...Indeed I, Paul, say to you that if you become circumcised, Christ will profit you nothing. And I testify again to every man who becomes circumcised that he is a debtor to keep the whole law**" (verses 2-3). In verse 4 Paul then said that any person who attempted to live under rules, and thus tried to establish his own righteousness, had "**fallen from grace.**"

How then are we to live? The principle we are to live by is Romans 8:2, "**For the law of the Spirit of life in Christ Jesus has made me free from the law of sin and death.**" The law tries to put sin to death in us. But does it succeed? It does not! In fact, it makes us sin more. Such 'self-righteousness' will inevitably make us sin more. Sin is only dealt with by grace inside, as we live according to the Spirit and realize that we died to sin in Christ. If we do not live according to the Spirit, then we have fallen from grace; and when we get to heaven, God will tell us where we went wrong!

Therefore beware of people who quote Scripture out of context! The Bible sometimes describes views that are incorrect and there are passages that can be misleading if quoted in isolation. For example, the words of a false prophet are lies.[2]

SCRIPTURE PASSAGES USED TO OPPOSE ETERNAL SECURITY

We will now consider some of the verses which can appear difficult to reconcile with an understanding of eternal security. I have divided them up into four main groups, with some miscellaneous scriptures at the end.

---

[2] If you take the words of a false prophet in isolation, you are actually quoting a false prophet who was talking nonsense, and you may fail to see that, in the surrounding verses, the false teaching was about to be corrected. The words of Job's three comforters, for example, should not be taken in isolation. These men were believers, but they completely misapplied certain truths, because they lacked understanding. They did not know the real reason for Job's suffering, and so they misrepresented God (see Job 42:7).

These groups demonstrate the four main ways in which scriptures are misinterpreted or misapplied in regard to the question of eternal security.

GROUP 1: PASSAGES DEALING WITH FRUIT AND THE JUDGMENT OF BELIEVERS' WORKS

People often quote verses that are about the fruit of a Christian's life or about the judgment of a believer's works, but apply them to salvation.

Once we are born again, we *should* bear fruit for God and be productive in our lives. Indeed, fruit is production. Some passages deal with this production of fruit and good works in a Christian's life and with the judgment of that production. They have nothing whatsoever to do with salvation. If we try to apply such verses to salvation, we will inevitably misinterpret them.

Consider this illustration: a farmer may keep chickens in order to produce eggs. If he grades the eggs, he is not grading the chickens. Similarly, someone may keep vines to produce grapes. Judging the grapes is not the same as judging the vine. In the same way, God may judge the works and the fruit of a believer's life, but this is completely different from His judging the believer.

The Parable of the Sower

The parable of the sower is an important passage. If we look at the version given in Matthew 13:3-9, it begins: **"Then He spoke many things to them in parables, saying: "Behold, a sower went out to sow...""** (verse 3). Jesus gave an explanation of the parable, which is recorded in verses 18-23. The main message is clearly about how people hear and understand the word of God. The seed is the word of the kingdom (verse 19), that is, the word of God (see Luke 8:11). There are four sections to this parable, corresponding to the types of ground where the seed fell—representing four conditions of the human heart. The whole parable concerns the effect of the word of God and the amounts of fruit it produces.

(1) **"And as he sowed, some seed fell by the wayside; and the birds came and devoured them"** (verse 4).

This first category is the seed that fell on the downtrodden path at the side of the field. In verse 19 we have Jesus' interpretation: **"When anyone hears the word of the kingdom, and does not understand it, then the wicked one comes and snatches away what was sown in his**

heart. This is he who received seed by the wayside." This hardened ground represents the hard-hearted unbeliever. The word of God comes, but it bounces off. And it is not long before the devil comes and takes away the seed, **"lest they should believe and be saved"** (Luke 8:12b). After the word of God bounces off, unbelievers usually become hardened to it even more.

It is important to notice that all of the next three cases are different in an important way—the seed was actually received into the ground. These three cases thus represent believers—who are born again of incorruptible seed, through the word of God (see 1 Peter 1:23-25). Once the seed has gone into the ground it does not lie there dormant; it starts producing. And we then have three types of production described. There are Christians in all three of these groups.

(2) **"Some fell on stony places, where they did not have much earth; and they immediately sprang up because they had no depth of earth. But when the sun was up they were scorched, and because they had no root they withered away"** (verses 5-6).

This category is seed that fell on stony, shallow ground, where there was not much depth of earth. **"But he who received the seed on stony places, this is he who hears the word and immediately receives it with joy; yet he has no root in himself, but endures only for a while. For when tribulation or persecution arises because of the word, immediately he stumbles"** (verses 20-21). This person **"immediately"** receives the word. Such Christians begin with a great spurt, but all of a sudden drop away and stop producing fruit. This may happen when they realize their friends do not like them any more, or when some other trouble or persecution comes. The first growth quickly withers. This should be a warning to us.

(3) **"And some fell among thorns, and the thorns sprang up and choked them"** (verse 7).

This third category is the seed that was choked by thorns. **"Now he who received seed among the thorns is he who hears the word, and the cares of this world and the deceitfulness of riches choke the word, and he becomes unfruitful"** (verse 22). This represents the type of Christian who continues to love what the world can offer. He still has some worldly ambition, or still desires riches or something else from this world. The production of fruit in his life slows down as these other cares grow and take over.

(4) **"But others fell on good ground and yielded a crop: some a hundredfold, some sixty, some thirty"** (verse 8).

Finally, some seed fell on good ground, and the result was great production! **"But he who received seed on the good ground is he who hears the word and understands it, who indeed bears fruit and produces: some a hundredfold, some sixty, some thirty"** (verse 23). This is the fruitful believer, who hears *and understands* the word of God. Luke's account also stresses the need for obedience and patience (see Luke 8:15). The production is vast, perhaps thirtyfold, sixtyfold or even a hundredfold.

The main message of this parable has nothing to do with salvation. It is primarily about the condition of people's hearts, the effect of the word of God and fruitfulness. Do not believe any person who takes it out of context and says, "Look, all except the last person fell away and lost their salvation!" Point out to such a person that *apart from in the first instance, the seed stayed in the ground, and it still had some root*. To interpret this parable as being about lost salvation is quite wrong.

Hebrews 6:7-10

Hebrews 6:7-10 requires careful reading, because it discusses not only fruitfulness, but also judgment. Here believers are represented by earth that can produce different types of crops.

"For the earth which drinks in the rain that often comes upon it, and bears herbs useful for those by whom it is cultivated, receives blessing from God" (verse 7). This describes the believer who is walking in the Spirit or 'in fellowship' as receiving showers of blessing.[3] Notice that it says **"often"**; God wants to pour blessings on us *often*.

This passage is again about production. The word translated **"herbs"** in verse 7 means 'vegetables'. The believer is therefore being pictured as a vegetable garden, bringing forth produce for God. However, the ground is also capable of producing thorns and briars: **"But if it bears thorns and briars, it is rejected and near to being cursed, whose end is to be burned"** (verse 8).

In Israel the land that bears thorns and briars is the desert, that is, the land which receives no rain. This is a picture of the believer who is not living in fellowship with God. It says that this land is **"rejected"** or, in some

---

[3] The term 'in fellowship' in these studies is used to describe the believer who is walking in agreement with God, without unconfessed sin, as discussed in the next chapter. The Bible describes the life of such a believer in terms of 'walking in the Spirit,' 'abiding in Christ,' 'walking in the light,' 'living by faith' and being 'spiritually minded'. In contrast, the believer who is not living in agreement with God, who does not walk in the light, is called 'out of fellowship' in these studies.

translations, "thrown out". However, neither of these translations is correct. The word in Greek is *adokimos*, which means 'not approved'. Earth which brings forth thorns and briars is *not approved* by God. Notice that the writer says such earth is only "**near to being cursed**"; he does not say that such earth "is cursed".

Why does it say this? It is because it is *unbelievers* who are ultimately going to be cursed, and they *inevitably* produce thorns and briars. The tragedy is that some Christians produce the same output as non-Christians. It is a disgrace for those who are ultimately going to heaven, and who are not of this world, to only ever produce worldly deeds. As we already know, believers will not be judged *themselves*. But their produce—that is, the thorns and briars they produce—*will* be judged.[4]

The verse concludes, "**...whose end is to be burned**", and the word "**whose**" refers to the earth. After every harvest, a farmer sets fire to his field. This burns up what is left (the stubble and weeds), but the field remains. Only the unwanted produce of the field is destroyed; the earth itself is not consumed. In the same way, the thorns and briars we produce will be burned up.

There will be some Christians who will try to enter heaven on the basis of their good deeds; but their 'good' deeds will be works of the flesh. God will burn up all the thorns and briars they have produced. "**For our God is a consuming fire**" (Hebrews 12:29). And such people will get into heaven "**as through fire**", as 1 Corinthians 3:15b tells us. Why? Because their so-called 'good' deeds, done not in faith and obedience but in an attempt to gain some 'reward' from God, are filthy rags in His sight; and God will say to them, "You can't come in here with those filthy rags. I've got to burn them off you first!" So the end of those Christians who produce thorns and briars is that the fire of judgment will remove all their unwanted produce.

The writer was not saying that the fruitless Christians would lose their salvation. In fact, in the very next verse he said, "**But, beloved, we are confident of better things concerning you, yes, things that accompany salvation, though we speak in this manner**" (Hebrews 6:9). The writer was assuring the Hebrew believers that they had good fruit (the fruit of the Spirit and genuine good works) in their lives. He was saying, "I know

---

[4] All works of the flesh are destined for judgment, whether such works are produced by Christians or non-Christians. The thorns and briars are a reference to works of the flesh. The writer was saying to the believers: "You are not going to be judged, but the world is; so don't therefore produce the same fruit as those in the world!" (Paul used a similar argument in Colossians 3:5-6).

that you are not like this desert land." Verse 10 makes it even clearer, **"For God is not unjust to forget your work and labour of love which you have shown towards His name, in that you have ministered to the saints, and do minister."** Therefore, in context, these verses were not written to the Hebrew believers to suggest they could lose their salvation, but rather to encourage them and assure them of God's blessing.

1 Corinthians 9:27

Another frequently misunderstood passage is 1 Corinthians 9:24-27. **"Do you not know that those who run in a race all run, but one receives the prize? Run in such a way that you may obtain it....But I discipline my body and bring it into subjection, lest, when I have preached to others, I myself should become disqualified"** (verses 24, 27).

The whole context is athletics. Some people actually think that Paul considered he could lose his salvation and end up in the lake of fire forever. But the word translated **"disqualified"** in verse 27 is the Greek word *adokimos* again, and it should be translated "not approved".[5] Paul wanted to ensure that he would be approved by God and not disapproved as far as his *works* were concerned. He was not worried about losing his salvation; rather, he wanted to be approved in all that he did and receive a reward.[6]

This first group of commonly misinterpreted passages therefore covers those dealing with the fruit of our lives, and the judgment of our works. Such verses, although often misapplied, are not about losing salvation at all. There are several other passages which also fit into this group.[7]

GROUP 2: PASSAGES ABOUT GOD DISCIPLINING BELIEVERS

Many people quote passages which concern God's fatherly discipline of His children, and wrongly interpret them by assuming they refer to losing salvation.

---

[5] The AV inaccurately translates it as being "made a castaway".

[6] In 2 Timothy 2:15, a familiar verse: "Be diligent to present yourself approved to God, a worker who does not need to be ashamed...", Paul used the opposite word dokimos for "approved". (The prefix 'a-' at the beginning of many Greek words makes them negative.)

[7] On the audio tape of BBS 11, Roger Price also discussed John 15:1-8 (Jesus' parable about the true vine) within this group. In view of the space necessary to fully discuss the various possible interpretations of this passage, it is not dealt with in this book. Again, it should be remembered that the main emphasis of the passage is fruitfulness. Jesus was teaching His disciples the necessity for union and communion with Him in order to be fruitful, as well as illustrating God's dealings with His people that they might produce much fruit for His glory.

It is important to remember that once we are saved we become "**children of God**" (1 John 3:1). God is a good father, and He immediately starts changing and disciplining us. His discipline does not mean we have lost our salvation. Quite the contrary: His discipline is *evidence* of our salvation, because it is a sign of His continuing care and fatherhood! A father does not discipline those who are not his children, but he does discipline his own children; and it is very important for their well-being that He does so.

There are two major passages on the discipline of believers: Hebrews 12:5-11 and 1 Corinthians 11:29-32. We will not go through them in detail here.[8] However, we need to look at the principle of *maximum* discipline or, as it is sometimes called, "sin unto death" (AV) or "sin leading to death." The verses about this cause some people a lot of difficulty.

"**If anyone sees his brother sinning a sin which does not lead to death, he will ask, and He will give him life for those who commit sin not leading to death. There is sin leading to death. I do not say that he should pray about that. All unrighteousness is sin, and there is sin not leading to death**" (1 John 5:16-17). We know from our studies so far that this "**sin leading to death**", which is committed by a believer, cannot be the same as the unforgivable sin, for we have seen what the unforgivable sin is. It may seem strange at first, but there can be a sin that causes a believer to die physically. What then is this "sin leading to death"? And why does a believer die as a result of such sins?

This refers to maximum discipline from the Father. God's discipline can become so severe that finally a person loses his or her life. For example, in 1 Corinthians 11:30, Paul said to the Corinthians, "**For this reason many are weak and sick among you, and many sleep**", and it is clear from the New Testament that, when a believer is said to "sleep" or to have "fallen asleep", he or she is physically dead.[9] Paul was telling the Corinthians that, because they were taking the Lord's Supper wrongly, without due respect for the Lord and His body, some of them were sick and some had even died.

---

[8] Hebrews chapter 12 is discussed briefly in chapter 12 of this book. Both passages are dealt with in detail in the Basic Bible Studies course Series 2, in BBS 21 to 23.

[9] See for example John 11:11-13, 1 Thessalonians 4:13, Matthew 9:24, Matthew 27:52. The term "sleep" really applies to the believer's dead body, since the soul is conscious in the presence of the Lord (see 1 Thessalonians 5:10, 2 Corinthians 4:8).

It is important to realize that this maximum discipline does not come unless the believer in question has been 'out of fellowship' continuously for a long time, has resisted all the discipline that God has already brought, and has disregarded many warnings from God and other Christians about the seriousness of his or her situation. Such believers have come to the place where they are being disciplined so severely that they are miserable, depressed or ill; and yet still they will not submit to the word of God or to the discipline of God. They go 'downhill' until, finally, they die. This is not a common thing at all. (I have only ever known a very few such cases.) It can take years and years, and God is all the time asking the person to submit to His discipline and not to resist it.

Ananias and Sapphira

There is a case given in Acts 5:1-11. Ananias and Sapphira lied to the Holy Spirit and died. We do not know the background to their situation; the actual sin referred to in the passage may well have been the final straw. The fact that they died, however, does *not* imply they lost their salvation. Rather, the very fact that they were still being disciplined at the point of their death is evidence that God was still their Father! God decided that, in view of the critical need for the Church to expand quickly and to exhibit His holiness, the wilful rebellion of Ananias and Sapphira made it better for them to be in heaven with Him immediately.

This may surprise us; but we need to realize that this life is not as important as eternity. Furthermore, there will be no pointing the finger at such people in heaven. By the time we meet Ananias and Sapphira in heaven, their dead works will have been burnt up, just like ours will have been burnt up.

King Saul

King Saul is an example in the Old Testament of a person who committed a sin leading to death. King Saul was a believer. He reigned as King of Israel for 40 years. For his first year, he was 'in fellowship' with God; but he then spent the next 39 years 'out of fellowship.'

Saul's final sin, which resulted in his death, was this: after having passed a law which said that all witches and mediums should be killed, he then secretly went to consult a witch from Endor because he needed guidance. Saul had turned His back on God. But instead of repenting and inquiring of the LORD, he decided to try to communicate with the prophet Samuel who was dead. Therefore God allowed Saul to be killed (as 1 Chronicles 10:13-14 tells us). The story is given in 1 Samuel 28.

In fact, God allowed Samuel to speak to Saul, much to the witch's surprise.[10] The words that Samuel said reveal some important things to us. **"Now Samuel said to Saul, "Why have you disturbed me by bringing me up?" And Saul answered, "I am deeply distressed; for the Philistines make war against me, and God has departed from me and does not answer me any longer, neither by prophets nor by dreams. Therefore I have called you, that you may reveal to me what I should do""** (1 Samuel 28:15).

Saul had not wanted to listen to Samuel when Samuel had been alive; but now that he was dead, Saul wanted to consult him and hear his advice! Note how Samuel said to Saul, **"Why have you disturbed me...?"** This tells us something wonderful—that Samuel was in perfect peace where he was![11] This should encourage us that there is no need to fear death! The place we will go to is much better than here on the earth.

Samuel then explained to Saul the dire situation he was in: **"Then Samuel said: "Why then do you ask me, seeing the LORD has departed from you and has become your enemy? And the LORD has done for Himself as He spoke by me. For the LORD has torn the kingdom out of your hand and given it to your neighbour, namely, David. Because you did not obey the voice of the LORD nor execute His fierce wrath upon Amalek, therefore the LORD has done this thing to you this day...""** (verses 16-18).

Saul had refused to execute God's judgment on the Amalekites and had disobeyed God (see 1 Samuel 13:1-14 and 1 Samuel 15). The judgment Samuel pronounced on Saul is given in verse 19: **"...Moreover the LORD will also deliver Israel with you into the hand of the Philistines. And tomorrow you and your sons will be <u>with me</u>. The LORD will also deliver the army of Israel into the hand of the Philistines."** Note the words, **"with me"**.

The Bible is a book of important prepositions. Even after this judgment, Saul was going to be in the same place as Samuel next day. He would be in Paradise! This reminds us of what Jesus said to one of the thieves crucified alongside Him: **"Assuredly, I say to you, today you will be**

---

[10] This is the only time ever that God has allowed a dead person to come back in this way. Today when mediums and spiritualists claim to communicate with the dead, they are communicating with lying, 'familiar' spirits and 'ventriloquist' spirits. Such activities need to be completely rejected.

[11] Samuel was in the place where all believers went when they died at that time: Paradise. This place of peace was also referred to as "Abraham's Bosom" (see Luke 16:23).

with Me in Paradise" (Luke 23:43). So today not only Samuel, but King Saul too, is in heaven.[12]

So what is a "sin unto death"? Is it loss of salvation? It is definitely not. In fact, it is a proof of salvation, and evidence of eternal security!

GROUP 3: PASSAGES OR VERSES TAKEN OUT OF CONTEXT

It is important always to look up a verse when someone quotes it at you, to check the context in which it appears.

Matthew 24:13

A verse which is often quoted by those who believe that we can lose our salvation is Matthew 24:13, **"But he who endures to the end shall be saved."** You will hear preachers say, "Unless we endure to the end, we will therefore not be saved"; and they quote this scripture to 'prove' it. But beware! The preacher might have got it from Scripture; however, he has also got it wrong from Scripture!

First, it is important to remember that the word 'saved,' in both Greek and English, does not only concern eternal salvation. 'Saved' also means to be 'delivered'—for example, saved from the hands of an enemy. The word is *sōzō* in Greek, which is translated "saved" or "delivered" in many places, as well as "healed" or "made whole." The way in which it should be translated is determined by the context.

Matthew 24 describes the stress that Jewish evangelists will be under in the Tribulation period, just before Jesus Christ returns. The land of Israel will be surrounded by enemies on every side; and these evangelists will have preached faithfully for up to seven years. Many thousands of Jews will have been killed.[13]

The Jewish believers in Jerusalem will remember this statement of Jesus, and will be encouraged. It is a promise. Jesus was saying to them, "You are not all going to die. If you are still there at the time I return, I will

---

[12] After Jesus died, He rose and ascended, and He took all the dead souls from Paradise (believers) up with Him into heaven; He emptied Abraham's Bosom. This subject is covered in more detail by Roger Price in Special Topic Study 39, which has been published as a book entitled "Explaining what happens after death" (Sovereign World).

[13] The same period is described in Matthew 10:22, and the same statement about endurance is made. This Tribulation period is described in Basic Bible Study BBS 56, "Evangelism in the Tribulation".

deliver you!" Jesus will return to Jerusalem and every single believer will be miraculously delivered.[14]

Matthew 7:21-23

Jesus' words in Matthew 7:21-23 are also often quoted by those trying to prove that we can lose our salvation. **"Not everyone who says to Me, 'Lord, Lord,' shall enter the kingdom of heaven, but he who does the will of My Father in heaven. Many will say to Me in that day, 'Lord, Lord, have we not prophesied in Your name, cast out demons in Your name, and done many wonders in Your name?' And then I will declare to them, 'I never knew you; depart from Me, you who practise lawlessness!'"**

The context is "**in that day**", and that day is the day of judgment. We know from Philippians 2:10-11 that "**at the name of Jesus every knee should bow.... and that every tongue should confess that Jesus Christ is Lord, to the glory of God the Father**"; and this will truly happen on judgment day (Romans 14:11). On judgment day even Satan is going to confess that Jesus Christ is Lord; every demon and every unbeliever is also going to confess Him as Lord. *Everyone* is therefore going to confess Jesus Christ as Lord *then*. But not everyone says, "Jesus is Lord" *now*— namely, the unbelievers.

However, some religious people call Jesus "Lord" today, although they are not born again. You have to be born again to enter the kingdom of heaven; it is not just what you say that counts.

In the last days there will be many false workers doing miracles, and there will be many false prophets and false messiahs (see Matthew 24:24) who will try to deceive, if possible, even the elect of God. These people, who will claim to have done miracles for Jesus, will be like so-called "white witches" or spiritualist healers today; they may have done many seemingly 'good' miracles, but they do not know Jesus. **"Unless one is born again, he cannot see the kingdom of God"** (John 3:3).

If we look at the context in which a verse or passage appears, therefore, its explanation often becomes clear.

---

[14] These believers will then go through into the Millennium (or kingdom), and will become the basis of the 'population explosion' that will take place during the Millennium. A description of the Second Coming of Christ and the wonderful way in which He will deliver the Jews is given in Basic Bible Study BBS 58. The Millennium is described in BBS 60-61.

Group 4: Passages exhorting believers to live in fellowship

Hebrews 6:1-6

This is a passage which exhorts believers to continue living 'in fellowship' with God and to grow to maturity. It is often quoted by opponents of eternal security, but it is a passage they really should leave well alone! It begins: "**Therefore, leaving the discussion of the elementary principles of Christ, let us go on to perfection, not laying again the foundation of repentance from dead works and of faith towards God, of the doctrine of baptisms, of laying on of hands, of resurrection of the dead, and of eternal judgment. And this we will do if God permits**" (verses 1-3).

The difficult verses are verses 4 to 6: "**For it is impossible for those who were once enlightened, and have tasted the heavenly gift, and have become partakers of the Holy Spirit, and have tasted the good word of God and the powers of the age to come, if they fall away, to renew them again to repentance, since they crucify again for themselves the Son of God, and put him to an open shame.**"

Before we look more closely at this passage, there is an important principle we must recognize: *if in a single passage a word (or phrase) is repeated, then the word (or phrase) has the same meaning each time.* Therefore, when verse 6 refers to "**repentance**", by referring to verse 1 we can learn that this is "**repentance from dead works**". The idea in view throughout this passage is thus repentance from dead works.

The writer was describing *Christians* who were 'out of fellowship' because of their dead works, who needed to repent from their dead works. The passage is therefore not talking about salvation, but about believers getting back in fellowship.[15] This is confirmed because the writer refers to those who were once enlightened, and have tasted the heavenly gift, and have become partakers of the Holy Spirit, and have

---

[15] An elementary principle that Christians need to know is how to be restored to living in fellowship with God when they are out of fellowship because of dead works. We should claim 1 John 1:9 and get back in fellowship quickly. There are believers who, having confessed their sins, still walk around as if they are under their sins. It is time to go back to the elementary principles! Sin should never defeat a Christian. We have an advocate in heaven—Jesus Christ (see 1 John 2:1). If your heart condemns you, God is greater than your heart (1 John 3:20). After we have confessed our sin, we should pick ourselves up, brush ourselves off, and, forgetting those things which lie behind, immediately press on. This is the subject of chapter 12.

tasted the good word of God and the powers of the age to come.[16] These are all things experienced by Christians.

The word "**tasted**" used in verses 4 and 5 is the same word used in Hebrews 2:9 of Jesus tasting death, and it implies a real personal experience of tasting. Jesus drank the cup God gave Him to drink; He did not merely sip it. To claim that these people had not truly experienced these things by personally tasting them is to imply Jesus did not truly experience death. The writer was therefore definitely talking about believers. Also, what could "**to renew them again to repentance**" mean unless he was referring to believers?

If, as some argue, these verses apply to those who have lost salvation, they present a real problem. If believers have fallen away and (as these people assume) lost salvation because of some sin, then these verses state that it is impossible to restore them. There is therefore no reason ever to try to restore such a person; you should just let him or her go! However, these same people often spend a lot of time quoting verses like these to try to restore such people! I, and many other Christians, can disprove this idea from personal experience. We have been away from the Lord for some time, and have come back to God 'glowing'! What then can this verse mean? In fact, it is a wonderful, wonderful verse.

Verse 6 begins, "**if they fall away...**" (literally, "having fallen away") and this is one of five aorist participles in the Greek of verses 4 to 6. It could therefore be placed at the start of verse 4 to give a slightly clearer translation: "Having fallen away, it is impossible for those who were once enlightened and have tasted of the heavenly gift and were made partakers of the Holy Spirit and have tasted the good word of God and the powers of the age to come, to renew them again to repentance, since they are crucifying the Son of God afresh."

If we regard the middle section as a parenthesis, we get the obvious statement that, "Having fallen away, it is impossible....to renew them again to repentance, since they are crucifying the Son of God afresh." If a believer is continually sinning, then it is impossible for him or her to live in fellowship with God. This is obviously true, because sin puts us out of fellowship.

---

[16] The Greek word translated "once" in verse 4 is hapax, which generally means 'on one occasion' or 'once and for all time.' In this context, where it is used with five participles, it may simply be translated 'after' to indicate that these things occurred in the past: that is, "It is impossible to renew to repentance those who, after they were enlightened, and tasted the gift from heaven....and fell away...." The participles are all aorist participles, meaning that the actions or experiences occurred in the past. An aorist participle precedes the action of the main verb.

The verb translated **"since they crucify"** in verse 6 could be translated "so long as they are crucifying" or "while they are crucifying". The writer was thus saying that it was impossible to restore those who were crucifying the Son of God afresh. He was saying to those who were sinning, "So long as you are constantly sinning and refusing to get back in fellowship, you cannot be restored; and no preaching, praying, or anything else will get you back in fellowship." Those believers who were sinning continually needed to be reminded how to get back in fellowship.

What sin were these Jewish believers committing? We can learn from history and from the context that, although these Jewish believers had truly believed on Christ, they had given in to the temptation to turn back to the rituals of Judaism; they had never truly given up their Jewish religious traditions, and were still sacrificing lambs in the Temple. This sin was putting them out of fellowship. The lamb represented Christ; and so every day, it was as if they were crucifying Christ again. But Jesus had died on the Cross once and for all as the Lamb of God.

Hebrews chapter 10

Hebrews 10 explains this more fully. **"By that will [God's will] we have been sanctified through the offering of the body of Jesus Christ once for all"** (verse 10). This verse says, **"we have been sanctified"**; and the verb form is passive, since God has sanctified us. (If the passive voice had not been used, it would imply there is something *we* have to do.) Jesus died for all our sins, and there is no other offering for sin.

Verses 12 and 14 emphasize this: **"But this Man, after He had offered one sacrifice for sins forever, sat down at the right hand of God....For by one offering He has perfected for ever those who are being sanctified."** Note that this says we have been perfected **"for ever"**.

If we try to keep the law religiously, we will keep failing; and our dead works will continually obstruct our fellowship with God. After the Cross, there is no longer any further offering that can be made for sin. It was Jesus Christ who died for our sins once for all; a lamb is of no effect. One sacrifice did it all. **"Their sins and their lawless deeds I will remember no more"** (verse 17). This again confirms our eternal security.

"Now where there is remission of these, there is no longer an offering for sin" (verse 18). If God has dealt with our past sins, then there is no offering that we need to make for our past sins. If He's dealt with our present sins, then no offering is required for them. And if He's dealt with our future sins, then why go back to animal sacrifices? It is the same sacrifice that covers all of these sins, and no other offering is necessary.

"**For if we sin wilfully after we have received the knowledge of the truth, there no longer remains a sacrifice for sins, but a certain fearful expectation of judgment, and fiery indignation which will devour the adversaries**" (Hebrews 10:26-27). These Jewish believers were wilfully going down to the Temple to offer sacrifices, even after receiving knowledge of the truth. The writer was saying to them, "Why turn back to lambs? They are not going to do you any good. Only one sacrifice counts—Jesus on the Cross!"

Is this not the most obvious interpretation of this passage when one considers the context?

From AD 66 to 73 the Romans massacred the Jews, and the Book of Hebrews was written just a few years before this terrible period. It was a final appeal to the Jewish believers to get back in fellowship with God; otherwise, they would die together with the rest of the Jews when the city was destroyed by the Romans in AD 70. (In other words, this would be their "sin leading to death".)

History reveals that those Jewish believers who were prepared to leave the Temple—who were living in fellowship with God—escaped and fled from Jerusalem. Those who stayed behind, because they considered that they could not leave the Temple, died along with the unbelieving Jews.

Understanding the context in the Book of Hebrews thus indicates that the writer was exhorting Jewish believers to stay in fellowship. If we study the text and background carefully, such passages as these thus present little problem.

Miscellaneous scriptures

There are two other passages often quoted by opponents of eternal security which do not fall into any of the groups discussed so far.

Revelation 3:5—'Overcomers'

Revelation 3:5 is sometimes quoted in arguments against eternal security, but I find it hard to see why. It is part of a letter to the church in Sardis from Jesus. In it, He said: "**He who overcomes shall be clothed in white garments, and I will not blot out his name from the Book of Life; but I will confess his name before My Father and before His angels.**"

Because it says, "**He who overcomes**" in this verse (as well as in others in Revelation chapters 2 and 3) some people presume there will be believers who will not overcome, who will not be clothed in white garments.

But who are overcomers? All Christians are! It was the apostle John who wrote Revelation; and it was the same John who in his first letter defined an 'overcomer': "**For whatever is born of God overcomes the world. And this is the victory that has overcome the world—our faith. Who is he who overcomes the world, but he who believes that Jesus is the Son of God?**" (1 John 5:4-5).

This should be no surprise to us. An overcomer is *one who has faith in Jesus Christ*: in other words, a born-again believer. The devil and the world thought they had overcome us, but then we believed on Jesus and, through our faith, we have overcome them! If we understand this, then we can see that Revelation 3:5 confirms eternal security. If you believe that Jesus is the Son of God, then you are an overcomer, and these promises are given to you:

1. you shall be clothed in white garments (that is, clothed in the righteousness of God in Christ);

2. your name will never be blotted out of the Book of Life; and,

3. Jesus will confess your name before the Father and His angels. Hallelujah!

I really do not know how this verse can be used by those who deny eternal security. It does not say, "If you do not overcome, you will have your name blotted out of the Book of Life." Instead, it says that if you *are* a believer, your name will *not* be blotted out—that is, eternal security!

2 Timothy 2:11-13

To end with, we will look at 2 Timothy 2:11-13, which is a glorious passage: "**This is a faithful saying: 'For if we died with Him, we shall also live with Him. If we endure, we shall also reign with Him. If we deny Him, He also will deny us. If we are faithless, He remains faithful; He cannot deny Himself.'**"

This is a quotation, probably from a hymn which was sung in the early Church. It actually contains a wonderful promise for us in verse 13. It is vital for us to understand it, and it should encourage us. However, verse 13 follows a difficult statement in verse 12: "**If we deny Him, He also will deny us...**". I am so glad that verse 13 is there; otherwise, people would read verse 12 and go wrong. It continues: "**...If we are faithless, He remains faithful; He cannot deny Himself.**" If someone asks you to explain verse 12, then ask him or her to explain verse 13!

The word for "**deny**" (*arneomai*) in verse 12 means 'to repudiate' or 'disown,' but it may also mean 'to deny someone a blessing or a benefit'.[17] Considering this latter meaning of the verb, if we deny God the blessing of having lordship of our lives and the joy of seeing us enduring and living holy lives, then He will deny us certain blessings too, such as peace and joy, as well as future rewards. We will be 'out of fellowship' and miserable. This should drive us back into the arms of Jesus.

Verse 13 deals with the one who temporarily loses his faith, or who is unfaithful to God. Does he lose salvation? It begins, "**If we are faithless...**", and Paul's assumption was that some Christians would indeed lose their faith. However, the verse goes on, "**...He remains faithful**". Salvation is the work of God, not the work of man. Therefore, so long as *God* remains faithful, we will be secure. And He *does* remain faithful, because "**He cannot deny Himself.**" There is no threat here!

The word for "**deny**" in verse 13 is the same as in verse 12. Here then is a glorious truth to end with: Jesus cannot disown us, because that would mean disowning Himself—He is in us and we are in Him. But also, Jesus cannot deny Himself the blessing He deserves; and part of that blessing is being with us for all eternity!

The Joy set before Him

We began our study of eternal security by considering how God's grace, revealed in the finished work of Christ, and the fact that He ever lives to make intercession for us should motivate us to live lives set apart for God and His purposes. But here is another aspect of these same truths which should also spur us on to live holy lives.

Jesus completed His work on the Cross with the knowledge and expectation that He would be the first-born of many brethren: "**When You make His soul an offering for sin, He shall see His seed... He shall see the travail of His soul, and be satisfied. By His knowledge My righteous Servant shall justify many, for He shall bear their iniquities**" (Isaiah 53:10b...11).

Jesus had His mind set on future joy and blessing when He endured the agony of the Cross: "**...Let us run with endurance the race that is set before us, looking unto Jesus, the author and finisher of our faith, who for the joy that was set before Him endured the Cross, despising the shame, and has sat down at the right hand of the throne of God**"

---

[17] See Luke 9:23 for example, where it is used in Jesus' exhortation: "If anyone desires to come after Me, let him deny himself, and take up his cross daily, and follow Me."

(Hebrews 12:1b-2). The joy set before Jesus included the joy of being seated at the right hand of God's throne in glory, but it also included the joy of seeing the fruit of His labours. Incredibly, therefore, He endured the Cross for the joy of seeing us made righteous, through what He would accomplish by laying down His life!

Jesus will not deny Himself His reward, and that is why He remains faithful! It is nothing to do with how good we are or anything else we do. If I am faithless, He is still going to have me as His reward. Praise God!

To me, this is a tremendous challenge to holiness. If I am to be Jesus' reward, I want Him to be rewarded *now*. I want holiness in my life and fruitfulness in my life now, in order to please Him. Jesus is faithful and He is lovely, and we ought to love Him with all our hearts, because He has loved us so much.

We should run the race set before us with our eyes fixed on Jesus, remembering that He is the author and finisher of our faith. He endured suffering for the joy set before Him, and we should follow His example. One day we too will be brought into the glorious presence of God where there will be great rejoicing!

Notice the confidence of these words in Jude 24-25, and the emphasis—not on us—but on God and *His* keeping power. Always bear this in mind. **"Now to Him who is able to keep you from stumbling, and to present you faultless before the presence of His glory with exceeding joy, to God our Saviour, who alone is wise, be glory and majesty, dominion and power, both now and for ever. Amen."**

NOTES

12. WALKING IN THE LIGHT WITH GOD — 1 JOHN 1:9

Having examined our salvation, we can now rejoice, knowing that we are saved, that we have not committed the unforgivable sin, that we are eternally safe, and that our salvation does not depend on us. There should be no anxious Christians. God is our Father and He is Lord of all the universe. He loves us, and nothing can separate us from His love. We are 'in Christ,' we share His life, and the barrier which separated us from God is gone.

Because Jesus died for every sin we would ever commit, the essence of the gospel is, **"Believe on the Lord Jesus Christ, and you will be saved"** (Acts 16:31). God demonstrated His great love for us by sending His only Son to die for us while we were yet sinners; and this love now becomes our motivation for living lives which are holy, worthy of our calling, and pleasing to Him.

WALKING IN AGREEMENT WITH GOD

In this study, we are going to move on from looking at our salvation to deal with another vitally important matter, which involves this question:

Q. HOW CAN A BELIEVER WALK IN FELLOWSHIP WITH GOD ?

We find essentially the same question expressed in more general terms in Amos 3:3, **"Can two walk together, unless they are agreed?"** The answer is no! Agreement *is essential*. Two can walk together only if they are in agreement.

The answer is not, "Two can walk together if they are *related*"—that would be the case with salvation. Christians are related to God forever: **"For you are all sons of God through faith in Christ Jesus"** (Galatians 3:26). But to be *related* to God is insufficient to ensure we will walk with Him for the rest of our lives. We need to remain in *agreement* with Him.

We can have fellowship with God because we now have His Spirit in us; we have been made spiritually alive. However, we are called to **"walk in**

the light" with Him, so that we might experience the fullness and joy of that fellowship with the Father, the Son and with other believers (1 John 1:1-7). I call this being 'in fellowship' with God.

God never changes; He always hates sin. Therefore, we cannot walk with God with known sin in our lives. Sin will not make us lose our salvation, but it does hinder our fellowship with God: it puts us 'out of fellowship.' This is a very important distinction. Sin can never cut us off from our family *relationship* with God; but it cuts us off from living 'in *fellowship*' with God.

How can sin affect our fellowship with God if Jesus died for every sin? The answer is that when Jesus died on the Cross, He dealt with the *legal requirements* of sin; He paid the penalty for our sin. However, we are now in a *family* relationship with God, and sin is a family business that has to be settled. We are children of God; and God is now our Father.

An example may help illustrate this. The story is told of a couple of newspaper journalists who came across a very odd circumstance indeed. A young man had committed a crime, and his case was due to come up in court. However, the judge for the trial happened to be the young man's father. The journalists decided to go to the court, to see if the case would be tried fairly. In court, the judge announced the verdict: the young man was found guilty, and he was fined £200. The journalists were satisfied. However, the judge then took out his cheque-book and paid the £200 fine for his son! The father thus paid the *legal* requirement of the law. But that was not the end of the story, as the son found out when he got home! The father surely disciplined him at home.

Using the same analogy, when Jesus died on the Cross God 'wrote a cheque' to pay the legal penalty for all of our sins in full. But our Father in heaven now treats us as sons. And, as Hebrews 12:7b says, "**What son is there whom a father does not chasten [discipline]?**" Sin obstructs our fellowship with God. And if we harbour sin in our lives, and do not address it, God our Father is surely going to discipline us; and this is *because* we are saved.

Has God provided for sin? Yes, He certainly has! He provided the Cross, on which Jesus Christ paid the penalty for our sins and satisfied the requirements of God's justice forever. But God has also provided the important principle given in 1 John 1:9, which is this: "**If we confess our sins, He is faithful and just to forgive us our sins and to cleanse us from all unrighteousness.**" If we apply this principle as Christians, God forgives our sins and cleanses us from any other unrighteousness, so that we can stay in unhindered fellowship with Him. However, if we get out of fellowship as a result of sins and we do not confess them, God will discipline us. This is a very important principle, and is greatly misunderstood.

THE DISCIPLINE OF A FATHER (HEBREWS 12)

Hebrews 12 describes the discipline God administers to us as our Father. God does not discipline us because He is a taskmaster, but He does so because—like any children—we *need* discipline and we need to be trained.

Verse 5 says, "**And you have forgotten the exhortation which speaks to you as to sons, "My son, do not despise the chastening of the LORD, nor be discouraged when you are rebuked by Him"**". We should not fight against the discipline of God. Many Christians do not hear what God is trying to tell them about their life through discipline, and they 'kick against the goad'.[1] God *has to* prod us sometimes, but we are naturally like wild oxen, and we tend to resist and fight; and that only means we get prodded more! However, God does not use up *His* energy; He simply continues to prod us until we eventually decide to confess our sin and admit that we are wrong. Then He stops and lays his goad aside. We need to learn that we cannot run away from God.

Notice the words, "**nor be discouraged**". (The AV says, "**nor faint**".) Discouragement is another thing that smites us as Christians. We tend to say to God, "This discipline is too much." But it never is, because God is omniscient and He knows exactly how far to go. He knows exactly how serious our sin is; He is the perfect judge of it. And He always disciplines us just the right amount, until we are willing to confess our sin and get back in fellowship. Then He says, "At last; now we can get on!"

God's discipline is in fact *proof* of His love for us: "**For whom the LORD loves He chastens, and scourges every son whom he receives**" (Hebrews 12:6). We tend to think that God must hate us when life seems really tough. But we should learn to rejoice when we are disciplined by God, because it proves that He is our Father, and that He truly loves us. If we understand this, it should give us great security and peace. Parents who do not discipline their children do them a great disservice. In the same way, firm teachers are always the best in a school; the children in fact prefer them, because they know where they stand.

---

[1] A goad was a long stick with a metal point on the end, which was used to prick a wild ox to get it in order.

"If you endure chastening, God deals with you as with sons; for what son is there whom a father does not chasten? But if you are without chastening, of which all have become partakers, then you are illegitimate and not sons. Furthermore, we have had human fathers who corrected us, and we paid them respect. Shall we not much more readily be in subjection to the Father of spirits and live?" (Hebrews 12:7-9).

What is meant in verse 9 by "**be in subjection**"? It means not kicking against God's discipline. When Jesus walked on the earth He did not kick against God His Father at all; He was meek and He did what His Father wanted at all times. As we go on with God, we are gradually changed by the Holy Spirit into the likeness of Jesus, and we too will become meek. It does not take as long as we might imagine to become like this if we are obedient to God and allow the Holy Spirit to mould us.

"**For they [our human fathers] indeed for a few days chastened us as seemed best to them, but He for our profit, that we may be partakers of His holiness**" (verse 10). If the Lord is disciplining us, we are heading towards holiness.

There is no quick way to escape God's discipline. We will all sin, because we still have an old sin nature inside us. But God, according to Romans 8:28, which says "**all things work together for [our] good**," uses even our sins to bring us into line with His holiness. He brings discipline to reveal His holiness in us, and He changes us from one degree of glory to another (2 Corinthians 3:18). When we see one another changing as the Lord deals with areas in our lives, it is very thrilling. It is always important to remember that God's discipline is "**for our profit**".

"**Now no chastening seems to be joyful for the present, but grievous; nevertheless, afterwards it yields the peaceable fruit of righteousness to those who have been trained by it**" (verse 11). Discipline is often hard. If we are able to smile through it, or if we find it easy, then the discipline may get harder, as it does for a child who grins when smacked by its parents. Next time, when the discipline is harder, we will not smile; but it will be worth it all in the end. In the words of the French singer Edith Piaf, who sang, "*Non, Je ne regrette rien,*" we need to get to the place where we can say, "I regret nothing, Lord," after all His dealings with us.

The Jews sometimes used to wear a little bottle around their necks, which contained their tears. These tears were precious to them, because they represented areas of their lives which had been dealt with. Their tears reminded them of the hard times and of God's gracious dealings.

Chastening always eventually **"yields the peaceable fruit of righteousness to those who have been trained by it."**

We need to submit to God's dealings with us. To 'submit' in both Greek and English is a term used in wrestling, meaning to 'give in' or 'yield.' For the rest of our lives we could choose to kick against God, but we would never have true peace or joy. But if we submit to and are **"trained by"** the discipline of the Lord, then we will have ever-increasing peace and holiness in our lives.

THE SPIRITUAL AND THE CARNAL CHRISTIAN

Two contrasting terms used to describe Christians in the New Testament are "carnal" and "spiritual" (see 1 Corinthians 3:1). The carnal Christian is not living in fellowship with God; God and this person are not in agreement. It is the carnal Christian who has to change, for God never changes! In contrast, the spiritual believer is living in fellowship with God and is able to enjoy the presence of the Lord at all times.

A carnal Christian can be as bad or even worse than an unbeliever in terms of behaviour. Legalistic Christians find this hard to understand, but with a little thought we should be able to see why this is the case.

An unbeliever has a functioning body and soul, and also an old sin nature; the human spirit of the unbeliever is dead. An unbeliever therefore inevitably lives according to his body, soul and old sin nature, and therefore can be called "carnal" or "natural".[2]

A believer also has a functioning body, soul and old sin nature; but the believer's human spirit is alive—it came back to life when he was born again—when the Holy Spirit came and indwelt him. The spiritual believer is one who lives according to the life of God's Spirit within.

An unbeliever can never be spiritual, because: "**...the natural man does not receive the things of the Spirit of God, for they are foolishness to**

---

[2] In some Bible versions the word 'fleshly' is used instead of 'carnal.' Both are translations of the Greek word sarkikos (from sarx = flesh). The 'flesh' in the New Testament does not simply mean the human body, which is fallen—just as the spirit and soul are fallen—but often refers to the sinful nature out of which man's natural wickedness, rebellion and lustful appetites originate. A carnal person is one who lives according to the flesh, that is, according to the old sin nature or principle of sin within. Such a person is at enmity with God (Romans 8:7).

The 'natural' or 'soulish' person (Greek psuchikos, from psuchē = soul, soul-life) lives according to the natural human soul-life, being ruled by the mind, emotions and will.

A 'spiritual' person, in contrast, is one who is ruled by the spirit. Since the Holy Spirit indwells Christians, a spiritual believer is one who is led by the Holy Spirit, who sets his mind on the things of the Spirit (Romans 8:5).

him; nor can he know them, because they are spiritually discerned" (1 Corinthians 2:14).[3] However, a believer can be carnal or natural (soulish), by living in exactly the same way as an unbeliever. Such a believer, instead of living by the Spirit, lives according to his body, soul and old sin nature. But the carnal Christian has an even worse time than an unbeliever, because he also receives the discipline of God. God disciplines His sons. Unbelievers are not His sons, and so God does not chasten them for their sins.[4] (As we have seen before, there is no such thing as a "universal brotherhood of man".)

Believers who fall away and then come back to God have testimonies galore of how God disciplined them and delivered them from terrible darkness. They were believers when they went away from God, and they recognize how God sought them out to bring them back into fellowship with Him. They were still sons of God throughout their period of rebellion (even if they would have denied it) and they are still sons of God at the end!

1 Corinthians was a very strongly-worded letter from Paul! The Corinthian Christians had done much wrong, and were getting out of hand. In chapter 3 Paul told them that, because they were so carnal, he was unable to discuss spiritual matters with them: "**And I, brethren, could not speak to you as to spiritual people, but as to carnal, as to babes in Christ. I fed you with milk and not with solid food; for until now you were not able to receive it, and even now you are still not able; for you are still carnal. For where there are envy, strife, and divisions among you, are you not carnal and behaving like mere men?**" (1 Corinthians 3:1-3). He was saying to them, "I couldn't come with spiritual information to you; you were—and still are—so out of fellowship that you wouldn't have known what I was talking about!"

They had not submitted to the Lord; so Paul had to deal with them like babes. They still needed baby milk (that is, foundational teaching) rather than meat (which refers to the deep things of the Word of God). Paul was saying to them, "Before, you could not take in what I wanted to share, and neither can you now. You have not grown up at all!" What a rebuke this was! When he said they were "**behaving like mere men**", he meant

---

[3] Unbelievers who try to cultivate spiritual activity are in grave danger of serious deception from evil spirits and often end up caught in occult practices.

[4] As discussed throughout this book, God does ultimately have to punish members of the human race who never put their trust in Jesus Christ for salvation. Occasionally, God may judge unbelievers in this life (Acts 12:23 for example). However, this is quite different from God's fatherly discipline in this life of His children.

they were indistinguishable from unbelievers. Paul was urging them, "Get back in fellowship, please!"

This brings us back to consider how we, as Christians, can start walking in fellowship with God again if we have sinned. We have already glimpsed the answer, found in 1 John 1:9.

1 JOHN 1:9—A GREAT PROMISE FOR US TO CLAIM

Two of the greatest promises in the New Testament, that are vital for us to understand and apply, are 1 John 1:9 and Romans 8:28. The first is the theme of this study. The second will be the subject of the next study.

We all sin, but in 1 John 1:9 we learn that, **"If we confess our sins, He is faithful and just to forgive us our sins and to cleanse us from all unrighteousness."** The lesson we need to grasp is this:

STAYING IN FELLOWSHIP WITH GOD IS AS EASY AS CONFESSING OUR SINS.

The example of David

David was saved, just like us, for he had believed in the Messiah who was to come, and his sins were forgiven in the same way as ours have been. In Psalm 32 David described the joy of knowing sins forgiven: **"Blessed is he whose transgression is forgiven, whose sin is covered. Blessed is the man to whom the LORD does not impute iniquity, and in whose spirit there is no guile"** (verses 1-2).

David then recalled an instance when he did not confess his sin: **"When I kept silent, my bones grew old, through my groaning all the day long. For day and night Your hand was heavy upon me; my vitality was turned into the drought of summer. Selah"** (verses 3-4). This was discipline from God. If we do not confess our sins, God, as a good father, will come along and discipline us—because we are His children.

But then David confessed his sin and he was forgiven. **"I acknowledged my sin to you, and my iniquity I have not hidden. I said, "I will confess my transgressions to the LORD," and you forgave the iniquity of my sin. Selah"** (verse 5). "Selah" probably meant 'Think on that!' David confessed his sin to God. It was as easy as that to get back in fellowship, even for David in about 1000 BC.[5]

---

[5] Various verses in the Old Testament, such as Leviticus 5:5 and 26:40, explained to the people the importance of confessing their sins, just as 1 John 1:9 explains it to us.

Repentance

There are two Greek words that we need to compare; they relate to the English verbs 'to repent' and 'to confess'.

The first word, which is always translated "repent" in the New Testament, is the Greek word *metanoeō*. It is made up of two shorter Greek words. The first of these is *meta*, meaning 'to change' (from which we get the English word 'metamorphose', meaning to change shape, etc.), and the second is *noeō*, meaning 'to think,' 'to perceive,' or 'to understand.' This latter word comes from the word *noos*, meaning 'the mind'. Thus, *metanoeō* means 'to change one's mind.' Repentance does not therefore mean or necessarily involve crying; indeed, this word has no emotional connotation at all. It means to change one's thinking or purpose, and implies a change for the better—a turning away from sin.

Sometimes, I used to try to make myself really miserable over my sins. But it is no good *trying* to make ourselves cry over our sins. As we grow up in God, however, we *will* tend to take sin more seriously and then we shall genuinely cry over our sins. When we are young Christians, God simply wants us to change our minds about our sin. God has made it so easy. He wants us simply to repent and to say, "God, I thought this was all right to do, but I've changed my mind. I now know it's wrong".[6]

A passage in 2 Corinthians 7 talks about both sorrow and repentance over sin. Paul referred back to the effect his first letter had on the Corinthians: **"Now I rejoice, not that you were made sorry, but that your sorrow led to repentance. For you were made sorry in a godly manner, that you might suffer loss from us in nothing. For godly sorrow produces repentance to salvation, not to be regretted; but the sorrow of the world produces death"** (verses 9-10).

After Paul's first letter to them, they had written back to say they were heartbroken. Paul was saying, "I'm not rejoicing because you started weeping about what I'd written, but because your sorrow led you to repentance." The important thing was that their sorrow had led them to *change their minds* about their own spiritual condition. In other words,

---

[6] It is interesting to note that the gospel message given to Jews in the New Testament was always, "Repent and be baptized", emphasizing the need to repent or change their minds. Why was this? It was because, although the Jews were looking for their Messiah, they were looking for a political Messiah who would immediately fight against Rome. They therefore needed to change their minds and see that Jesus of Nazareth was indeed their Messiah, but that He had not come to be a political deliverer; instead, He had come to die for their sins. The Gentiles in general did not have such preconceptions about the Messiah. They simply needed to hear the gospel, turn from their sins and believe on Christ.

godly sorrow is the kind of sorrow that produces repentance, and such sorrow is not regretted later.[7]

If we weep out of self-pity, then we are still thinking about ourselves. That is not repentance. We may weep, but the important thing is that we change our minds; then God is pleased. God allows us to go through sorrow so that eventually we will change our minds, not so that we might say, "I feel a lot better now that I've had a good cry," and then start doing all the same old things. We must be honest about the source of our grief, because God wants us to repent of our sins.

CONFESSION

The second Greek word we need to look at is *homologeō*, which is translated "confess". It means 'to agree,' 'to acknowledge,' or literally 'to say the same.' Again, there is no emotion implied. It was a legal word, used in a court of law. For example, someone would be asked, "Do you confess that you are...?" and the person would reply, "Yes, I confess that I am." You certainly did not have to weep to acknowledge your name! The question simply sought *agreement*. To 'confess' thus means 'to say the same thing' as someone else.

John says, "**If we say that we have no sin, we deceive ourselves, and the truth is not in us**" (1 John 1:8). We all have an old sin nature, and if we say we don't then we are fooling ourselves. We *are* going to sin—at the very least, sometimes.[8] But verse 9 reveals God's way of escape for us: "**If we confess our sins...**". If we acknowledge our sins, then we are immediately forgiven and cleansed. If we do not, we should expect discipline at any time. We are to *confess* our sins, and this means to agree with God that our sin is indeed sin. We therefore need to *name our sins*. This verse does not say we have to weep over them.

---

[7] There is another Greek word meaning 'to regret,' 'to have sorrow,' or 'to have remorse' (with tears)—metamelomai—but it does not mean to change one's mind. The word translated "not to be regretted" in verse 10 is ametamelētos, the same word used in Romans 11:29. These words were discussed in chapter 10.

[8] Some Christians believe in "sinless perfection now"—that a Christian can and should reach a point where he or she will never sin again. But this is not possible. We will only know true perfection after we die or after the Lord returns, because that is when the old sin nature will be removed from us. In Romans 7, Paul described how the old sin nature was still present in him, in his life as a believer, and the battle he fought against it. The old sin nature is still in us, and we all have to fight against it. We can have victory only by walking in the Spirit, in faith, knowing that we died to sin in Christ.

As we name every sin that we know, we have the promise that God will then deal with every sin that we have forgotten to mention as well. Our unhindered fellowship with God will immediately be restored. If we sin and then confess that sin, our fellowship is fully restored. If we commit a sin 100 times and confess it 100 times, then we are just as much 'in fellowship' at the end as beforehand.

We will need to acknowledge the truth and lay hold of the promise in 1 John 1:9 again and again. As we do so, we will remain in fellowship with God and grow. How fantastic this is! We do not need to make promises to God such as, "I'll never do that again," or, "I hate that sin." (If we do, then we have just committed another sin—that of lying!)

Neither must we live by our emotions. It is not necessary to walk to the front in a meeting or to plead with God for forgiveness. No, we simply need to *confess* our sins *to God*, not to an evangelist or any other minister.

Our emotions and our hearts are deceptive. If we commit a sin, Satan wants to immobilize us and to make us flounder over that sin for months at a time. But God is faithful and just, and He will forgive us. 1 John 1:9 is a promise. It is *God* who is faithful, not us.

When we fall, we should pick ourselves up, brush ourselves off (by applying 1 John 1:9) and press on! We will find that God changes us as we go on with Him, and He will soon have a particular sin dealt with. *The important thing is that we continue to live in fellowship with Him.*

I was once taught that I had to 'labour with sin.' Therefore, I used to concentrate on my sin, and pray a lot about it. But the sin just seemed to get bigger and bigger! God does not want us to sit under our sins or to allow them to block our fellowship with Him. Rather, we should confess them, forget them, and immediately carry on in fellowship with God, concentrating on loving and serving Him, and knowing that He has cleansed us from all unrighteousness.

Jesus died on the Cross for our sins and, therefore, God does not want us labouring under them. He wants us to cast our burden on Him (Psalm 55:22, 1 Peter 5:7), and that is done through applying 1 John 1:9. Sin should no longer be an anchor or a hindrance in our lives; we should confess our sins quickly and press on, **"forgetting those things which are behind and reaching forward to those things which are ahead..."** (Philippians 3:13b).

Many Christians become bogged down by their sins and cannot raise themselves up above them. This is not right. God knew that we would have weaknesses and problems when He saved us; and that is why He gave us a simple way out. As we go on with the Lord, we shall grow to love Him more and more, and we *will* begin to hate sin more. And *He* will change us to become more like Jesus.

It is vital to realize that we cannot go on with God and grow unless we are in fellowship with God. If we live in fellowship, then He can change us. Staying in fellowship with God is therefore the key; and it simply involves applying the principle of 1 John 1:9.

THE PARABLES OF LUKE 15

The parables in Luke 15 concern a lost sheep, a lost coin and a lost son. They involve stories about restoration of people to right relationships or property to a rightful owner. They reveal the heart of God towards repentant people, and His joy in welcoming them back to Himself.

"Then all the tax collectors and the sinners drew near to Him to hear Him. And the Pharisees and scribes murmured, saying, "This man receives sinners and eats with them"" (verses 1-2). There were thus two groups of Jews to whom Jesus spoke these parables.

Jesus' main audience comprised the "**tax collectors and the sinners**" ("publicans" in the AV means tax collectors). The "**tax collectors**", such as the apostle Matthew had been, were the lowest of the low in Jewish society. They were the ones who had sided with the Romans, and everyone hated them. The "**sinners**" were those who were not trying to keep the law.

The "**Pharisees and scribes**" were thoroughly religious men; but they were almost all *unbelieving* religious men. They were the ones who attacked Jesus more than any other group. They kept the law (or more accurately, *their* interpretation of it) down to the very last detail. As far as the *law* was concerned, they considered themselves blameless: when Paul described his life before he was saved, he said, "**concerning the law, [I was] a Pharisee....concerning the righteousness which is in the law, [I was] blameless**" (Philippians 3:5-6).

So here were two groups of Jews; one group kept the law and the other did not. Jesus had chosen to talk and eat with the tax collectors and sinners. Around them, the Pharisees and scribes were murmuring and giving Him trouble for this, but He reached out to all those who had gathered to hear Him. Among them were undoubtedly a few who had believed on Him and many who had yet to believe.

"**So he spoke a parable to them, saying...**" (Luke 15:3). Now the word translated "**parable**" (*parabolē*) denoted something laid alongside something else. (Our English word 'parallel' includes the same prefix *para*, meaning 'beside'.) A parable is therefore a story which, if it is laid alongside a particular truth, helps explain that truth to us.[9]

The essential truth that Jesus wanted to convey was that He had come to call sinners to repentance. He would also show the Pharisees and scribes how, because of their self-righteous attitude, they did not understand God's abundant grace.

The Parables of the Lost Sheep and Lost Coin

In the parables of the lost sheep and the lost coin, Jesus clearly emphasized the heart of God in seeking out the one who is lost. God's heart is always towards the repentant sinner and is filled with joy at his return. This principle applies not only to God seeking out His lost people in Israel, but also to all sinners today—unbelievers and believers.

"**What man of you, having a hundred sheep, if he loses one of them, does not leave the ninety-nine in the wilderness, and go after the one which is lost until he finds it? And when he has found it, he lays it on his shoulders, rejoicing. And when he comes home, he calls together his friends and neighbours, saying to them, 'Rejoice with me, for I have found my sheep which was lost!' I say to you that likewise there will be more joy in heaven over one sinner who repents than over ninety-nine just persons who need no repentance**" (verses 4-7).

This parable tells us that *the Lord seeks after His lost sheep*. Notice that the lost sheep did not find the Lord; the Lord found the sheep. When the man found his sheep, he rejoiced! The friends and neighbours represent the angels in heaven. 'Heaven' rejoices when we repent and are restored to a right relationship with God. In case that parable was not enough, Jesus told another.

---

[9] It is possible to misinterpret parables, however, by laying them alongside the wrong bits of truth. Then, it becomes necessary to ignore major parts of the parable in question, or to move parts around. Some preachers say, "Beware of parables...and don't consider the details too carefully." But when a parable is applied correctly, it tends to be very precise, and most, if not all parts of it, will be significant. Jesus taught in parables to help make certain truths easier for us to understand. For unbelievers, however, parables may obscure the truth (see Matthew 13:13).

The most misapplied parable must surely be the Parable of the Ten Virgins (see Matthew 25:1-13). Incredible ideas are laid alongside it and the story is twisted to make it fit! (This parable is covered in Basic Bible Study BBS 27, entitled "The Wise and Foolish Virgins.")

"Or what woman, having ten silver coins, if she loses one coin, does not light a lamp, sweep the house, and seek diligently until she finds it? And when she has found it, she calls her friends and neighbours together, saying, 'Rejoice with me, for I have found the piece which I lost!' Likewise, I say to you, there is joy in the presence of the angels of God over one sinner who repents" (verses 8-10).

The woman in this parable rightfully owns the silver coins. Again, the lesson is that the Lord seeks us out. His Holy Spirit (possibly represented by the candle) draws us back to God, and shows us our need for repentance and confession. I always used to misread verse 10 and assume it was just the angels who were joyful. But who is in the presence of the angels? God the Father is! This verse therefore suggests that our heavenly Father is excited and joyful when even one sinner repents!

The Parable of the Prodigal Son

The story of the prodigal son is the *'pièce de résistance'* of Luke 15. Jesus told this parable not only to emphasize God's fatherly heart of grace towards sinners, represented by the prodigal son, but also to expose the ungracious attitude of the religious Jews, portrayed by the elder brother. This parable thus applied to the two groups of Jews listening to Jesus, who both needed to come into a right relationship with God.

"Then He said: "A certain man had two sons"" (verse 11a). If we recall that Galatians 3:26 says, "**For you are all sons of God through faith in Christ Jesus**", this immediately suggests that this story is also applicable to believers, whose Father is God. When we wander off from a life in fellowship with God, we need to 'return' to our Father with the same broken, repentant attitude as the prodigal son. Since the themes of grace and our need for repentance and confession permeate Jesus' teaching and are also taken up by the writers of the epistles, we may legitimately consider how this parable applies to us.

"A certain man had two sons. And the younger of them said to his father, "Father, give me the portion of goods that falls to me." So he divided to them his livelihood" (verses 11-12). Note that it was the *younger* son who requested his inheritance immediately, and who later became prodigal—that is, wasteful. Sometimes this is what happens with immature believers; while they are still young in the Lord and self-centred, sin causes them to squander the inheritance they have received in Christ. But note as well that *both* sons received their inheritance.

For us, this inheritance represents the things we receive as Christians: the presence of the Holy Spirit inside (Romans 8:11), "**joy inexpressible**

and full of glory" (1 Peter 1:8b), "**the peace of God, which surpasses all understanding**" (Philippians 4:7), various gifts, and so on. If we take these things for granted or misuse them, we will be unable to enjoy them any more, and gifts we have might slip away. This is one important lesson for us from this parable: *we have gifts as our inheritance, but we must use these gifts for the Lord and invest them in His service.*

"**And not many days after, the younger son gathered all together, journeyed to a far country, and there wasted his possessions with prodigal living**" (verse 13). The younger son took his inheritance and wasted it. There is no point in listing his sins, because the list might miss out one of yours! His sins included every sin that we commit. Through self-indulgence the son wasted everything that his father had given him.

As believers, we might renounce God, or waste our life, but we will not lose our salvation. However, we may get a big shock when we die; Jesus might say, "Oh Foolish man! You've wasted and squandered your life, which could have been used for Me." If we are not living in fellowship with God—if we are 'far away' from God—then we cannot be truly fruitful for Him. Our sins, which take us out of fellowship, can therefore lead us to waste our inheritance. What happened next?

"**But when he had spent all, there arose a severe famine in that land, and he began to be in want**" (verse 14). A famine came to the land. This represents discipline. A Christian should be content; but this son had want. He had want for peace inside, as well as for money and food.

"**Then he went and joined himself to a citizen of that country, and he sent him into his fields to feed swine. And he would gladly have filled his stomach with the pods that the swine ate, and no one gave him anything**" (verses 15-16). We can tell that this son was far from home, because the Jews never wanted to be near pigs, and certainly never touched pigs; pigs were unclean to them. The owner of the pigs would not even waste good pig swill on him, suggesting that he valued the pigs more than he valued the prodigal son. The son had thus been reduced to a state that any self-respecting Jew would have abhorred.

This is the condition of a Christian becoming 'worse that an unbeliever.' As we have discussed earlier, out-of-fellowship Christians sometimes behave in ways that even most unbelievers in the world would consider to be awful. Legalistic believers look at such people and say, "Oh, they were never saved!" But this is not true. Such people are simply terribly out of fellowship and being disciplined by God. God will bring them home, just as in this story. They will be disciplined and they will return, perhaps many years later, just as sheep tend to come home eventually.

"But when he came to himself, he said, 'How many of my father's hired servants have bread enough and to spare, and I perish with hunger! I will arise and go to my father, and will say to him, "Father, I have sinned against heaven and before you, and I am no longer worthy to be called your son..."'" (verses 17-19a). Verse 17 says "**he came to himself**"; in other words, he *repented* and changed his mind. Other versions say he "**came to his senses**" (NASB, NIV). He decided to *confess* his sin and admit he had done wrong—that's 1 John 1:9.

Then he was going to add something: "**...Make me like one of your hired servants**" (verse 19b). However, it was not necessary for him to say this; his emotions were stirred. A son can never be a servant. That would be ridiculous! Similarly, when we confess our sins to God we do not need to say this. God has made us His sons; and we can never be like hired servants of His. (We should recognize, however, that none of us is ever worthy to be God's son; God has made us His sons by grace!)

"**And he arose and came to his father. But when he was still a great way off, his father saw him and had compassion, and ran and fell on his neck and kissed him**" (verse 20). The father saw him a great way off. He had been constantly watching for his son to return. He was not waiting for apologies; he *loved* his son, and he was *longing* for him to return. If we foolishly stay out of fellowship and are a long way off from God our Father, He is constantly watching for us to return.

Notice one thing: the son had not come back because he was sorry. He wasn't primarily sorry; he was just starving hungry! He would have stayed away longer if he had had more money. But the father was still thrilled to see him. His son had come home to be fed! It is often the same with Christians. Whatever our motive for returning to God, we can come back on the basis of 1 John 1:9, not on the basis of feeling sorry or anything else. (Of course the father would have been delighted if his son *had* said he wanted to weep about what he had done—if his son had been more mature.)

The father ran to greet him anyway. This is what grace is all about; it is undeserved. And this tells us how thrilled God is whenever we get back in fellowship. He is thrilled whenever any of His children 'come home,' and there is joy all round.

"**And the son said to him, "Father, I have sinned against heaven and in your sight, and am no longer worthy to be called your son." But the father said to his servants, "Bring out the best robe and put it on him, and put a ring on his hand and sandals on his feet. And bring the fatted calf here and kill it, and let us eat and be merry; for this** my son was dead and is alive again; he was lost and is found." And they began to be merry" (verses 21-24).

The father interrupted his son; his confession was good enough. He did not let his son carry on and say, "Make me like one of your hired servants." No! Rather, the father said, **"Bring out the best robe..."** He did not say to bring out the second best in view of his son's past foolishness.

This robe shows us the father's complete acceptance of his son and speaks of a new righteousness.[10] God loves us more than we can imagine! The ring speaks of belonging and is a sign of authority; and the shoes speak of our ministry. When we come back to God, then we can go on with our ministry, as ambassadors for Christ. The moment we turn back to God and confess our sins, we receive all these things, which are lavished upon us by God our loving Father.

That was the account of the younger son: he went away from his father and then he came back. The account continues by describing the elder brother: **"Now his older son was in the field. And as he came and drew near to the house, he heard music and dancing. So he called one of the servants and asked what these things meant. And he said to him, 'Your brother has come, and because he has received him safe and sound, your father has killed the fatted calf'"** (verses 25-27). The older son was now about to get out of fellowship! He had been in fellowship all the time until this point. Note that he was in the field; this suggests he had been working very hard.

If you are a legalistic believer, you will find it very hard when someone gets back in fellowship. You will be thinking, "I've always led such a good life; it's about time God blessed *me*." And then you might see someone who has been out of fellowship, who is restored to fellowship and is thrilled with the Lord, overflowing with everything God gives. A legalistic person finds this very hard to swallow. Sometimes it is very hard to see others being blessed when we feel that we are not being blessed. But we need grace in our hearts.

"But he was angry and would not go in. Therefore his father came out and pleaded with him. So he answered and said to his father, "Lo, these many years I have been serving you; I never transgressed your commandment at any time; and yet you never gave me a young goat, that I might make merry with my friends. But as soon as this

---

[10] This reminds us of the new robe Joshua the High Priest received in Zechariah chapter 3.

son of yours came, who has devoured your livelihood with prostitutes, you killed the fatted calf for him'" (verses 28-30). The older brother was angry rather than thrilled, and refused to go into the house to celebrate. But his father came out and pleaded with him; this also was grace. The older brother then slandered his younger brother, saying he had been with prostitutes—he probably did not know this for sure. This was another sign of his legalism; he was putting the worst interpretation on things.

His father then spoke gently to him and said in effect, "Why be angry?" **"And he said to him, "Son, you are always with me, and all that I have is yours. It was right that we should make merry and be glad, for your brother was dead and is alive again, and was lost and is found'"** (verses 31-32). The father had to teach his legalistic son about grace.

CONCLUSION

The clear message of 1 John 1:9 is that when our sins obstruct our fellowship with God, we should confess our sins and God will welcome us back. Indeed, He accepts us back with open arms. No sin is too big to stop God our Father from welcoming us back. Therefore, there is no excuse for us to be out of fellowship.

We need to be honest with God about our sins and apply 1 John 1:9. When we fall into sin, we should confess it quickly, and then pick ourselves up, brush ourselves off and start all over again! This way we can enjoy constant fellowship with God and grow up into maturity. Hallelujah!

NOTES

NOTES

13. ALL THINGS WORK TOGETHER FOR GOOD — ROMANS 8:28

The aim of all these studies is to give us peace and stability so that we might be effective witnesses for Christ. But the subject of this study is probably the most helpful of all, because it deals with how to live a peaceful life. Indeed, a sub-title could be "How to live a peaceful life" or "How not to get upset at the smallest thing." It deals with the very important principle found in Romans 8:28.

Worrying is a sin, and is a major obstacle to effective witnessing for Jesus, because it makes us self-centred. To worry, you have to think about yourself and the things coming against you rather than about the Lord and the things that come from Him. Worrying is in effect saying, "God, You are not quite big enough to cope with my circumstances," and the thought behind it is, "If I don't worry about this, then things will not work out; I've got to see all the ins and outs of the problem in case I miss something."

As Christians, we should understand that God is omniscient, and that He knows not only every problem that we have, but every part of every problem. There is nothing He overlooks.

ANTICIPATING DIFFICULTIES

We all have difficulties. In fact, Jesus told us to expect them: **"In the world you will have tribulation; but be of good cheer, I have overcome the world"** (John 16:33).

Before I was a believer, a Christian had once said to me, "The great thing about being a Christian is that all your problems disappear." I now realize that this person was not mature in the Lord. It is only during difficulties in our lives that we come to understand the depth of the provision available for us in the Lord. Unless we have had testing experiences like those of Elijah, Daniel or Paul, for example, we cannot truly know the sufficiency of God's grace in every trial.

The trials of Elijah[1]

Elijah's experience is related in 1 Kings chapters 17 to 19. The account begins with him declaring to Ahab, King of Israel, that a great miracle was about to take place. Elijah asked God to stop the rain, and God did so (see James 5:17): there would now be no dew or rain except at his word. Elijah must have wondered what to do, because he knew he would not be popular! Then God said to him, "You will be all right because I'm going to lead you to a little stream called Cherith. Go and hide there." God gave Elijah directions, and he set off. God told Elijah that he could drink from the brook, and that the ravens would feed him there.

Now if the rainfall stops in any place, a few months later, of course, the streams and rivers will dry up too. God knew that, but I don't think Elijah did. (I, as a geographer, would have worried about this.) Elijah arrived at the stream, and indeed it soon dried up. The situation was now dry and barren, but he knew God had led him there.

Why had God led him there? It was because God was able to do exceeding abundantly above all that Elijah could ask or think (see Ephesians 3:20). Elijah had already seen God's provision—God had miraculously commanded ravens to come and feed him. But then suddenly there was no longer a stream. Elijah now *had to* go on with the LORD. There was no turning back. He knew God had led him to this point, and now he had to trust God to solve his problem.

The Lord will lead us into certain predicaments too. We will know that He led us into those circumstances, but, when we are in the middle of them, things seem to dry up around us. It is then that our maturity (or lack of it) will show! Peace in the midst of difficulties is a sign of maturity. If we can be peaceful when things seem to be collapsing around us, then we are mature. It is easy to be peaceful if everything is going our way, but the moment things change, our maturity is going to show forth.

In Elijah's case, more testing was to come. The LORD then sent him to dwell in Zarephath, saying, **"See, I have commanded a widow there to provide for you"** (1 Kings 17:9). Yet when Elijah arrived, the widow's flour and oil had almost run out, and the widow was preparing a final meal for herself and her son. Elijah could have murmured to himself, "Why did the Lord bring me here?", yet he believed the word of God and God showed him what to do. As a result, Elijah, the widow and her son were all sustained by a miracle; neither the bin of flour nor the jar of oil

---

[1] This section has been expanded compared with the audio tape, to clarify the order of events in Elijah's life and to emphasize how God led him and used him.

was exhausted. When subsequently the widow's son died, instead of despairing, Elijah cried out to God, who heard his prayer and revived the child. At the end of these trials, this widow was able to say to Elijah, **"I know that you are a man of God, and that the word of the LORD in your mouth is the truth"** (1 Kings 17:24). Soon Elijah was ready to confront Ahab and the prophets of Baal, and he won a great victory over them (see 1 Kings 18).

We could conclude that Elijah was such a great man of God that he must have had no further problems or doubts. But he had one major problem: he was scared of Ahab's wife Jezebel! Fear of any person brings us into bondage; and Elijah was scared of this woman. Despite having seen many miracles and winning a total victory on Mount Carmel, he said to himself, "Lord, they'll be after me; and that woman Jezebel will be after me!" Instead of trusting the LORD, he ran for his life, and then prayed that he might die (see 1 Kings 19:1-4).

The rest of Elijah's story is told in 1 Kings 19 and 21, and in 2 Kings 1 and 2. God continued to provide for him and to use him. God taught Elijah how He was always with him, even if it appeared that He had led him into an impossible situation.

Simon Peter's denial of Jesus

Satan may also try to lead us into difficult circumstances, and we can cause our own difficult circumstances too. But God is bigger than our situation, and He can give us peace.

Jesus knew that Simon Peter would deny him. He even warned him of what would happen beforehand, and reassured him, "Don't worry. I have prayed for you." **"Simon, Simon! Indeed, Satan has asked for you** [the apostles]**, that he may sift you as wheat. But I have prayed for you** [Simon]**, that your faith should not fail; and when you have returned to Me, strengthen your brethren"** (Luke 22:31-32). Peter did deny the Lord, but he went on to become one of the most dynamic Christians there has ever been! This is the heritage of all believers.

THE PROMISES OF GOD

One of the reasons why God has given us His Word is to produce faith within us. Romans 10:17 says, **"So then faith comes by hearing, and hearing by the word of God."** There are promises in the Bible especially for us. They are like armchairs for us to sit in, whatever kind of situation we are in, or whatever type of weariness we may have. In the

Psalms, the truth of God is described as **"a shield and buckler"** (Psalm 91:4). A shield was huge, and you could hide your whole self behind it. A buckler was a small hand-held shield. The promises of God are like these various types of defences to us.

There are promises in the Bible for our big problems as well as our small ones. There are promises that cover the whole world, as well as promises which cover our smallest concerns. For example, the promise, **"I will never leave you nor forsake you"** (Hebrews 13:5; Joshua 1:5; Deuteronomy 31:6,8) is one of the biggest shields we can 'hide behind.' It covers a whole host of problems. We can claim such a promise in every circumstance of our lives.

Have you noticed how sometimes, despite claiming a particular promise, there is still turmoil inside. Don't worry! Carry on trusting God's promise, and the Word of God will eventually produce faith inside. You might claim that promise and think nothing is happening, but then, as other problems come along, you will suddenly realize that the truth of the promise is now real to you, and then you will experience peace inside.

In relation to gossip, for example, I needed to come to believe Romans 12:19, **"'Vengeance is mine, I will repay', says the Lord."** Gossip is a sin and it is a great and destructive problem in the Body of Christ. I needed to see that *God* would defend me and vindicate me if others maligned me. At first when people attacked me, I couldn't sleep. But eventually, as I repeatedly claimed this promise, I had great peace. I believe it now, and I can still sleep soundly even if I know of terrible gossip about myself. We must not avenge ourselves, but, rather, leave any intervention to God. The important thing is what *God* thinks of us. Jesus is our defence lawyer. Imagine that! Jesus is looking after us, so we do not have to defend ourselves. This should certainly give us peace.

Another example is 1 Samuel 17:47, **"For the battle is the LORD's..."** This must mean that *we* do not have to fight. But how hard it is to stop spending our time gathering ammunition and getting ready to fight and defend ourselves!

We must practise claiming the promises of God—the big and the small ones. If we do so, it will not be long before we stop needing to stockpile ammunition. The Word of God will have produced faith inside. And as we acknowledge God in every situation, we will find that He will direct our paths (Proverbs 3:6).

We can see from the lives of various characters in the Old Testament and the New Testament how the promises of God produced faith in them and gave them peace.

The example of Moses

In Exodus chapter 14 we read how God directed Israel to camp by the Red Sea. He spoke to Moses to give them the following promise: **"...I will gain honour over Pharaoh and over all his army, that the Egyptians may know that I am the Lord"** (verse 4b). Thus, despite their apparently vulnerable situation, Moses was able to say to the Israelites, **"Do not be afraid. Stand still, and see the salvation of the Lord, which He will accomplish for you today. For the Egyptians whom you see today, you shall see again no more for ever. The Lord will fight for you, and you shall hold your peace"** (verses 13-14).

Wouldn't it have been ridiculous if Moses, having come to the Red Sea, had begun giving the Israelites swimming lessons, or boat building lessons, to help them get across! But that is exactly what we tend to do very often.

Moses was a mature believer. He was not worried by the Egyptians at all. He had learned that *he* could not do anything; but *God* would keep His promise. If God had said He was going to take the people out of Egypt despite Pharaoh, then they were going out of Egypt! Moses knew that he was just a vessel and that God had all the power necessary. Moses was like a pylon, that does not carry electricity itself, but which enables the power to flow. Because he believed God's promise, Moses could stand there and say, "Thank you, Lord!" and he could be at peace, knowing God would do it all.

Unfortunately, throughout their journeys in the wilderness, the children of Israel tended always to look to Moses instead of to the Lord. Moses therefore had to cope with two million people who wanted food and water. Could Moses produce food and water? Of course he couldn't. But the Lord could! Moses knew that God would provide for His people, and so he looked to God who could supply what they needed.

Romans 8:28—All things work together for good

In the previous chapter, we looked at the great promise of God's faithfulness and forgiveness in 1 John 1:9.

Here we will look at a second important promise, found in Romans 8:28: **"And we know that all things work together for good to those who love God, to those who are the called according to His purpose."**

The Greek word for "**know**" here means 'to have knowledge from experience,' 'to know in detail' or 'understand.' We should be able to say, "Amen!" to this verse. It does not say that all things are good; in fact, many things that happen are often bad. But this verse promises that all things WORK TOGETHER FOR GOOD.

To whom does this promise apply? It applies to **"those who love God, to those who are the called according to His purpose."** This tells us that it applies to *all believers*. People sometimes think that this verse is limited to a special group of Christians, such as missionaries. But *all* Christians are called.

Romans 1:6 confirms this. The letter to the Romans was written to the *whole* Roman church, and Paul wrote to them, **"...you also are the called of Jesus Christ"**. So when Paul said **"the called"** in Romans 8:28 he had already defined this term in the same letter in Romans 1:6; **"the called"** meant all the believers. In Romans 1:1, Paul had said that he was **"called to be an apostle"**. All believers are not called to be apostles, but we are all called according to God's purpose; and we are all called saints (Romans 1:7).

Therefore, the promise of Romans 8:28 is a promise to all of us who are believers. We are all predestined to be conformed to the image of Jesus Christ (see Romans 8:29-30); God has called us to this. Therefore, everything works together for our good, *to this end*. If everything looks bad—if our house has been burgled, or we have no job or no money—what should we do? *Whatever* situation we find ourselves in, we should acknowledge and praise God, because Romans 8:28 still applies. Good and bad circumstances alike all work together for our good. This promise should therefore give us peace in EVERY circumstance.

If you have a revelation of Romans 8:28 then, even if everything seems to be going wrong in your life, you can have the same peace as if everything was going 'right'. Sometimes, when things are very easy in our lives, our lives are powerless spiritually. We naturally tend to put our trust in money, in our peaceful home life, and so on. But God may allow these to be disturbed. Maturity often comes by persevering through such problems. It may be the only way.

The example of Simon Peter again

Peter denied the Lord. But he was humbled and he matured after he had confessed his sin. He realized his human frailty, and grew through the experience. It was not good that he denied Jesus, but it worked for good.

In chapter 1 of Peter's first epistle, he wrote, **"...now for a little while, if need be, you have been grieved by various trials, that the genuineness of your faith, being much more precious than gold that** perishes, though it is tested by fire, may be found to praise, honour, and glory at the revelation of Jesus Christ..." (verses 6-7). Our faith *will* be tried and, by enduring such faith trials, we will grow to maturity. God wants us to understand the truth of Romans 8:28 so that we might have *peace* even in the difficult trials, as well as in all of the other circumstances in our lives.

THREE PRINCIPLES THAT APPLY TO ALL BELIEVERS

There are three principles that we can identify in the lives of many characters in the Bible, and which apply to every single believer today.

1. *God is always faithful.* God's faithfulness depends on Him and not on us. "**If we are faithless, He remains faithful; He cannot deny Himself**" (2 Timothy 2:13). God never changes. He was faithful yesterday, and He is going to be faithful to us today and in the future. This should give us great peace and assurance.

2. *God turns cursing into blessing for a believer.* You cannot, as a believer, stay under cursing for too long. God eventually turns cursing into blessing. "**Christ has redeemed us from the curse of the law, having become a curse for us**" (Galatians 3:13). Balaam was not able to curse God's people, because God had blessed them (see Numbers 23:8, 20).

3. *The Romans 8:28 principle*: "**All things work together for good to those who love God, to those who are the called according to His purpose.**"

These principles are founded on God's faithfulness and the fact that He is *for* us (Romans 8:31). We should keep them in mind when studying any particular character in the Bible. As we look at characters such as Elijah, Elisha, Isaiah, Jacob, David, and so on, we should be able to identify how these principles are in fact the essential message God wants us to learn from them.

It is hard to choose just one example of someone in the Bible, to see how the Romans 8:28 principle worked for them, because there are so many good examples. My favourite examples are Daniel and Joseph. We do not know too much about Daniel's early life, and how he came to be a spiritual believer; so here we will consider Joseph. In the Book of Genesis, we can see how the promise given in Romans 8:28 was worked out not only in the life of Joseph, but also in the lives of the other members of his family.

THE ROMANS 8:28 PRINCIPLE SEEN IN THE LIVES OF JOSEPH AND HIS FAMILY

"**Now Jacob dwelt in the land where his father was a stranger, in the land of Canaan**" (Genesis 37:1). Canaan was the land of promise. God had promised Abraham that his descendants would inherit the land (see Genesis 12:7; 17:8 etc.). Jacob, Abraham's grandson, was now living there—but only temporarily—for God had also told Abraham that before his descendants could have it, they would be captives in Egypt for 400 years (see Genesis 15:13-16).

Jacob's sons were a very motley bunch, from the oldest son, Reuben, to the youngest son, Benjamin. They were amazing characters, as can be learned from reading Genesis chapter 49.

Reuben

Reuben, for example, was unstable and very weak, despite acting nobly at times. (In fact, only Reuben and Joseph were good sons.) Reuben was the firstborn, and the firstborn in those days automatically received three things:

1. The rulership in the family among the children (and after the parents died).

2. The priesthood; for example, he would make sacrifices on behalf of the family (this was before the Levitical priesthood).

3. The double portion of the inheritance when the father died (which helped ensure that he retained the rulership).

Reuben was in line to get all three of these privileges. However, because he was so unstable, he lost them all.

1. He lost the rulership to Judah. Later, Jesus the Messiah, the King of Israel, came from the line of Judah. If only Reuben had known what he was losing!

2. He lost the priesthood to Levi (a miraculous story, as explained below).

3. Finally, he lost the double portion to Joseph. A portion was later given to *both* of Joseph's sons, Ephraim and Manasseh, thus passing the double portion to the tribe of Joseph.

The details of these events can be found in Genesis or can be traced throughout the Old Testament. The lesson for us is that Reuben was a noble person, but his instability caused him to lose these three great things. We must beware lest we lose part of our inheritance in the Lord or miss out with the Lord because of instability. There are many people with good intentions, whose hearts are 'right' with the Lord, yet they miss out because of instability. That is why the principles of 1 John 1:9 and Romans 8:28 are so vital to us. They can help us grow up to be stable and mature. We need God's promises to be effective in our lives.

Simeon and Levi

Levi began as a terrible man, one of the most mean and cruel in the whole history of Israel. Simeon was perhaps the second most shocking. On one occasion, to get revenge on someone, they killed him and his father (see Genesis chapter 34). They also hamstrung an ox because of their self-will. This meant they cut the animal's muscles in half; the animal would not die directly, but it would experience great pain and be unable to reach food or water. It was a cruel, pointless act.

Jacob cursed Simeon and Levi's anger (Genesis 49:7), and told them they would be scattered in Israel. Yet Levi became a miracle of grace. In His grace, God turned this curse into a blessing. God chose to give Levi the priesthood, and his tribe became a tribe of priests in Israel. That meant they did not need any land, because all the other people would provide for them (see Numbers 18:20-21)!

Judah, Issachar, Dan and Benjamin

Jacob described Judah as **"a lion's whelp"** (Genesis 49:9a), that is, a lion cub. This meant he had great potential which wasn't yet developed. He had potential as a leader, for example.

Issachar was described as **"a strong donkey, lying down between two burdens"** (Genesis 49:14). This meant he was very lazy.

Dan was called, **"a serpent by the way, a viper by the path"** (Genesis 49:17a). He was terrible, and he never confessed his sins.[2]

Benjamin was not so good either. Everyone tends to have a soft spot for Benjamin, because he was the youngest of the 12 sons of Jacob, but he grew up to be quite a 'monster'!

Jacob faced the facts, and that is why we have Genesis chapter 49 in the Bible. This chapter provides us with the descriptions Jacob gave of each of his sons just before he died. The stories of their lives and of the 12

---

[2] Dan was so bad in fact that when, during the Tribulation, 144 000 Jewish evangelists will go forth to preach the gospel, there will be no one from the tribe of Dan (see Revelation 7:4-8).

tribes that came from them can all be traced throughout the Bible and can teach us many important principles.

This is the kind of teaching that should be expounded in our churches every week. We need to learn about these stories, because they teach us about God's grace, and because the lessons they contain will make us grow. 1 Peter 2:2 says, **"Desire the pure milk of the word, that you may grow thereby."** The simple truths of the Word of God make us grow. A man's thoughts will not make us grow in faith; but the Word of God will.

The story of Joseph

The story of Joseph begins in Genesis 37. He was a young lad of just 17 at the start of the story, being the second youngest of Jacob's 12 sons. Benjamin his brother was the youngest.[3]

"This is the genealogy of Jacob. Joseph, being seventeen years old, was feeding the flock with his brothers. And the boy was with the sons of Bilhah and the sons of Zilpah, his father's wives; and Joseph brought a bad report of them to his father. Now Israel (Jacob) loved Joseph more than all his children, because he was the son of his old age. Also, he made him a tunic of many colours" (verses 2-3).

The Hebrew suggests Joseph was literally shepherding the sheep *and* his brothers too! These brothers were all older than Joseph, yet the account implies that only Joseph could be trusted. Jacob therefore used to send Joseph to keep an eye on his brothers, and Joseph reported back to his father. You can imagine the brothers' reaction to this!

The sons of Bilhah were Dan and Naphtali, and the sons of Zilpah were Gad and Asher. Joseph was therefore with four of his brothers, and he brought a bad report about them to Jacob. The four brothers were evidently not looking after the sheep properly; they'd been messing about.

It obviously did nothing for the unity of the family for Jacob to give Joseph, who was only 17, responsibility for his older brothers. It was unwise and foolish of Jacob to show this preference for one of his sons above the others.[4] He was treating Joseph wrongly. The phrase "**son of**

---

[3] At the time Joseph was 17, some evidence suggests that Benjamin was not yet born. If this was the case, Joseph's second dream had an added significance, as explained in footnote 6.

[4] Note that it is not necessarily wrong for a parent to have a greater affinity for one child than another; in fact, it is natural. However, it is extremely unwise to show it. A parent is responsible for bringing up all his or her children equally.

his old age" was an idiom meaning Joseph was the *wisest* son; in other words, Joseph had the wisdom of old age. It did not simply mean that he was the youngest son—Benjamin was. Nor did it mean Jacob was *very* old; Jacob was still to live for many more years, and he fathered Benjamin after Joseph.

This may shatter some illusions, but the final phrase in verse 3 should probably be translated, "a long coat (or tunic) with sleeves." The usual idea that Joseph was given a coat of many colours is not in the Hebrew at all; it would be meaningless. A long coat, however, signified a high position and authority: the longer someone's coat was, the more authority he had.

By favouring Joseph, Jacob was making a fool of Reuben, his eldest son. He had also put Joseph in a ridiculous position; and it was bound to lead to trouble. The next few verses show how Joseph's brothers grew to despise him, because they saw how their father loved him the most: "**they hated him and could not speak peaceably to him**" (verse 4); "**...they hated him even more**" (verse 5); "**...they hated him even more for his dreams and for his words**" (verse 8); "**And his brothers envied him...**" (verse 11). Joseph's brothers thus had sinful attitudes.

These are in fact some of the worst kinds of sins: they are sins inside the head. Mental sins are just as real as physical sins, and in fact are a greater problem because they are easier to ignore or cover up. But God sees such sins, and they too prevent us from living in fellowship with Him.

We should be aware of and ashamed of our inward sins, and confess them to God—not simply embarrassed if they show forth. Such sins do affect us. If we are jealous of someone, for example, we cannot look him straight in the eye or treat him as a normal brother in the Lord . Also, our envy, jealousy and hatred may cause us to commit other terrible sins, as was the case in this true story.

As the hatred of Joseph's brothers grew and grew, they eventually began to plot against Joseph until "**they conspired against him to kill him**" (verse 18). They ridiculed him because of his dreams (verse 19) and, finally, they discussed how to kill him secretly (verse 20). It is interesting to trace the events which unfolded as a result of this growing hatred.

Going back to verse 4, it was "**when his brothers saw that their father loved him more than all his brothers**" that "**they hated him, and could not speak peaceably to him.**" They should not have had to see Jacob's favouritism. But because they saw it, they were unable to give Joseph the usual greeting, "Shalom," meaning, 'Peace (to you).'

"Now Joseph dreamed a dream, and he told it to his brothers; and they hated him even more. So he said to them, "Please hear this dream which I have dreamed"" (verses 5-6). Things began to get worse when Joseph began to have dreams. It is no wonder his brothers could not receive Joseph's first dream: "There we were, binding sheaves in the field. Then behold, my sheaf arose and also stood upright; and indeed your sheaves stood all around and bowed down to my sheaf" (verse 7). Joseph was saying to his brothers, "You will all bow down to me one day." His brothers could not accept the dream—especially in view of the fact that they already hated him so much.[5]

The effect of this is easy for us to imagine. Nevertheless, the dream *was* from God. One day Joseph would indeed rule the family; God was speaking through this dream. Jacob had already seen this, but he had acted too hastily and was trying to make Joseph the ruler already. (If God speaks to us in a situation, it is to give us peace, not for us to try to run ahead of Him.)

Then Joseph had a second dream and told his brothers: **"And this time, the sun, the moon and the eleven stars bowed down to me"** (verse 9b). Who was this referring to? The sun referred to Jacob; the moon referred to Joseph's mother Rachel, or to Leah;[6] and, the eleven stars referred to Joseph's eleven brothers.

"So he told it to his father and his brothers; and his father rebuked him and said to him, "What is this dream that you have dreamed? Shall your mother and I and your brothers indeed come and bow down to the earth before you?" And his brothers envied him, but his father kept the matter in mind" (verses 10-11). It is amazing that Joseph had the cheek to tell this second dream to his father and brothers. The brothers of course rejected it totally. However, Jacob was wiser and

---

[5] I have sometimes ministered things that other people could not receive. In some cases, they could not accept the message because our fellowship had been broken. Sometimes, however, the message itself was the main problem. In this case, the brothers' hatred of Joseph made the message of the dream extremely unwelcome.

[6] Jacob's rebuke in verse 10 suggests that Rachel was still alive at this time, which would mean Benjamin was not yet born. If this was the case, the eleventh star in the dream indicated that God knew another son would be born by the time the dream would be fulfilled. Jacob may not have known it; Rachel may not have known it; but God knew it. When God gives a vision or dream it is always perfect! However, "your mother" in verse 10 might refer to Leah, who would have assumed the role of mother to all 12 sons after Rachel's death.

Revelation 12:1 refers to "a woman clothed with the sun, with the moon under her feet, and on her head a garland of twelve stars." This is a much misunderstood passage, yet by referring to Genesis 37, we can see that it refers to the family of Jacob, that is, the Jews. The Bible is its own commentary.

more mature, and he took note of it. "Lord, perhaps this is from You," he thought. He later forgot it, however. We believers have not changed a bit!

"**Then his brothers went to feed their father's flock in Shechem. And Israel (Jacob) said to Joseph, "Are not your brothers feeding the flock in Shechem? Come, I will send you to them." So he said to him, "Here I am""** (verses 12-13). Jacob was worried about what Joseph's brothers might get up to, so again he sent Joseph to report on them. They had already had one bad report, and another would do them even more damage.

"**Then he (Jacob) said to him (Joseph), "Please go and see if it is well with your brothers and well with the flocks, and bring back word to me." So he sent him out of the Valley of Hebron, and he went to Shechem**" (verse 14). Joseph went to Shechem, but his brothers had left.

"**Now a certain man found him, and there he was, wandering in the field. And the man asked him, saying, "What are you seeking?" So he said, "I am seeking my brothers. Please tell me where they are feeding their flocks." And the man said, "They have departed from here, for I heard them say, 'Let us go to Dothan.' " So Joseph went after his brothers and found them in Dothan**" (verses 15-17). Joseph's brothers had moved on to Dothan. They had perhaps got bored and decided to move on. Joseph followed them, because this was precisely the type of thing he had been sent to check up on.

Joseph's brothers knew they would be harmed by another evil report, so they conspired to kill Joseph rather than have him report back to their father. "**Now when they saw him afar off, even before he came near them, they conspired against him to kill him. Then they said to one another, "Look, this dreamer is coming! Come therefore, let us now kill him and cast him into some pit; and we shall say, 'Some wild beast has devoured him.' We shall see what will become of his dreams!"**" (verses 18-20). Notice that they not only plotted to slay Joseph, but they mocked his dreams and wanted to prove them to be untrue. However, nothing can ever break the word of God—not even the greatest conspiracy.

Reuben, who was noble in heart, tried to come to Joseph's rescue. However, he was too weak to resist his younger brothers, despite having the authority to do so as the eldest son. He therefore decided to trick his brothers, and he devised a plan. "**But Reuben heard it, and he delivered him out of their hands, and said, "Let us not kill him." And Reuben said to them, "Shed no blood, but cast him into this pit which is in the wilderness, and do not lay a hand on him"**—that he might deliver him out of their hands, and bring him back to his father" (verses 21-22). Reuben stopped his brothers killing Joseph at that time and tried to ensure Joseph was thrown into a pit alive. He intended to rescue Joseph later, without his brothers knowing. But the other brothers were to ruin Reuben's plan. God had used Reuben's intervention, but He did not need Reuben's help to rescue Joseph; He was quite able to do so on His own!

"**So it came to pass, when Joseph had come to his brothers, that they stripped Joseph of his tunic, the tunic of many colours that was on him. Then they took him and cast him into a pit. And the pit was empty; there was no water in it**" (verses 23-24). There was no water in this pit, which was probably a deep well. This is a good example of Romans 8:28 because, if there had been water in the well, Joseph might have drowned. God had known all about Joseph's predicament long before this happened, and had made sure there had been no rain for a long time, so that the well would be dry.

This is an example of how God prepares for our problems in advance. He knows the problems we will get two weeks or two years from now. And already something is happening somewhere that is going to be just perfect for helping us through that particular problem and for overcoming our predicament.

Joseph did not react like Daniel who, when he was thrown into the lions' den, was quite calm. Joseph did not yet know the principle of Romans 8:28, being only 17, whereas Daniel was about 90 years old when he was put in the lions' den. Joseph wailed in anguish; he was crying and begging and pleading for his life. (We know this because in Genesis 42:21, when Joseph was ruler of Egypt some 20 years later, Joseph's brothers reflected on how he had been down the well begging for their help: "**We are truly guilty concerning our brother, for we saw the anguish of his soul when he pleaded with us, and we would not hear.**") If Joseph had been mature, he would have been able to sit in the pit, quietly praising the Lord; instead, he was in great anguish and pleading for help.

The brothers' review of these events in Genesis 42 continues, "**And Reuben answered them, saying, "Did I not speak to you, saying, 'Do not sin against the boy'; and you would not listen? Therefore behold, his blood is now required of us"**" (verse 22). Here, some 20 years on, Reuben was telling them off and saying, "I told you so"—but he should have had the fortitude to insist they did not sin against Joseph 20 years earlier.

This whole situation is an example of Romans 8:28. It was not good that Joseph's brothers hated him, nor that they threw him into the pit. But it all worked for good in the end. Joseph would not have become ruler of Egypt if he had not been thrown down that pit. God used the bad situation to fulfil His glorious plan!

The account in Genesis 37 continues: **"And they sat down to eat a meal..."** (verse 25a). While Joseph was down in the pit, his brothers ignored Joseph's cries, and continued with what they were doing—which was sitting down and eating a meal. So while Joseph was in deep anguish, they were busy having a picnic! They truly were a rotten bunch!

"Then they lifted their eyes and looked, and there was a company of Ishmaelites, coming from Gilead with their camels, bearing spices, balm, and myrrh, on their way to carry them down to Egypt" (verse 25b). Here we see how God stepped in. These Ishmaelites were medicine carriers (the Bible refers to the "balm of Gilead" for example). It 'just so happened' that this pit was by a main road! This was Romans 8:28 again. And what is more, at the exact moment that the brothers were sitting down to eat their meal and deciding what to do with Joseph, a camel train came by! It was timed to perfection—another example of Romans 8:28. This camel train must have set out several weeks before. Perhaps it had been delayed at some point, or a camel had broken its leg? Whatever happened, God had planned it to arrive at this precise moment! The lesson for us is this:

JOSEPH WAS IN GOD'S HANDS, EVEN AT THE BOTTOM OF THE PIT.

The same applies to us as well. Joseph did not realize it; we often do not realize it. But Romans 8:28 tells us that everything will be all right in the end, because God works everything for our good. We are always in God's hands and He is working out His purposes in our lives. We therefore need to learn to have peace in every situation.

"So Judah said to his brothers, "What profit is there if we kill our brother and conceal his blood? Come and let us sell him to the Ishmaelites, and let not our hand be upon him, for he is our brother and our flesh." And his brothers listened" (verses 26-27). Judah spoke up. His question concerned how much money they would make. Why not sell him to the Ishmaelites? (The Ishmaelites were descendants of Abraham, and distant cousins of Jacob's family.)

"Then Midianite traders passed by; so the brothers pulled Joseph up and lifted him out of the pit, and sold him to the Ishmaelites for

twenty shekels of silver. And they took Joseph to Egypt" (verse 28). They sold Joseph for 20 pieces of silver to Midianite merchants, who were part of the caravan. He was later sold on in Egypt to Potiphar, one of the Pharaoh's officers. Let us stop here and consider:

Q. Was it good that Jacob had treated Joseph wrongly?

A. It was not good, *but it worked for good.*

Q. Was it good that Joseph's brothers hated him?

A. No. It was not good, *but it worked for good.*

Q. Was Reuben's suggestion good?

A. Yes, it was good, *and it worked for good.*

Q. Was Judah's suggestion to sell Joseph good?

A. No, it was very bad, *but it worked for good.*

Q. Was it good that the Ishmaelites and Midianites came along at that time?

A. Yes. It was very good, *and it worked for good.*

Q. Was it good that Joseph was sold as a slave?

A. No. It was not good, *but it was going to work for good.*

Q. Was it good that Joseph was going to be sold into the house of Potiphar?

A. Yes. It may not have seemed to good to Joseph at the time, *but it was going to work for good.*

Most of these events were not good; some were terrible, while others were slightly better. But the important thing for us to recognize is that ALL these events worked for good in the end.

Let us read on to the end of Genesis 37. "**Then Reuben returned to the pit, and indeed Joseph was not in the pit; and he tore his clothes**" (verse 29). Reuben waited until all his brothers had gone, and then returned to carry out his plan; but he was horrified to find that Joseph was gone. (It seems the other brothers never told him where Joseph was.) But God did not need Reuben to rescue Joseph!

"**And he (Reuben) returned to his brothers and said, "The boy is no more; and I, where shall I go?" So they took Joseph's tunic, killed a kid of the goats, and dipped the tunic in the blood. Then they sent the tunic of many colours, and they brought it to their father and said, "We have found this. Do you know whether it is your son's tunic or** not?" And he recognized it and said, "It is my son's tunic. A wild beast has devoured him. Without doubt Joseph is torn to pieces." Then Jacob tore his clothes, put sackcloth on his waist, and mourned for his son many days. And all his sons and all his daughters arose to comfort him; but he refused to be comforted, and he said, "For I shall go down into the grave to my son in mourning." Thus his father wept for him.**

Now the Midianites had sold him in Egypt to Potiphar, an officer of Pharaoh and captain of the guard" (verses 30-36).

Later, further bad events were to happen to Joseph (read Genesis chapters 38 to 41). Potiphar's wife was going to fall in love with Joseph and desire him. Joseph was going to reject her, and she was going to start spreading lies which resulted in his being put in prison. But this time, there was no crying or complaining from Joseph; he had learned something! And, amazingly, his being put in prison was what God used to cause Joseph to become the ruler of Egypt under Pharaoh!

Some 20 years later, when Joseph had been raised up to rule Egypt, he helped his brothers, who had earlier put him in the pit (read Genesis chapters 42 to 45). His being in Egypt during a famine at that time was not only a blessing to himself; it became a blessing to the very brothers who had plotted to kill him, because Romans 8:28 applied even to them!

CONCLUSION

Whether our circumstances are good or bad or indifferent, they will all work together for good, because God has made a covenant with us in love. When we were God's enemies He 'gave us the best.' Now that we are His children, we receive 'better than the best'—for not only will the good things that happen to us bless us, but the bad things will bless us too! This means that everything in our lives is a blessing to us. What an amazing thing this is!

Joseph could have had peace throughout his ordeal if he had known the principle of Romans 8:28; but he was too immature to appreciate it at the time he was thrown into the pit. However, later on he did learn this principle and he did learn to have peace in every situation.

All things worked together for good, not only for Joseph, but also for his brothers and parents. They also were called according to God's purposes. Romans 8:28 applied to them all. Their actions towards Joseph, although awful, were overruled by the principle of Romans 8:28—and they worked for their good, as well as for Joseph's ultimate good.

When you get problems and feel down, do not worry. Rather, learn from your mistakes, and learn to claim the promises of the Word of God in every situation. Learn to have Romans 8:28 so living inside you that you will know it is true in every circumstance. It is no wonder the apostle Paul could say, "**In everything give thanks**" (1 Thessalonians 5:18). He knew that for those in Christ all things work together for good!

NOTES
---

14. THE RICH YOUNG RULER

This is the final study in this first series of Basic Bible Studies. I have aimed to lay a foundation upon which we can go on to build a thorough understanding of the Bible. The basics are essential; without them we could get into a terrible mess later. This series has been aimed at giving God's people stability and leading them on to reach maturity. I hope that no Christian who has gone through this series still doubts his or her salvation, or thinks that he or she might have lost it or committed the unforgivable sin. By now we should not be anxious about these things, but should know where we stand, and should be able to explain these issues to others. There is no reason for anyone to lose 'flying time' in the Spirit. The time when Satan could make us anxious and deter us from moving on with the Lord should be finished once and for all.

In this final study, we are going to turn out attention to how to witness effectively for the Lord.

THE IMPORTANCE OF LIVING A GODLY LIFE

It is important to realize that it is primarily the quality of *our lives* that will preach the gospel to the world. Therefore we who are Christians must make sure that our lives match up to what our mouths profess. I think that many non-Christians are seriously disturbed by the fact that, when they look at the lives of some Christians who give them the gospel message, they cannot *see* the gospel coming out.

People should be able to see the difference in our lives resulting from having God with us and in us. For example, it is no good if we crumple under the slightest pressure at work and become moody. As soon as we have an opportunity to tell the gospel to our colleagues, they will remember what we have been like, and say, "If you've got God and we haven't, why then is there no significant difference between us?" It is time we called the devil's bluff and started *living* the Christian life.

The Holy Spirit is in us for one main purpose: *to reveal Jesus Christ in us*. He indwells us, and so we have God's very life within us, enabling us to live as God intended. God desires to change us so that, wherever we may be, Jesus might be seen. And the Word of God is very important in this process, because the Holy Spirit uses it to renew our minds and make us grow.

The world desperately needs *Jesus*. It does not need *our* philosophy or *our* ideas, but it needs *Jesus* and *His* ideas. Every time we are questioned, we should give the thoughts of Jesus to the world. The Chinese, for example, used to give out the thoughts of Chairman Mao. We should be able to give the thoughts of Jesus to people, and should effectively *be* Jesus to the world. It should be the case, if we allow Jesus to be revealed in us, that when people need comfort, security, love and so on, they will come to us, because they recognize Jesus in us.

I am convinced that the thing closest to the Father's heart is the salvation of any sinner. I will never forget the day when I realized that the Father was more thrilled with my salvation than I was! It was then that I began to realize what saving souls is all about.

I also believe that God loves us so much that He would rather we were with Him in heaven right now. The reason we are still here is that we might be ambassadors of Christ on the earth: living epistles—that is, a 'talking book'—revealing Jesus in everything that we say and do. This is the essence of the Christian life, and our Father's will and desire.

How to Witness

When we meet unbelievers, we need to know how best to present the gospel to them. It is no good just automatically handing out a tract, giving a testimony, or churning out the same old phrases. It is essential to discern their individual needs.

For example, if you give your testimony to someone in this godless world, and say that Jesus has 'enlightened' you, then that person might give you a testimony about what drugs have done for them, or Hare Krishna or Christian Science. Some people *do* need to hear your testimony; but other people need you to emphasize some other point. We all need the Holy Spirit to guide us as to how to witness. Every person we meet is an individual and has a different background. Everyone has different problems and needs. Everyone has been affected differently by things in their past. Jesus has *and is Himself* the answer for every person, but we need to present the answer in a way that is appropriate.

In this study we will look at Jesus' encounter with a rich young ruler. We will see how Jesus met an individual and got straight to the root of his problem. I once spoke to a man whose fundamental problem was that he could not accept the Word of God. It was no good talking to such a person about every other subject under the sun. *That* problem had to be addressed first. Jesus always addressed the real problem, as we will see in this story.

THE RICH YOUNG RULER

This is one of those incidents that is recorded in all three of the "Synoptic" gospels: Matthew (19:16-22), Mark (10:17-22) and Luke (18:18-23). We will look at the account given in Mark. The three accounts are all slightly different, but this should not surprise us. Three accounts of a story or a conversation made by three people can all be slightly different and have different emphases, and yet still be accurate. In fact, it is to be *expected* that three such accounts would vary slightly. If we combine them, we get a fuller picture than from just one account.

For example, I have called the central figure of these accounts "the rich young ruler," although Mark 10 simply states that "**he had great possessions**" (verse 22). Mark calls him neither young nor a ruler. However, Matthew tells us he was a "**young man**" (Matthew 19:20); and the Greek word he used meant someone who was out of boyhood, but who was not yet in full manhood. Therefore, this rich man was in his late teens or twenties, or perhaps early thirties. It is Luke who tells us that he was a "**ruler**" (Luke 18:18). This word (*archōn*) was used in many ways, such as for a ruling judge or magistrate, or even a certain group of angels. But in this context in the New Testament it usually meant a ruler of the synagogue or a member of the Sanhedrin. The rich young man was thus a religious leader, and probably a high-ranking Pharisee. He was therefore not just any young man coming to Jesus; he was probably a 'millionaire' and someone with a very prominent position in society. Praise God for His omniscience. Jesus knew all about this young man's life![1]

"Now as He was going out on the road, one came running, knelt before Him, and asked Him, "Good Teacher, what shall I do that I

---

[1] God's omniscience is thrilling. When we meet Him face to face, we will not shock Him! He is not going to find out some dreadful truth that He didn't already know about our lives, and cast us out. The woman caught in adultery must have had a revelation of this (see John 8:1-11). I think she realized that Jesus knew everything about her. As she looked into Jesus' eyes, which were full of love and compassion, there was not one scrap of condemnation or hatred. I think this changed her life. Looking at those eyes meant she was never the same.

The same applies to us today. If we catch just one glimpse of the eyes of Jesus, we will come to understand the truth of Romans 8:1, "There is therefore now no condemnation to those who are in Christ Jesus." I think one such glimpse is enough to make any person just get up out of the grime and dirt of their lives and be transformed.

may inherit eternal life?"' (Mark 10:17). Jesus saw this rich young ruler and knew all about his life. But Jesus also saw that he was simply a helpless sinner in need of salvation. This was a man genuinely seeking after truth: his kneeling shows us that he was sincere. He came and knelt and asked a question of Jesus; and his one brief question speaks volumes. Jesus was to know from this question what his problem was and how to deal with him, how to counter his erroneous ideas and the best way to give him the gospel.

First, it is important to note that the word translated "**Teacher**" ("**Master**" in the AV) was simply the usual word for a *human* teacher. Sometimes in the gospels we read of those who addressed Jesus as "Lord," which implied they believed Jesus to be the Messiah and God.[2] But this man did not say, "Lord"; instead, he said, "**Good Teacher**". It was similar to calling someone "Professor" today. This shows us that the rich young ruler was impressed by the scholarship and teaching of Jesus, but that he did not think Jesus was the Messiah or that Jesus was divine. In his opinion, Jesus was simply an excellent teacher and no more.

The rich young ruler's use of the word "**Good**" (*agathos* in Greek) and the rest of his question revealed where he was wrong. The word *agathos* meant 'excellent' in any respect, 'distinguished,' 'good in character,' 'morally good.'

This rich young ruler understood Jesus to be a *human* teacher, yet he suggested that Jesus was morally good. He would probably have called other people "*agathos*" too. Jesus of course was indeed a good man—the only One—but the rich young ruler did not realize this. He also assumed that Jesus, being just a normal man, was able to gain his own salvation by good works, and could help him do the same.

He asked Jesus, **"What shall I do that I may inherit eternal life?"** This question exposed the error in the rich young ruler's thinking. It tells us that he did not know anything about the Fall of Man. He evidently believed that a man could be good and thereby gain his own salvation.

Note the rich young ruler's question in Matthew's account: **"Good Teacher, what good thing shall I do that I may have eternal life?"** (Matthew 19:16). He was basically asking, "What good (*agathos*) thing can I *myself* do to ensure that I will be saved?" He evidently believed that he, as a member of the human race, had some intrinsic goodness in him

---

[2] See footnote 4 in chapter 6.

and so could do some work (or works) to guarantee his salvation. He was totally wrong.

I hope that no one who has gone through this first series of Basic Bible Studies will make the same error. The Fall of Man is one of the bases of our faith. As we have discovered, when Adam sinned, he not only fell himself but he dragged the whole of humanity down into a completely fallen state. This is a very important principle; and it is the basis of everything evil we see in the world today. However, most people do not believe in the Fall, but instead wrongly believe that man is fundamentally good. The truth is that all people need a saviour because they are fallen.

The Fall implies two things:

1. We all deserve judgment. Many people ask questions such as, "How can God 'unfairly' exercise judgment on 'good' people?" But God is never unjust; we *all* deserve to be judged.

2. There is nothing at all we can do to impress God or to earn favour with Him. All the works of a fallen person are fallen works. God is not fallen, and so all our works achieve nothing as far as God is concerned.

We have looked at many passages before which state that we are not saved by anything *we* do (such as Ephesians 2:8-9 and Titus 3:5). This rich young ruler needed to realize that no one can do anything to be saved except to believe and accept the gift of God's grace. Every single time a person is saved it is by God's grace alone. We will meet many people who are in exactly the same state as this rich young ruler, who think that by their own good works they will be able to enter heaven. We need to learn from the way Jesus answered him.

Jesus' response to the young man's question is most interesting: "**So Jesus said to him, "Why do you call Me good? No one is good but One, that is, God""** (Mark 10:18). Although *agathos* was used of people or things in general, Jesus took him up on his use of the word and chose to re-use the word differently, pointing the rich young ruler to its ultimate meaning. Jesus was not saying that He Himself did not deserve to be described as "good." Rather, Jesus was making the same assumption as the man. He was questioning him, "*If* I am just a human teacher, then why are you calling Me good?"

Jesus then stated a great truth: **"No one is good but One, that is, God."** He was saying to the man, "Only God is good. Therefore, no man is good in comparison or can naturally do good!" Jesus thus got straight to the root of this young man's problem: his totally wrong idea about man. He lifted the word 'good' on to a divine level, and spoke of God being good in respect of His being perfectly good.

Recall the barrier for a moment. God was on one side, absolutely holy and righteous, and absolutely good. Fallen man was on the other side, churning out more and more filthy rags. The solution came when Jesus dealt with our sins, and with our filthy rags too, through the Cross. But then God had to bring Himself and man together.

As we have seen, God achieved this by *imputing* His own righteousness to us. I, as a fallen human being, could not meet God; but Jesus bore all my sins and paid the penalty for them. And then God gave me His righteousness as a gift as well; He did not just leave me neutral! "**For He (God) made Him who knew no sin (Jesus) to be sin for us, that we might become the righteousness of God in Him**" (2 Corinthians 5:21). We have been given the righteousness of God in Christ. This means I am now covered with a robe of righteousness. I am able to meet God face to face if I die right now. God is absolutely righteous, but I have been given the same absolute righteousness in Christ!

This rich young ruler had no conception of this at all. Jesus therefore asked him, "Only God is good, so how do you think *you* can possibly impress Him?"

This young man was thoroughly religious; therefore, he thought he understood and was obeying the law. In fact, however, he believed in a perverted view of the law, because the Pharisees and other religious leaders took the law completely out of context and changed it so that they could manage to live under it. Jesus knew all about this hypocrisy.

THE RELIGIOUS LEADERS AND THE LAW

It is important to remember that the one thing which stood out more vividly than anything else when the law was given on Mount Sinai was God's holy presence. The people could not touch the mountain when Moses received the law, because of the holiness of God.

When the law was given, it was thus given by the LORD in an appropriate way. It was only later when religious people 'got their hands on' the law that people forgot how it was originally given. Let us remind ourselves of the details.

After Moses recounted to the people of Israel how God had given them the Ten Commandments (Deuteronomy 5:1-21), he continued by describing the scene: "**These words the LORD spoke to all your** assembly, in the mountain from the midst of the fire, the cloud, and the thick darkness, with a loud voice; and He added no more. And He wrote them on two tablets of stone and gave them to me.

"So it was, when you heard the voice from the midst of the darkness, while the mountain was burning with fire, that you came near to me, all the heads of your tribes and your elders. And you said: 'Surely the LORD our God has shown us His glory and His greatness, and we have heard His voice from the midst of the fire. We have seen this day that God speaks with man; yet he still lives. Now therefore, why should we die? For this great fire will consume us; if we hear the voice of the LORD our God any more, then we shall die. For who is there of all flesh who has heard the voice of the living God speaking from the midst of the fire, as we have, and lived? You go near and hear all that the LORD our God may say, and tell us all that the LORD our God says to you, and we will hear and do it'" (verses 22-27).

Clearly, when the law was given, absolute separation occurred. The people knew they could not approach God. God was present in all His holiness, and man was unable to come near.

As we have seen before, the law was given to show man that he is utterly sinful. No one can keep the law in the way it was meant to be kept. As soon as a person came up against the Ten Commandments, for example, and broke one of them, a second aspect of the law became applicable: the *ceremonial law*. This part of the law was full of rituals and sacrifices.

How wonderful it is that God put this second part in. It shows us that He knew that His people would surely break the law!

We are familiar with what the people in Israel had to do when they committed a sin. They had to sacrifice an innocent lamb or young goat. The guilty person's sins were symbolically put on the lamb, which was then killed. The lamb which died was meant to represent Christ and lead people through to find Christ. Galatians 3:23-24 says this: "**But before faith came, we were kept under guard by the law, kept for the faith which would afterwards be revealed. Therefore the law was our tutor to bring us to Christ, that we might be justified by faith.**" The law was thus a "**tutor**" or guide to lead people to faith in Christ.

Paul made it clear in Galatians 3 that absolutely no one was ever justified through keeping the law (Galatians 3:11). He had earlier argued like this: if anyone *had* been justified through keeping the law, then that person would not have needed faith, and Christ would have died for no reason: "**...For by the works of the law no flesh shall be justified....For if** righteousness comes through the law, then Christ died in vain" (Galatians 2:16b and 21b).

What had the Pharisees done? They had taken the law and toned it down, so that it might become manageable. The Pharisees were then able to strut along the road saying to people, "I keep the law completely, you know." They had lost sight of the whole purpose of the law: **"...for by the law is the knowledge of sin"** (Romans 3:20b).

That is why, when Jesus came, He constantly reaffirmed the law. However, He taught it in a way which was radically different from that of the Pharisees: **"You have heard that it was said to those of old....But I say to you..."** (see Matthew 5:21-48). By doing this He was expounding the full requirements of the law about murder,[3] anger, adultery, divorce, swearing, and so on, not emphasizing merely external adherence to rules, but highlighting the fundamental issues of the heart. Jesus thus raised the law back to the original level that God had intended for it.

JESUS SHOWED THE RICH YOUNG RULER HOW HE WAS BREAKING THE LAW

When Jesus told the rich young ruler that only God was good and questioned how he could call Him, **"Good Teacher"**, Jesus had probably surprised and confused him. He had taught the man a lesson about divine goodness. But now He was coming on to talk to him about the law, and this would be even more of a shock to him!

The young man believed that he could keep the law and be justified on the basis of keeping the law. In order to reply to his question, **"What shall I do that I may inherit eternal life?"**, Jesus assumed that he was right. But Jesus then began to show the man that not even he, a leading religious Jew, could keep the whole law. (Recall that James 2:10 says, **"For whoever shall keep the whole law, and yet stumble in one point, he is guilty of all."**)

Jesus answered the rich young ruler, **"You know the commandments: 'Do not commit adultery,' 'Do not murder,' 'Do not steal,' 'Do not bear false witness,' 'Do not defraud'..."** (Mark 10:19). Jesus began to list some of the Ten Commandments. He listed the seventh, then the sixth, then the eighth. The rich young ruler was probably ticking them off

---

[3] Note that the law forbade "murder" (Exodus 20:13); the word was not 'killing.' There is a difference. All killing is not murder—for example, in a time of war. (This is explained more fully in the Special Topic Studies 60 to 62, entitled "The Doctrine of War.")

in his mind; he knew them well. He had been brought up knowing these commandments, and must have been listening and saying to himself, "No, I've never done that, nor that, nor that..." Then Jesus listed the ninth and the tenth commandments.

Suddenly, the rich young ruler was jolted. Jesus did not stop on the tenth commandment, but He went back to the *fifth* commandment, **"...'Honour your father and your mother.'"** Usually, all the Ten Commandments were read or recited in order. But Jesus knew that this man's weakness was the fifth commandment, and He wanted to show him that, even according to one of the most basic laws, he was not righteous. This commandment was the weakness of the Pharisees and, as usual, Jesus zoomed right in on the problem. He always did.[4]

The fifth commandment identified the very thing the rich young ruler was doing wrong, and the reason behind it: he was not honouring his father and his mother, and it was because he loved money. The Pharisees and religious leaders conveniently took the fifth commandment to mean honouring your parents *with your lips*. But in the Bible, to honour parents means not only to obey them when you are young, but also to provide for them when they are old or infirm.[5]

They should have interpreted the commandment, **" 'Honour your father and your mother' "** to include providing for their parents, caring for

---

[4] On another occasion, described in Luke 10:25-37, Jesus was tested by a lawyer, who asked a similar question to that of the rich young ruler: "And behold, a certain lawyer stood up and tested Him, saying, "Teacher, what shall I do to inherit eternal life?"" (verse 25). He said, "Teacher", exactly like the rich young ruler did. Jesus asked that lawyer, "What is written in the law? What is your reading of it?" (Luke 10:26). The lawyer began to recite, " 'You shall love the LORD your God with all your heart, with all your soul, with all your strength, and with all your mind,' and 'your neighbour as yourself.' " The lawyer was a very religious man, and a very proud man. When he got to this second statement Jesus stopped him and told him to go and do it: "And He said to him, "You have answered rightly; do this and you will live"" (verse 28). Jesus was telling him, "Go on, then—go and love your neighbour as yourself!"

Jesus knew that the lawyer had hang-ups: he only liked people who were like himself! There were other people whom he did not like—in particular, the Samaritans, whom he hated. So Jesus was saying to him, "Right, we'll stop at this command," and He zoomed in on it. The lawyer came up with the usual get-out, and asked, "Who is my neighbour?" The Pharisees used to say this frequently—"We do not have to help that person because he is not our neighbour"—a neighbour was only someone like themselves! Jesus then told the lawyer the parable of the "Good Samaritan." It was a cutting story. The good Samaritan was the hero, whereas a priest and a Levite failed to do their duty. This was very pointed stuff. Jesus was implying to the lawyer not only that any needy person he came across was his neighbour, but also that a Samaritan could fulfil the law!

[5] The Bible also says to honour elders, especially those who labour in the Word and in doctrine (see 1 Timothy 5:17). This means that when ministers are invited to speak in our churches, we should not only listen to their ministry, but we should also provide them with hospitality and money. This is all part of honouring them.

them, and sharing their homes with them. But the Pharisees had a clever way out of their responsibilities, which I call "the Corban gimmick".

"The Corban gimmick"

This was a simple ruse, and Jesus described it in Mark 7:9-13. "**And He said to them, "All too well you reject the commandment of God, that you may keep your tradition. For Moses said, 'Honour your father and your mother'; and, 'He who curses his father or mother, let him be put to death.' But you say, 'If a man says to his father or mother, "Whatever profit you might have received from me is Corban (that is, dedicated to the Temple)"'; and you no longer let him do anything for his father or his mother, making the word of God of no effect through your tradition which you have handed down. And many such things you do."**" (We should never ignore or invalidate the Word of God because of our tradition. If the Word of God says something, it does not matter what we have been used to before, we must obey the Word and put it into practice.)

If for example, a young Pharisee had £100 000, he would know that he might have to support his parents for perhaps 20 years in their old age. So he would give £10 000 to the priest, and ask him to declare his remaining £90 000 and his property as "Corban", that is, a gift to the Temple. If his parents then asked him for any money, he would say, "I'm terribly sorry, but I do not have any money. I've given it all to God." If the parents called in the priest to mediate, the priest (who had £10 000 in his pocket) would agree with the Pharisee and say, "He's right; he does not have any money because he's given it to God." According to this system, the priests got rich, and the Pharisees preserved their wealth for themselves.

The Pharisees were therefore hypocrites. This rich young ruler had almost certainly done this trick, and so Jesus focused in on it. This man had made money his god and was looking for treasure on earth.

The rich young ruler was also self-righteous: "**And he answered and said to Him, "Teacher, all these I have observed from my youth"**" (Mark 10:20). According to the standards of the Pharisees, he probably *was* 'righteous', and had done nothing wrong. He therefore considered himself to be righteous according to the law. But he was not righteous according to *God's* standard.

The glorious thing is that this man knew that he was not saved; that was why he had come to Jesus and asked how to inherit eternal life. Generally, I have found that religious people know they are not saved. When they feel down, they realize they are uncertain of their salvation.

That is when we should take the opportunity to tell them the wonderful truth of assurance of salvation.

Jesus' challenge to the rich young ruler

"**Then Jesus, looking at him, loved him, and said to him, "One thing you lack..."**" (Mark 10:21a). I love this verse. I imagine those eyes of Jesus melting into the man. The Greek translated "**loved him**" literally implies Jesus 'responded with love for him'. I think Jesus probably kept this man in his heart after this occasion. We do not know if this man was ever actually saved; but he had seen the eyes of Jesus, and conviction must have begun in his heart from this time on.

The rich young ruler worshipped money, and that was the reason why he was failing to honour his father and mother. And so Jesus pointed out this one great weakness to him: "*You* think that you will be saved by your actions; but here is one thing that you have not done—honoured your parents—and one thing that you cannot do—sell everything!" Jesus wanted to convict the man of his need, and therefore he ended with this last series of instructions, "**One thing you lack: Go your way, sell whatever you have and give to the poor, and you will have treasure in heaven; and come, take up the cross, and follow Me**" (verse 21b). The young man must have thought to himself, "Oh dear; this is the one issue I hoped He wouldn't put His finger on."

If salvation was by works, then the implication would be that *we* have to do the works. But no human being is capable of doing the works. Some people today think they will be saved so long as they do good to everyone. But there is almost certainly one person they simply cannot do good to and whom they detest. It is *that* person who needs to be pointed out to them to bring them under conviction.

Jesus wasn't saying to the man that if he did sell everything he would automatically be saved. Rather, Jesus knew that, for this particular young man, the issue of possessions was what he had to face up to. The rich young ruler must have come under great conviction. Oh that he had fallen flat on his face and said, "Lord, forgive me!"; but he did not—he loved money too much at this time. He had made a choice. He worshipped treasure on earth more than he wanted treasure in heaven; and so he went away sad: "**But he was sad at this word, and went away grieved, for he had great possessions**" (Mark 10:22).

The thing we should particularly learn from this passage is the way Jesus approached this young man. It was up to the rich young ruler whether or not he would believe on Christ, but Jesus had clearly presented the relevant issues to him and knocked the ground away completely from under his feet. Jesus did not get into some complex theological discussion with him. Instead, He simply pointed out the very line of weakness in the man. The young man "**was sad**"—and the word used here (*stugnazō*) meant 'overcast' or 'gloomy.' (It was a metaphor for a sky covered with storm clouds.) He was 'stormcloud-like'; it was as if a dark cloud was over him. He now knew for certain that he was not saved, even according to his own terms. The choice was now his.

Lessons for Jesus' disciples

Jesus never missed an opportunity to drive a message home to His disciples. He was always teaching them. The disciples must have been absolutely astonished. Here was a rich influential young man, and Jesus had turned him away!

"**Then Jesus looked around and said to His disciples, "How hard it is for those who have riches to enter the kingdom of God!"**" (Mark 10:23). Jesus caught their eye. His disciples were believers, but they were just as wrong in their thinking as the rich young ruler was. (Similarly, many Christians today, despite being born again, are enemies of the Cross of Christ in their thinking.)

The statement, "**How hard it is for those who have riches to enter the kingdom of God!**" is certainly true. People who are rich in any area of their lives (not just in possessions, but in personality, relationships, success in business, and so on) find it hard to recognize their need of salvation. Lonely people, for example, find it easier to seek for God than those who are satisfied in relationships, because they realize they need a relationship with someone. Rich people can go 'out on the town' every night or are able to do all sorts of other things to try to fill the void they have inside.[6]

"**And the disciples were astonished at His words**" (verse 24a). Why were the disciples so astonished? It was because, in those days, people considered that, if you were rich, then you were blessed by God. It is

---

[6] Incidentally, there is a passage in 1 Samuel 22:2 about the people who gathered to David, which is a beautiful picture of salvation. "And everyone who was in distress, everyone who was in debt, and everyone who was discontented gathered to him. So he became captain over them. And there were about four hundred men with him." This is generally applicable to the Body of Christ. The lesson is this: it is the 'messers' who come to God. The rich tend to cover up or not realize their need.

often the opposite today, and many think that the poor or the deprived cannot sin; they think the poor are always good and that the rich are always bad. However, the Bible makes it clear that both rich and poor alike are wretched miserable sinners who need Jesus.

"But Jesus answered again and said to them, "Children, how hard it is for those who trust in riches to enter the kingdom of God! It is easier for a camel to go through the eye of a needle than for a rich man to enter the kingdom of God"" (verses 24b-25). Jesus repeated His point. The idiom about a camel passing through the eye of a needle simply meant *impossible*.[7]

"And they were astonished beyond measure, saying among themselves, "Who then can be saved?"" (verse 26). The disciples thought to themselves, "If the rich cannot be saved, how then can a poor person who is a nobody like me ever be saved?" They were accustomed to thinking that the rich were those most likely to be saved.

"But looking at them, Jesus said, "With men it is impossible, but not with God; for with God all things are possible"" (verse 27). It may be impossible *with men* for any to be saved, but not *with God*. With God all things are possible. Hallelujah! A rich person can give up all his or her riches and still not go to heaven. But God has made a way. For *all* people, there is one way: to believe on the Lord Jesus Christ!

THE ISSUE OF REWARDS

Peter and the other disciples did not understand Jesus' teaching at all. **"Then Peter began to say to Him, "See, we have left all and followed You.""** (verse 28). Matthew's account tells us that Peter also asked, **"Therefore, what shall we have?"** (Matthew 19:27b). Despite Jesus' words that **"with God all things are possible"**, Peter was confused as to why Jesus had called them to follow Him. They had each given up so much. They were worrying, "If we have given up all these things for You, Lord, what will we receive?"

Jesus reassured His disciples and taught them a new principle: although their sacrifice did not bring salvation, there were *rewards* for those who

---

[7] This idiom was not referring to a small gate within a bigger gate, for example. Other writings used this same expression, but said "an elephant" instead of a camel. Some people make an illustration out of this idiom and say a camel could only fit through a small gate (a "needle") in the city gate if its baggage was unloaded. But that would imply that if a rich man gave all his money away he would be saved automatically; this is just not true. The idiom simply meant impossible. The needle meant a literal needle.

gave up things for His sake: "**So Jesus answered and said, "Assuredly, I say to you, there is no one who has left house or brothers or sisters or father or mother or wife or children or lands, for My sake and the gospel's, who shall not receive a hundredfold now in this time— houses and brothers and sisters and mothers and children and lands, with persecutions—and in the age to come, eternal life""** (Mark 10:29-30). This was a marvellous promise. Giving up things for the sake of Jesus and the gospel would not save them; but they would be rewarded—both in this life, and in the life to come.

They would receive rewards in *this* life as well as in the life to come, because "**all the promises of God in Him (Christ) are Yes, and in Him Amen**" (see 2 Corinthians 1:20). All the promises of God have been secured for us in Christ, and we can begin to enjoy our future inheritance even now.

Paul said that if there was no resurrection, then he was a fool, because he'd given up *everything* for Jesus (see 1 Corinthians 15:12-19). But praise God, there *is* a resurrection! Paul was not serving the Lord in vain. Similarly, Peter and the other disciples were not serving the Lord in vain. And neither do *we* serve the Lord in vain!

Conclusion

The world may laugh at us when we give up things for the sake of following Jesus. But they will have to give up all of those same things when they die; they will not take anything with them! We who are believers, and who serve the Lord now—we are the ones who have good sense. We will receive things back again a hundred times from God. That is why Jim Elliot, who was killed by the Auca Indians in Ecuador in 1956, together with four other missionaries, wrote, "He is no fool who gives what he cannot keep to gain what he cannot lose."

A lesson Jesus' disciples learned, and that we should learn, from this rich young ruler is that God is no respecter of persons. Salvation is by grace. No one can ever earn it or deserve it. And everyone who gives up things to follow Jesus shall receive a reward. Moreover, we should not be deceived into analysing who will ultimately be rewarded by God on the basis of their position now. As Jesus said at the end of His answer to His disciples, **"But many who are first will be last, and the last first"** (Mark 10:31).

Whether you are rich or poor, influential or a 'nobody', high or low, churchman or not, atheist or agnostic, you need Jesus! Everyone around us needs Jesus. Your employers and those you meet at work need Jesus. Lords and ladies need Jesus, kings and queens—they all need Jesus. It is *salvation*, not death, that is the great equalizer, for we are all fallen creatures in need of salvation. All our good deeds are like filthy rags. There is nothing any of us can do to gain salvation ourselves.

But what is impossible for me is possible with God! The message is the same for us all: "**Believe on the Lord Jesus Christ, and you will be saved**" (Acts 16:31), and there are no further conditions at all. "**For by grace you have been saved through faith**" (Ephesians 2:8). Praise His wonderful name! This is the message we have to give out. High or low, we are all the same. We all need Jesus; and salvation is *by grace*, and it is *through faith* in the Lord Jesus Christ.

I pray that God will, by the Holy Spirit, reveal to us how we should speak to our non-Christian friends and neighbours, so that we won't simply repeat platitudes, but will identify the issues affecting them and deliver to them the glorious gospel of Jesus Christ. Praise God!

NOTES

Appendix 1
The Original Languages of the Bible

Hebrew [1]

Hebrew is one of the world's oldest living languages. It has been spoken since the time of Abraham (c.2000 BC), or possibly earlier, and it is the official language of Israel today. It was one of the northwestern Semitic languages, along with Phoenician and Aramaic etc. It also has considerable affinity with Arabic, a southern Semitic language. ('Semitic' peoples were those descended from Noah's son Shem after the Flood.)

Writing is thought to have first developed in the ancient civilization of Sumer (Shinar) in lower Mesopotamia, from where God later called Abraham. Other ancient peoples also devised writing, including the Chinese, Hittites and Egyptians. However, these ancient writing techniques were very cumbersome, using numerous symbols that represented objects and ideas. Sumerian cuneiform writing, for example, involved some 600 characters, and writing in ancient Egypt some 700 hieroglyphs. Consequently, the ability to read and write was probably restricted to the educated few.

Hebrew was one of the very first languages to have an *alphabet*, probably around 1500 BC, which in the providence of God made it available for recording His written revelation. (In alphabetic writing words are broken down into their component parts, and a *small* number of characters are used to represent *sounds*, rather than objects or ideas.) Such a *phonetic* system of alphabetic writing facilitated widespread literacy, since significantly fewer elements needed to be mastered.

Nations other than Israel also developed alphabets, but national literacy in the ancient world was known possibly only in Israel. The Old Testament Scriptures, which were the rule of life, provided the necessary incentive for the skills of reading and writing to be taught.

Hebrew is read from right to left, and uses an alphabet of 22 letters, all of which are consonants (the shapes of which possibly signified objects originally). Hebrew words are formed from roots, usually comprising three consonants, which are altered by the use of vowel sounds, as well as by

---

[1] Principal Reference: "World History and Cultures—in Christian Perspective" (A Beka Book Publications, USA; 1992). Used with permission.
   Other References: "Brief notes on the Historical and General Background of the Bible" by L.A.T. Van Dooren (Capernwray Press, UK), "The Zondervan Pictorial Encyclopedia of the Bible" (Zondervan, USA), "Biblical Hebrew" by R.K. Harrison (Hodder and Stoughton, UK; 1981), and "The Interlinear Bible: Hebrew-Greek-English" (General Editor and Translator Jay P. Green, Sr., Hendrickson Publishers, USA).

prefixes and suffixes. Although ancient Hebrew was written without vowels ("unpointed script") and pronunciation relied on the reader's memory, a system was later devised in which the pronunciation of each consonant was indicated by various "vowel points" and accents.[2]

Hebrew is relatively uncomplicated, lacking the precision in tenses of Greek, Latin and many other Indo-European languages. However, it possesses qualities of purity, simplicity and starkness which make it a very effective vehicle for narration and poetic expression. It has a dynamic, emotive, penetrative force, and the ability to soar quickly to sublime heights in beautiful poetry, exalted prose and eloquent prophecy. Hebrew was thus a very appropriate medium for conveying fundamental spiritual truths, being ideal not only for reaching the intellect, but for profoundly stirring the emotions and will of man.

It is impossible to bring out in any English translation the many shades of thought carried by the original Hebrew. Also, no translation can fully do justice to the emotional intensity and rugged beauty of the Hebrew verse, or duplicate its shifting moods. Many people consider that only the King James Version in English comes close to capturing the majesty and rhythm of the Hebrew Old Testament.

The Old Testament text abounds with vivid idioms and forthright utterances. All speech is reported in direct form; anthropomorphisms are used regularly to describe God (eg. Exodus 31:18, 33:23); nations or groups of people are frequently personalized (eg. Jacob, Edom); and, extreme language is employed for emphasis (eg. Malachi 1:3).

Hebrew has passed through three major periods of development:

1. **Biblical** (classical) Hebrew (c.1500 to 300 BC), during which the Old Testament was written;

2. **Rabbinic** (or Mishnaic) Hebrew (c.300 BC to 500 AD), during which time the Jewish oral laws and traditions (the *Mishna*) were written and collected in the *Talmud*; and,

3. **Modern** Hebrew (since c.1850 AD). Hebrew scholars aimed to create a modern tongue which would combine the majesty of Biblical Hebrew with the concise style of Rabbinic Hebrew. Modern Hebrew includes many words borrowed from modern European tongues, as well as from Yiddish—a language derived from medieval High German and spoken by Central and East European (Ashkenazi) Jews.

---

[2] The original manuscripts of the Bible lacked punctuation, and upper and lower case letters were not distinguished. The Hebrew manuscripts were later supplied with punctuation by a group known as the Masoretes (6th Century AD onwards), leading to the authoritative Ben Asher text in the 12th Century.

Original Languages — Appendix 1

It is important to note that there is almost no difference between the language of the oldest and latest parts of the Old Testament. Thus, critics who try to date the writings based on the language alone cannot do so with any certainty.

Aramaic[3]

The name 'Aramaic' comes from *Aram*, the Hebrew word for Syria. The Aramaic language is sometimes inaccurately called "Chaldaic" or "Chaldean". The first biblical occurrence of Aramaic is found in Genesis 31:47, when it was used by Laban, who lived at Padan Aram in the land east of Canaan (Syria).

In the 8th Century BC, Aramaic was adopted as the language of diplomatic communications in the Assyrian Empire (c.1100 to 612 BC): see eg. 2 Kings 18:26. It was then widely used in the Near East during the successive empires: the Neo-Babylonian or Chaldean empire (612 to 539 BC); and, the Medo-Persian empire (539 to 330 BC). It continued to be the diplomatic language until the Greeks overthrew the Persians around 330 BC. (It is interesting that those sections of the Book of Ezra written in Aramaic mostly comprise official correspondence.)

The Book of Daniel was written when many Jews were exiled in Babylon, who would have adopted Aramaic during their captivity. Aramaic was therefore appropriate for Daniel's message about the rise and fall of Gentile empires, since the exiles, as well as people in the surrounding nations, would have been able to understand it.

Upon their return, the Jewish exiles brought Aramaic back to the land of Israel, and probably found that it had also largely been adopted by those who had remained there. Many born in exile may never have learned Hebrew. Therefore, although Hebrew remained the ecclesiastical language, in the post-exilic days few of the common people would have known it (this could be alluded to in Nehemiah 8:2-3,8). It thus supplanted Hebrew as the customary spoken language of the Israelites.

Aramaic was probably used in Israel (Palestine) until the Arab conquest in the 7th Century AD, and thus would have been used by Jesus and His disciples, and by the early Church in Israel. Many words of Aramaic origin appear in the New Testament, such as 'Abba,' 'Marana tha,' and 'mammon' (see also Mark 5:41, 7:34, 15:34). If Aramaic was the common tongue in Israel at the time of our Lord and the New Testament writers, the question thus arises, "Why was the New Testament not written in Aramaic?"

---

[3] Based on: "Brief notes on the Historical and General Background of the Bible" by L.A.T. Van Dooren (Capernwray Press, UK). Used with permission.

New Testament Greek [4]

"Old Testament revelation was committed particularly to one nation as a trust (Romans 3:2) and was therefore recorded in that nation's language. New Testament revelation was not intended to be restricted but to be committed to all nations (Luke 2:30-32; 24:47). The most appropriate language, therefore, would be the one most widely known. In God's providence a suitable language lay ready to hand—Greek."

As Alexander the Great extended the Greek empire, he carried the Greek language throughout the then-known world. *"The differences between the various Greek dialects were by this process slowly eliminated. In the last three centuries B.C., Hellenistic Greek, the 'common speech' or koinē dialektos became the most widely known language. It was the official language of the empire into which the Grecian Empire was divided after Alexander the Great's death in 323 BC.*

"The Roman Empire which followed was bilingual, with Latin being the language of the Army in all parts, and Greek the common language of the streets, sports arena, trade and foreign intercourse. Palestine became incorporated into the Roman Empire in 63 B.C., as part of the province of Syria. To the educated, classical Greek was the language of culture and ancient classics. To the lower classes and slaves, the common tongue, colloquial Greek, was the language of their birth."

Koine Greek was a *"language rich in style, elegance, idioms and exact expression, which gives it a place of eminence amongst languages and made it very suitable for the communicating of God's revelation to men."*

Both Greek and Latin, as well as Aramaic, would thus have been used in the land of Israel in the 1st Century AD, and the Jews would also have used Hebrew, particularly in religious contexts. Jesus and His disciples would thus have spoken Greek and Aramaic in everyday life. They would have been familiar with the Hebrew used in the synagogue (that is, Rabbinic or Mishnaic Hebrew), and may have known some Latin.

The conciseness of Koine Greek

In its capacity for expressing the whole range of human experience and thought, the Greek language was very versatile. It is highly inflected, having verb forms for each person, each tense, each mood and each voice. Thus much meaning can be encapsulated in a single word, resulting in a highly compact language which pin-points meaning in brevity, making for quick

---

[4] Italics denote text quoted directly from: "Brief notes on the Historical and General Background of the Bible" by L.A.T. Van Dooren (Capernwray Press, UK). Used with permission.

Original Languages   Appendix 1

and immediate impact. Thus, Koine Greek could be described as a "precise" language, although "concise" or "compact" are perhaps better descriptions.

Quite apart from verbs, the various cases of nouns (nominative, accusative, dative, genitive and vocative) make the same quick impact without the need for prepositions, such as 'of' (genitive) or 'to'/ 'for' (dative).

The special impact created by the brevity of Greek verb forms

The use of the imperative mood in Greek illustrates well the conciseness of the language, since a command may be given for an immediate single action or for a continuous permanent obligation. In English we might say "Knock!" (meaning "Do it now") or "Keep on knocking!" (meaning "Don't stop after a few attempts"); but we have to use extra words to show that we require extended or continuous action.

Not so in Greek! One word only is used in each instance. The present tense of the imperative mood is used for an extended or continuous command, and the aorist tense of the imperative is used for a single or an immediate command. (Roger Price referred to this in the first study, when he mentioned how a soldier could tell from the Greek verb form whether he was expected to fire once or continuously.)

The following quotations from the gospels demonstrate how admirably the conciseness of the Greek verb in either the present imperative or the aorist imperative gives the meaning which the writer or speaker intended:

Present imperatives

Luke 11:9	*aiteite*	=	*keep* asking!
	zēteite	=	*keep* seeking!
	krouete	=	*keep* knocking!
Mark 11:24	*pisteuete*	=	*always* believe!
Mark 11:25	*aphiete*	=	*always* forgive!

(in both these latter examples, Jesus is speaking of recurring situations).

Matthew 7:1   *mē* (negative) *krinete*   =   do not make a practice of *always* judging!

Aorist imperatives

Matthew 25:28	*arate*	=	take away (the talent)!
	dote	=	give it! (ie. immediately)
Luke 6:42	*ekbale*	=	cast out (the beam)!

Aorist and present imperatives together

The following examples illustrate the difference between the tenses in the imperative:

221

John 2:16   *Arate tauta enteuthen. Mē poieite ton oikon tou Patros mou oikov emporiou* = Take away (*Arate*, aorist) these things from here! Do not make (*poieite*, present) the house of My Father a house of [the] market!

The imperative *poieite* is in the present tense, and so an enlarged translation that contrasts the continuation of this order with the immediacy of the previous order is, "Take these things away from here immediately! Do not make a practice of making My Father's house a market-house!"

John 5:8   *aron ton krabbaton sou kai peripatei* = take up (*aron*, aorist) your pallet and walk (*peripatei*, present)!

The man only had to pick up his pallet (ie. his mattress or bed) once, but then he had to walk and continue walking from then on (present tense).

The numerous verb forms in Greek

Being highly inflected, a Greek verb (comprising only one word) can express the finest shades of thought with subtlety and precision.

There are indicative, subjunctive and imperative moods in Greek, as well as infinitives; and there are other rarer ones besides, such as the optative. There are active, middle and passive voices. There are six main tenses found in the New Testament (present, imperfect, future, aorist, perfect, pluperfect) as well as other rare ones (eg. future perfect occurs once). If we add participles (which being adjectives have 3 genders, 4 cases, singular and plural, and thus they have 24 possible endings), then we amass a large collection of possible verb forms acting as statements, possibilities, wishes, commands etc., in active, middle and passive voices.

A typical regular verb may thus be found in more than 600 variations, each of which will be just one word. Of course many verbs will not be fully used; but this statistic does show the one-word-compactness of Greek. English verbs, in contrast, usually have only four basic forms: loos*e*, loos*es*, loos*ed*, loos*ing*. Auxiliary verbs have to be brought in to construct various tenses (eg. I shall have loosed, I had loosed, etc.) or moods (eg. I was loosed).

A further benefit of referring to the original Greek

Our English translations of the New Testament may use a single word to translate several different Greek words. For example, more than 10 different Greek verbs are translated as "see" in many versions, representing a whole range of ideas covering all aspects of inward or outward perception of abstract and material things. By looking at the original Greek verb, therefore, much can be learned about whether the writer meant literally 'to see with the eyes,' or rather to 'perceive,' 'recognize,' 'observe,' 'behold,' 'discern,' 'apprehend,' 'understand,' etc.

Appendix 2
Conditional sentences in Greek[1]

In Koine Greek, a verb has different forms not only according to *tense*, *number* and *person*, but also for *voice* and *mood*. There are four main moods: the *indicative* mood is the mood of reality (which is used to assert facts, for example, "Jesus died"); the *subjunctive* mood is the mood of possibility, potentiality or uncertainty (perhaps yes, perhaps no); the *imperative* mood is used in commands; and, the *optative* mood is the mood of wishfulness or doubtful assertion.

Conditional sentences have two parts. Most commonly and simply, they are statements of the type, "If....then....", that is, "If condition A is fulfilled, then B follows." The conditional clause (the 'if' clause) is called the "*protasis*," and the main clause (the 'then' clause) is the "*apodosis*."

The inference to be drawn from the conditional clause in Koine Greek depends on two things:

- the tense and mood of the verb following the word for 'if', which can be εἰ or ἐάν (*ei* or *ean*); and,
- the presence or absence of the word ἄν (*an*) in the apodosis, which is an untranslatable particle.

All one has to do is check the tense and mood of the verbs and look for the word ἄν, and then one can tell what type of 'if' statement it is.

In English we can give exactly the same kind of conditional patterns, and we also work out the meaning of the English from the mood and tense of the verbs. However, we have to use rather more words! Additional meaning can thus sometimes be learned from the original Greek sentence in the New Testament than comes across in translation.

There are various types of conditional statements. Some conditions are factual, some are contrary to fact (that is unfulfilled or impossible), and some look to the future. It is helpful to group them together in this way. They are classed under four main headings below, corresponding to the four cases described by Roger Price in BBS 1. Even this analysis gives only the simplest forms.

---

[1] Bibliography: Lesson 39 in "The Elements of New Testament Greek" by J.W. Wenham (Cambridge University Press, 1981). Most of the examples discussed by Roger Price on the audio tape of BBS 1 have also been incorporated in the latter sections.

Appendix 2 — Conditional Sentences

Types of conditions

Case 1. Factual conditions

In conditions of fact, a statement is made on the assumption that the given condition was or is factual, or that it will be fulfilled. These sentences are introduced by εἰ in the protasis and use the indicative mood.

(a) for past facts

εἰ + aorist indicative in the protasis, and aorist indicative (or another indicative tense) in the apodosis.

eg. If God loved us, we must love. (As in the English, the writer assumes that God did indeed love.)

eg. If he did this, he sinned.

(b) for present facts

εἰ + present indicative in the protasis, and present indicative (or perhaps imperative) in the apodosis.

eg. If God loves us, we must love. (Again it is assumed that God does indeed love.)

eg. If he is doing this, he is sinning.

eg. If You are the Son of God, throw Yourself down! (This uses an imperative in the apodosis.)

Case 2. Conditions contrary to fact (unfulfilled conditions)

In conditions contrary to fact, a statement is made recognizing that the given condition was not or is not fulfilled. These also have εἰ in the protasis and use the indicative mood, *but the word ἄν is in the apodosis.*

(a) Past unfulfilled conditions

These use the <u>aorist</u> tense:

εἰ + aorist indicative in the protasis, and aorist indicative + ἄν in the apodosis (what would have been in the past).

eg. If you had believed Him, you would have believed Me. (It is clear that the writer assumed they had not believed Him.)

eg. If he had done this, he would have sinned. (But he didn't!)

(b) Present unfulfilled conditions

These use the <u>imperfect</u> tense:

εἰ + imperfect indicative in the protasis, and imperfect indicative + ἄν in the apodosis (what would otherwise now be happening).

Conditional Sentences — Appendix 2

eg.   If you believed Him (now), you would believe Me. (But you do not believe Him.)

eg.   If he were doing this, he would be sinning. (But he isn't!)

eg.   If I were you, I would be feeling shame. (But I am not you!)

Note that the forms of the Greek and English sentences are quite different here in respect of the *tenses*.

A sentence might also be 'mixed' in respect of tenses, and refer to past action in one clause and present action in the other:

eg.   If you had believed Him, you would believe Me.

Note that the only difference in Greek between cases 1(a) and 2(a) is the presence of ἄν in the apodosis of 2(a). Likewise, 1(b) is absolutely factual, because there is no ἄν in the apodosis, while 2(b) is not factual, because there is ἄν in the apodosis—which shows what *would* be happening if things were other than they are. However, when we look at present conditions, there is another difference between factual and unfulfilled conditions: case 1(b) uses the present tense, whereas case 2(b) uses the *imperfect* tense.

Case 3. Future possible (open) conditions

Future conditions have ἐάν and the subjunctive in the protasis. Fulfillment of the condition is hypothetical but possible. They use ἐάν + present/aorist subjunctive (or occasionally εἰ + future indicative for extra emphasis) in the protasis, and future indicative in the apodosis.

eg.   If I only touch His garment, I shall be made well.

eg.   If he does this, he will sin.

eg.   If you keep doing that, then there'll be trouble!

The ἐάν introducing the protasis shows that a future condition is being expressed, the subjunctive being not yet a fact. Although these conditions are sometimes referred to as "future factual" conditions, the subjunctive mood reflects the element of doubt in most future conditions. Fulfillment of the condition may or may not happen; but if the condition is indeed fulfilled, then the statement made in the apodosis will also be fulfilled.

Case 4. Remotely possible conditions in the future

There is also another type of future condition which expresses only remote possibility. This uses the optative mood. However, this mood, though used commonly in classical Greek, is rare in the New Testament.

Such sentences have εἰ + present/aorist optative in the protasis. The apodosis would have present or aorist optative + ἄν, but this construction does not appear in the New Testament. In 1 Peter 3:14 (see below) only the protasis follows this pattern.

eg. If he were to do this, he would sin.

eg. Teachers might say to their pupils, "If you would work harder, you'd get some results." This could be written in the optative mood in Greek—if the teacher was implying there was only a remote possibility of the pupils working harder.

In conditional sentences, therefore, the mood of the verb is always indicative except in future conditions. Future conditions use the subjunctive mood in the protasis, or occasionally the optative if the condition is only remotely possible.

There are other ways in which these types of conditional sentence could be grouped. The above analysis groups them according to factual, unfulfilled and two types of future conditions. Because both factual and unfulfilled conditions can be past or present conditions, the analysis really gives us six basic divisions. It would have been equally possible to group the sentences according to past, present and future, with past and present conditions subdivided into factual and non-factual, giving the same six divisions.

Sentences could also be grouped solely according to mood or tense, but this would not tell the whole story. Looking only at the *mood* of the verb following εἰ or ἐάν does not take you as far as in the above analysis, since 9 out of the 12 verb forms (protasis and apodosis in six divisions) can be indicative. Similarly, arrangement according to *tenses* only does not reveal all of the information.

The best approach is to look for what follows the word for 'if' in the protasis (that is, εἰ for past or present, or ἐάν for the future), and then to link this with information in the apodosis. Although the tense and mood of the verb in the protasis are important, therefore, it is the apodosis which seals the meaning. What leads to clarification is the 'wedding' of protasis and apodosis, the presence or absence of ἄν in the apodosis for the unfulfilled past and present conditions, and ἐάν and subjunctive in the protasis for future factual (open) conditions.

Examples from the New Testament

In these examples, the numbers 1(a), 1(b), 2(a), 2(b), 3 or 4 denote the six divisions just described.

Case 1(a). Past factual condition

"**If God so loved us, we also ought to love one another**" (1 John 4:11). This uses the aorist indicative in the protasis and has the present indicative in the apodosis. John was assuming God did so love us.